# IN THE
# MAINSTREAM

# IN THE MAINSTREAM

## The Jewish Presence
in
Twentieth-Century American Literature,
1950s–1980s

### LOUIS HARAP

*Published in cooperation with the*
*American Jewish Archives*

FOREWORD BY JACOB RADER MARCUS

Contributions in Ethnic Studies, Number 19

GREENWOOD PRESS
*New York • Westport, Connecticut • London*

*810.9*
*H25 in*

**Library of Congress Cataloging-in-Publication Data**

Harap, Louis.
    In the mainstream.

    (Contributions in ethnic studies, ISSN 0196-7088 ;
no. 19)
    "Published in cooperation with the American Jewish
Archives."
    Bibliography: p.
    Includes index.
    1. American literature—Jewish authors—History
and criticism.   2. American literature—20th century—
History and criticism.   3. Jews in literature.
I. Title.  II. Series.

PS153.J4H37     1987        810'.9'8924        86-19459
ISBN 0-313-25387-0 (lib. bdg. : alk. paper)

Library of Congress Catalog Card Number: 86-19459
ISBN: 0-313-25387-0
ISSN: 0196-7088

First published in 1987

Greenwood Press, Inc.
88 Post Road West
Westport, Connecticut 06881

Printed in the United States of America

The paper used in this book complies with the
Permanent Paper Standard issued by the National
Information Standards Organization (Z39.48-1984).

10  9  8  7  6  5  4  3  2  1

# Contents

# Series Foreword

The Contributions in Ethnic Studies series focuses on the problems that arise when people with different cultures and goals come together and interact productively or tragically. The modes of adjustment or conflict are various, but usually one group dominates or attempts to dominate the other. Eventually some accommodation is reached: the process is likely to be long and, for the weaker group, painful. No one scholarly discipline monopolizes the research necessary to comprehend these intergroup relations. The emerging analysis, consequently, is of interest to historians, social scientists, psychologists, psychiatrists, and scholars in communication studies.

For centuries Jews everywhere have been the victims of prejudice and discrimination while preserving many of the main tenets of their culture and religious beliefs. In these three volumes the treatment of Jews in fiction, serious journals, drama, and poetry by Jewish and non-Jewish authors in the United States during the twentieth century is vividly portrayed. In each case, a concise, arresting, critical summary of the story, plot or theme follows the salient, biographical details concerning the writer himself or herself. The reader thus either can nostalgically recall a book or character he once read or knew, or else he can be stimulated to pursue for the first time a literary experience by dipping or plunging into the publications of a popular or scarcely known writer.

We have in these pages an opportunity to view the impact of changes within American society upon the depiction of Jewish characters and indeed of anti-Semitism among gentile and Jewish authors. In the earlier part of the period conditions in the slums of East Side New York City, for example, impelled many Jews to join the forces supporting unions and the American version of socialism. Then the rise of Nazi ideology in the 1930s and later the depictions of the Holocaust caused Jews and non-Jews alike to appraise anew their own Jewish stereotypes. In addition, as readers we are challenged by a philosophical and social issue that still confronts Jews as well as other minority ethnic groups: should or how can we choose between the now less popular melting-pot objective for these groups, or have we really come to tolerate or favor cultural pluralism?

Louis Harap emphasizes quite rightly what he calls the problems of acculturation and assimilation of Jews as described in the literature and by the writers of the period, particularly when he examines differences between older and younger generations of Jews and also when he analyzes alienation generally in our society. The fiction and other literary creations, therefore, have never been wholly fictitious; perhaps more than scholarly tomes they depict the struggles and the satisfactions of Jews as well as unfriendly and friendly appraisals by other Americans. Simultaneously, moreover, they influence the views of a very large public. We are thus offered a most compelling documentation of the significant interaction between literature and what we too easily call reality: accurately or not, literature both reflects and affects us, or at least some of us.

Leonard W. Doob

# Foreword

There are minds which insist on literature as pure artifice, and there are minds which see in literature a reflection not only of literary tradition but also of history and sociology. Louis Harap belongs—has long belonged—to this latter company. Literary merit is not the sole value he seeks when he confronts a work of the imagination. He looks for social value as well. It is important to discern and appreciate in him an accomplished social analyst of literary effort, a scholar who tends to concentrate unfailingly on the (not always so clearly discernible) nexus between a work of literature and the social or psychosocial context in which it was composed.

Dr. Harap is not a literary critic or literary theorist. He is an historian and draws on literature for his work as an historian. He is, more emphatically, a social historian, an historian devoted to the study of social reality with literary expression as a major instrument for his research.

Now to say this is not to suggest the lack in Dr. Harap's work of a *Tendenz* or ideological preference. His work does evince bias and offers a left-of-center perspective—but he is certainly not to be thought of as an ideologue in his judgments. It is Dr. Harap's sensitivity to social experience, not any ideological commitment he may have, that gives his thought a large interest for those concerned, as I am, to find in American-Jewish literary expression some index to how Jews have found their way through the labyrinths of American life.

What Dr. Harap offers in these three new volumes are erudite, forthright, incisive discussions of fiction, discussions which are consistently "socioliterary"—that is, art-for-the-sake-of-art, the purely esthetic, is never his goal or preoccupation. No, it is something else, awareness of the socioeconomic and psychic context, which governs his understanding of the stories and novels he examines so intelligently.

I think worth noting also Dr. Harap's readiness to consider women writers and women characters a major factor in the web of literary expression documenting American-Jewish life. It is impressive to see him calling our attention to Clara Yavner in Abraham Cahan's 1905 novel *The White Terror and the Red*; Clara, he observes, "is among the distinctly new figures ... in all American fiction" and is "of special interest because she anticipates the new place of the Jewish woman in radical fiction of the first decades of the century—the courageous, effective, able Jewish woman labor organizer and socialist." Dr. Harap notes with approval James Oppenheim's incorporation into his 1911 novel *The Nine-Tenths* of a "recognition that the waistmakers' strike in 1911 had brought forward perhaps for the first time in the United States the 'New Woman,' the active and heroic participant in labor struggles and the struggle for a better world." The illumination of Jewish women by non-Jewish writers is not overlooked. He takes into account, for instance, Albert Edwards (*né* Arthur Bullard), who in 1913 published *Comrade Yetta*, a novel about Jewish radicalism, and speculated about Jewish "single-mindedness and consistency of purpose" in contrast to "Anglo-Saxon ... compromise and confused issues."

In general, it may be said, Dr. Harap is fully and commendably alive to the documentary potential, the documentary implications, of fiction by non-Jewish writers. He is as much interested in Judeophobic writers like Frank Norris, Owen Wister, Edith Wharton, Jack London, and David Graham Phillips as he is in more sympathetic fictionists like Mark Twain, William Dean Howells, O. Henry, Thomas Nelson Page, and Dorothy Canfield Fisher. He understands that, "to achieve a comprehensive picture of the status of the Jew in our literature ... it is not enough to study how the Jewish writer regarded his own Jewishness." He wants us also to "look at the way ... non-Jewish writers depicted the Jew and met the challenge of anti-Semitism." As Dr. Harap points out, "the responses varied widely."

Readers may rely on Dr. Harap for formidable learning, and also, it is a pleasure to add, for a most accessible expository style. It is an honor to help bring these volumes to print; they will in time to come, I am confident, be recognized for the classics they are.

Jacob Rader Marcus
American Jewish Archives
Hebrew Union College–Jewish Institute of Religion
Cincinnati, Ohio

# Preface

This work is conceived and organized around the concept of Jewish presence in American literature. The study of Jewish development as refracted in the nation's literature in the present century flows out of this concept. In this context literature is viewed as a social manifestation whose meaning extends beyond the "literary" in the specialized sense, essential as this literary aspect is to the total grasp of a work. Thus to trace the Jewish presence is to follow the rapid changes in the Jewish situation, in the material and social status of Jews, and in the conditions of their life as these form the generative basis for literary expression as well as the mode in which Jews make their appearance within that expression by both Jews and non-Jews. The content of the ensuing work is then the literary rendering of the acculturation process, the making of the texture of American-Jewish social life in the specific historic circumstances of this period of mass immigration and its aftermath.

The centuries-old history of the Jew as alien in Christian civilization and the strong inertial power of anti-Semitism and discrimination, the temptation to use the Jew as scapegoat in time of trouble, the traumatic effect of the necessary transition from the largely hermetic East European milieu to the contrasting mores and atmosphere and language of the "land of the free"—all these provided, willy-nilly, the ground of Jewish life in this country. Significantly, then, Jewish presence in the first half of the century and even beyond is a name for the acculturation of the main body of American Jews.

Jewish presence in literature is a complex phenomenon. Within it is the basic dichotomy of the Jew as writer and as subject or character. A Jew is no less Jewish when presented by a non-Jewish author than when included in work by a Jewish writer, regardless of the varying degrees of intimacy between author and subject. It is especially important to consider the release of the Jew in literature from the age-old stereotype, which prevailed in most writing of the past century. As the new century progressed, we find more sophisticated treatment of Jews as rounded individual characters. In such changes we can perceive the close connection between the strictly literary and the social, since the literary change from a cliché to a fresh creation reflects both more knowledge and, usually, a related new attitude. Throughout the century attitudes toward the Jew, as depicted in literature, are largely dependent on the status of the Jew in society. The non-Jewish author's attitude toward anti-Semitism is important in determining how he will present his Jewish characters. Hence, were one to omit examination of non-Jewish treatments of the Jew, the ensuing account of the Jewish presence in literature would be severely truncated.

The wider the arc of inclusion of elements of Jewish relevance in work by both Jewish and non-Jewish authors, the fuller the emergent picture of Jewish status at a given time will be. Our inquiry here is by no means strictly literary; one might best, perhaps, term it socioliterary. We have therefore given considerable attention to the development of the social situation during the century, and specifically to its anti-Semitic manifestations, whether those are presented by the story material alone or shared or condemned by the author. Our aim has been to achieve the most comprehensive view of the situation of the Jew in each period as adduced from the information available in the various components of presence. Indeed the entire work has been organized to bring out the various elements of presence. While all genres are subject to the same basic social conditions, out of which they all spring, each has its own special problems relating to its specific public and its internal formal requirements. In view of these differences, the variety of talents each calls upon, and the favorable or unfavorable social atmosphere for their evocation, the genres develop at different rates and with different qualities. These factors will be suggested in each case.

The evolving picture calls for a chronological periodization. It has seemed helpful to divide the first half century roughly into decades. The two decades from the opening of the century to the end of World War I form the first division; the 1920s, second; the Depression 1930s a third; the 1940s, the war decade, a fourth; the 1950s and beyond, a period of relatively full acceptance of the Jew in life and in the literary mainstream, the last. Within each period for the most part we examine separately the work of non-Jewish and Jewish writers. During the first three decades we find three important recurrent fictional themes: (1) the progress of acculturation fiction, (2) the radical novel, and (3) the manifestations of anti-Semitism in the work of non-Jewish authors as well as their own attitudes toward it. Within this third theme of anti-Semitism there are several striking phenomena which are discussed in separate chapters. First is the anti-Semitic attitudes in Jewish writers and in their Jewish characters, which illustrate what has been called "self-hate." Second, the war novels of World War II by both Jewish and non-Jewish writers are studied with a focus on the widespread anti-Semitism in the armed forces that they reveal.

Among the new developments in the nation after World War II we find, together with an increase in the number of important woman writers and the emergence of many impressive Black writers, the movement of Jewish authors into the central currents of American literature. The 1950s saw so many widely read novels, both popular and sophisticated, by Jewish writers and/or with central Jewish characters that it is no exaggeration to call this the "Jewish decade." We explore the genesis of this emergence in the 1920s and 1930s. A chapter is devoted to a number of Jewish literary critics who participated in these developments; Delmore Schwartz and Isaac Rosenfeld are discussed as harbingers of much postwar writing, and a chapter is devoted to each of four major Jewish novelists—Saul Bellow, Bernard Malamud, Philip Roth, and Norman Mailer. The return to religion in postwar writing is discussed, as well as the literary relations of Blacks and Jews.

Our study appears in three volumes. The first covers fiction from 1900 to the 1940s; the second resumes with the fiction in the 1950s, which we have designated "The Jewish Decade" for reasons there stated, until the 1980s; and the third takes up a survey of the drama from 1900 to the post–World War II period, as well as poetry and humor from 1900.

As any student of American literature must be aware, aspects of the Jew in literature as both author and subject, particularly in the latter half of the present century, is an area under increasing critical and historical scrutiny. There are already numerous studies of many themes and tendencies as well as of individual authors, groups of authors, and literary periods. However, of the present work, as of my earlier volume, it is, I think, true that no study so comprehensive has yet appeared. The abundance of material has, of course, made it necessary to be highly selective, and other scholars will inevitably differ in choices or in emphases as well as in general outlook. Yet they will, I hope, find their tasks easier for the broad survey here presented.

# Acknowledgments

After publication of *The Image of the Jew in American Literature: From Early Republic to Mass Immigration* (1974), I turned to reading and writing on other, though related, topics. Toward the end of the Preface to that volume I had written, "We leave the proliferation of literature by and about Jews in our century to other, younger hands." But the respite proved brief. I was strongly encouraged by the late Oscar Cohen, by then retired program director of the Anti-Defamation League, to continue my research on Jews in American literature from the cut-off date of the earlier volume, 1900, to the present. I soon found myself committed to the second part of a comprehensive study of the Jew in American literature from the days of the early Republic to our own time. I am indebted to Oscar Cohen for his stimulus to continue on this project and for his many kindnesses.

My thanks also are due to several libraries and their helpful personnel: New York Public Library and its Library of the Performing Arts, the Bobst Library of New York University, the Harvard University Library, and the Hebrew Union College–Jewish Institute of Religion Library in New York City. The dedicated staff of the Southwest Regional Library of the Vermont State Library system responded most helpfully to my numerous requests for books on interlibrary loan, thus enabling me to work in my mountain home.

A portion of chapter 6, "From *Shlemihl* to *Mentsch*: Bernard Malamud," previously appeared in *Jewish Currents* (November, 1986) and is reprinted with permission.

I wish to thank Jacob Sherman, of Rutland, Vermont, who devotedly typewrote the manuscript at various stages so accurately and together with his wife Madeline helped with other kindnesses relating to the preparation of the manuscript, as also did a Jewish group in Rutland. My thanks are also due to Joan Wright, who typewrote the final draft for the press.

Morris U. Schappes kindly loaned me his valuable files on several current authors. Professor Ellen F. Schiff, of North Adams (Mass.) Community College, read the material on drama and made helpful suggestions.

Most particularly I wish to thank Dr. Annette Rubenstein for her careful, critical scrutiny of the entire manuscript, for her editorial suggestions, and for her copy-editing at several stages of the writing. We did not always agree, but she was ever sensitively aware of the distinction between difference of interpretation and indefensible error on my part. My debt to her is very great.

However, full responsibility for the entire work, mistakes and all, is of course mine alone.

# IN THE MAINSTREAM

# 1

# Thread of Influence: From *Menorah Journal* to *Partisan Review* to *Commentary*

By the end of the 1950s it became unmistakably clear that Jewish writers of fiction and literary criticism had moved into the literary mainstream, taking their place with the leading figures in both popular and serious fiction. Among the most important critics were Lionel Trilling, Philip Rahv, Alfred Kazin, Leslie Fiedler, and Irving Howe. Among the numerous Jewish fiction writers attention was focused on the poet Delmore Schwartz, Saul Bellow, Bernard Malamud, Norman Mailer, and Philip Roth. In retrospect we can now see that William Dean Howells was correct in his unusual insight concerning the future of Jewish and American literature. In opposition to the prevailing bigoted view that Jews were incapable of fully grasping English and American literature he wrote in 1915, "Very possibly there may be at this moment a Russian or Polish Jew, born or bred on our East Side, who shall burst from his parental Yiddish, and from the local hydrants, as well as from the wells of English undefiled, slake our thirst of imaginative literature."[1] Consider: Delmore Schwartz was born in Brooklyn in 1913, Bernard Malamud in Brooklyn in 1914, Saul Bellow in Lachine, near Montreal, in 1915, Alfred Kazin in Brownsville, a section of Brooklyn, in 1915, Arthur Miller in Manhattan in 1915.

By the end of World War II large numbers of the second generation like these had become acculturated; they matured and entered the cultural mainstream. The burst of creativity in the 1920s had been prepared by the break with the genteel tradition by such critics as Randolph Bourne and Van Wyck Brooks and modernist poets like Ezra Pound and T. S. Eliot, as well as James Joyce, which merged with postwar disillusionment. Likewise, the emergence of major Jewish writers of the 1950s had its origins in the Great Depression of the 1930s, the spiritual exhaustion following World War II, the ever-present awareness of the Holocaust, and the struggle to establish

Israel. The second generation now had a large pool of literary talent, and the literary, political, and social antecedents determined the directions in which those talents would be exercised. We may unravel the complex set of influences that issued in the recognition by the 1950s of Jewish writing as part of the major American literature by examining three elements, the Jewish, the political, and the literary, in three journals that were their main bearers, *The Menorah Journal* of the 1920s, *Partisan Review* of the 1930s and beyond, and *Commentary* from the late 1940s to about 1970.

In the first few decades of the century the dominant trend among the second generation was assimilationism. The parochialism of much Jewish life, as well as the entire structure of ritual and millennial customs seemed to this generation alien to the larger world in which they lived outside of the home. There was a tendency to cast off the traditional ghetto attitudes as these Jews were educated in the public schools, learning English and non-Jewish Western modes of life and thought. Jewishness seemed irrelevant to their interests and life among their peers in the larger American world. No doubt the fear of anti-Semitism and an effort to evade the undoubted religious and economic ineligibilities of Jewishness in the general community were also a prime motive for assimilationism.

But this assimilationist trend was not universal among the second generation. Many writers drew on their own experience in the Jewish milieu for their material. Others sought to cultivate their Jewishness as a valid aspect of their life as Americans by eschewing parochialism.

Perhaps the most important manifestation of this latter trend, except for Zionism, was the formation of the Intercollegiate Menorah Society of Harvard in 1906 to serve as a vehicle for the promotion of Jewish identity and culture among college students. That the organization answered a felt need was indicated by the fact that by 1920 the society already had eighty chapters in American colleges. In 1915—Howells' significant year—the *Menorah Journal*, a secular and cultural organ of the society, first appeared under the editorship of Henry Hurwitz, who remained editor until his death in 1961, only a year before the demise of the journal. The magazine was intended to establish an intellectual center which called upon Jewish resources to lend validity and status to Jewish intellectual efforts in the larger intellectual community and to legitimize a Jewish humanist and national identity.

The first fifteen years of the magazine were its more innovative and significant; after that it continued, as Robert Alter has written, "to flicker through a strange half-life for three decades." But the magazine was, he wrote in his epitaph, "surely one of the most exciting episodes in the history of the American-Jewish intellectual community," and it yielded "a fascinating record of the varying efforts of this community to preserve a meaningful attachment to Jewish culture while participating fully in American intellectual life."[2]

The magazine was "exciting" not only because its literary as well as its intellectual level was high, but also because of its non-parochial tone. It was permeated with the sense of simultaneous residence in both the Jewish and the larger American communities: this was its distinctive quality, unique among Jewish publications until the post–World War II period. At the end of its first decade an editorial in the February, 1925 issue articulated the aims of the magazine. Without false modesty or exaggeration the magazine could assert that it had become the foremost Jewish publication in English and "now holds a position in the front rank of American magazines." The working premise of the magazine was to place the Jew in a "thoroughly American context," avoiding both "self-adulation" and "self-effacement" while exercising "honest self-criticism" as well as "self-expression," defying both "chauvinists and assimilationists." The statement emphasizes three aims of the magazine: to "illuminate" and "reconquer" the Jewish past "in the light of modern research and psychology" as a "broadly humane interest"; to discuss the contemporary life and problems of Jews in both the United States and the world in an "open forum"; and finally "to foster, stimulate, bring out the works of Jewish creative writers and artists in all fields."[3] The actualization of these aims was what made the magazine so exciting.

In the same month and year Elliot Cohen emerged as managing and de facto editor. From this nuclear fact much literary history follows. Cohen was a brilliant student, a Yale graduate in 1917 at the age of eighteen. His interest and aspiration was to teach English literature, but the current academic disbelief in the capacity of Jews to understand this literature and rigid college discrimination against Jews, especially in English departments, made him abandon hope for such a career. He was president of the Yale Menorah Society and in 1923 published his first article in *Menorah Journal*, in which he argued that Jews should be full participants in the context of society rather than remaining isolated in the Jewish community, essentially the approach that was to underlie the Jewish intellectual and literary renaissance a few decades later. Indeed, this is essentially what is projected in the editorial in the issue in which Cohen was announced as managing editor. (He had been associated with the journal since 1923, listed as an associate editor.) As editor Cohen initiated a remarkable period. He was not primarily a writer but had an extraordinary talent for selecting writers and editing their work. He made the magazine a forum for a group of young Jewish writers who were to influence the course of the nation's literary life. In the more than six years of his editorship the magazine became a leading intellectual organ. He attracted a number of second-generation Jewish poets, fiction writers, and critics as well as social and political analysts. Among the literary figures were Lionel Trilling, Albert Halper, Tess Slesinger, Clifton Fadiman, Isidor Schneider, Kenneth Fearing, Alfred Kreymborg, Mike Gold, Waldo Frank, and Meyer Levin. Among the political analysts were some who became well known in the 1930s but are largely forgotten today, such as Herbert Solow, Felix Morrow, Anita Brenner, and Louis Fischer. In 1928 and 1929 Ludwig Lewisohn's autobiographical *Mid-Channel* was published serially in the *Menorah*. Cohen put into practice his projected editorial aims in a broad, non-parochial outlook on Jewishness and the place of the Jew in modern society, which proved attractive to the writers he drew to the journal.

An exchange of letters between Cohen and Isidor Schneider shows how explicitly aware they all were of what they were doing. On November 27, 1929, Cohen wrote to Schneider that the magazine was in danger because the Board of Governors might withdraw their financial support owing to the drain on funds caused by the Arab riots in Palestine and by losses in the stock market crash a month earlier. Cohen asked if Schneider would write a letter, which could be shown to the governors, indicating the value of the magazine. At that time Schneider was a socialist and an aspiring poet—in the 1930s he was to become a leading Communist writer. He had as a boy, he wrote Cohen, been a Zionist, but since then, "Jewish matters . . . seemed to me narrow." Dedication to socialism and literature were now more important to him. He had become "antinationalist politically and antitraditional culturally," an attitude he thought "common and almost inevitable in the intellectual evolution of thinking people in our time." He saw "the intellectual life of the English-speaking section of American Jewry" as "trivial and exasperating." There was, he thought, greater vitality in "Yiddish-speaking Jewry"; he had even considered learning Yiddish for that reason but realized that English was his "native tongue." His Jewish awareness was "kept alive" by the existence of great ones like Einstein, Freud, and Marx, but he sustained his cultural hopes on such figures as James Joyce and Marcel Proust. However, he continued, his work in publishing had brought the *Menorah* to his attention, and he felt pride in its quality and agreed that it was a leading American cultural magazine. He had been glad, he then said, to accept Cohen's invitation to write for it. He firmly regarded it as having "great importance as a focus for intellectual consolidation and the only organ that a self-regarding Jew can turn to, to reach a Jewish audience." It was, he concluded, "the one force existing that can capture" the interest of intellectuals "whose interests led them away from the Jewish center." And he pointed to the "unnoticed" service it performed for American letters by its stimulus to creativity. In addition, the magazine attracted "a large number of Gentile writers"—and readers, too (like its later successor, *Commentary*, we may add). Finally, he observed that in the magazine "Jewish life faces Gentile life . . . in one of its finest aspects."[4]

Schneider here spoke for the whole generation, which was rejecting the apartness of the ghetto mentality and wished to shape their Jewish consciousness in a reciprocal relationship with general intellectual and cultural life. Indeed, his letter aptly states in essence the point of view of many of the writers who treated Jewish subject matter in their fiction several decades later. His letter is witness to the emergence of Jews as fully American writers, without loss of Jewish identity, an emergence that was to mature several decades later and achieve full acceptance by the general American public in the 1950s. And indeed there was continuity with the *Menorah* idea in the work of not only Cohen, who resumed his efforts in this direction in 1945 when he became the founding editor of *Commentary*, but also Lionel Trilling, who published short stories and reviews in the *Menorah* and was assistant editor there for a brief period. Trilling has since written of the motivation of the *Menorah* group. It

was the idea of Jewishness. This had nothing to do with religion; we were not religious. . . . Chiefly our concern with Jewishness was about what is [1966] called authenticity, . . . that the individual Jewish person recognizes naturally and easily that he *is* a Jew and "accepts himself" as such, finding pleasure and taking pride in the identification. . . . [We suggested that] the Jewish present . . . was not only as respectable as the present of any other group but also as foolish, vulgar, complicated.

The group were less interested, for instance, in anti-Semitism as such, much less in counteracting it, than in not allowing it to skew their characters or diminish "acceptance of themselves."[5] One requirement for such acceptance was in subjecting the vulgar and philistine aspects of organized Jewish life— that is, the "bourgeois" stratum—to a stringent critique, which the magazine did.

Trilling's contributions to the journal between 1926 and 1931 were numerous and all were related to Jews in literature. His judgments of current fiction and poetry by Jews were severe and unsparing. Of Ludwig Lewisohn's novel *Random Harvest*, Trilling wrote, "To his account of the progress of unsophistication Mr. Lewisohn has brought neither poetry nor imagination."[6] Reviewing the same author's play *Adam* and his novel *Stephen Escott*, Trilling grants that in advancing the propagandist intent in the play (to heighten the sense of Jewishness), the author "is justified in sacrificing ultimate artistic merit to immediate emotional effect." But the novel has "essentially the same faults and suggests no pragmatic excuse for them." Lewisohn seems unable "to create character," but is "vivid and convincing" when he deals with "concepts and institutions."[7] In Trilling's review of Louis Untermeyer's book of poems, *Burning Bush*, he said categorically that Untermeyer "is not a good poet, American or Jewish." He is simply "a bad poet" and "pretentious."[8] A reading of Robert Nathan's *There Is Another Heaven* and a few of his other novels led Trilling to conclude that Nathan oversimplified life and virtue. He reminded the author that "there are others besides children in the kingdom of heaven."[9] The music critic Paul Rosenfeld's "novel of adolescence," *Boy in the Sun*, Trilling thought a "rather complete failure," which he ascribed to Rosenfeld's "preoccupation with music," which in this case leads to a "disagreeable pulpiness of prose."[10]

Not all of Trilling's judgments were so harsh. He thought that Charles Reznikoff's immigrant novel, *By the Waters of Manhattan*, was "remarkable and original" and the best of its kind because it was not "false" and was written with "the greatest delicacy and distinction."[11]

Like most of the best writers of the time, Trilling became radicalized in the latter 1920s. However, his early reviews show little evidence of this. A few book reviews did show sensitivity to the sociopolitical aspects of fiction. In discussing Hannah R. London's handsome book of reproductions of portraits of early American Jews, he found the information it contained about the "eminence of Jews" interesting and conducive to "pride." But he is sharply critical of the editor's "uncritical spirit" and "resents" her evocations as "abstractions" which he calls the "Absolute Jew." She discussed Jews as if they were absolutely good. He finds woefully lacking any mention of crucial aspects of their relations with gentiles. She lacks, he says, "true proportion" by her total omission of "the mass of poor and insignificant Jews that must have existed in the Colonies." Indeed, she seems to leave "the impression that the Colonies were almost exclusively controlled by Jews." He ends by asking, "Is a Jew a Jew without a pogrom in the middle distance?"[12]

Trilling's last review in the journal was of Lion Feuchtwanger's *Success*, "a novel about injustice" in Germany. The book, he thought, "was almost completely successful" and was "history beautifully constructed." At the same time it was "propaganda in the cause of political decency." Against those who denied propaganda any artistic function, Trilling declared himself opposed to readers who view literature as "a solace, an escape, a high amusement." Contrarily, Trilling argued that literature had "always been opposed to the evil, the greed, the blindness and stupidity of the world." Such proponents of "expressing important ideas" in literature are animated not only by esthetic, but "political" considerations against "obscurantism," against everything that is "symptomatic of the greed and injustice of our world, dangerous for the hope of amelioration of that world." One result would be the "destruction not only of a literature of ideas but of all art no matter how 'pure.' "[13] The existence of art itself was at stake, he said, and the artist must therefore make it at least a part of his function to be a political propagandist for political decency and against injustice.

The note for a politically purposive art struck in Trilling's last review for *Menorah* shows how the Jewish and literary origins of the postwar burgeoning of Jewish writing must also be sought in politics. This aspect was at least as important as the literary during the Cohen period of the magazine, whether its ultimate expression after the 1930s was embrace of politics or revulsion from it. In the group of political and social analysts that Cohen attracted to the magazine the leader was Herbert Solow, who became an assistant editor. The leftward movement among writers begun in the latter 1920s was, of course, greatly accelerated by the onset of the Great Depression. By 1931 the pro-Communist sympathies of Cohen and his group had become so pronounced that the magazine's wealthy and conservative sponsors were upset. Together with Henry Hurwitz, who had never relinquished the formal editorship, the sponsors made Cohen's position intolerable, and he resigned. With Cohen virtually the entire group he had brought onto the magazine left, and most of them never again appeared in its pages. The magazine suspended publication after Cohen's last issue (June, 1931) and did not reappear until the following spring. It then came out sporadically and finally only as a quarterly until its end in 1962.

The Cohen group turned their energies and sympathies toward the Communist party, though few actually joined and became politically active. Some contributed to *New Masses*. They helped form the National Committee for the Defense of Political Prisoners, of which Cohen later became executive secretary, which worked in tandem with the Communist International Labor Defense. They joined the defense of the miners in Harlan County, Kentucky, and in 1932 some of the group signed the manifesto of the League of Professionals in support of the presidential and vice-presidential candidacy of William Z. Foster and James W. Ford on the Communist ticket. But their differences with the Communists kept mounting. They sharply disapproved of the sectarian position of the party toward the Socialist party, which was condemned as "social fascism." Antagonism culminated in February, 1934, when the Communists broke up a Madison Square Garden meeting held to protest the armed attack on the Karl Marx workers' housing project in Vienna because the meeting had been called by the Socialist party. A protest against the disruption composed by Cohen and a colleague was signed by twenty-five writers and intellectuals, including some of the *Menorah* group. At this time some had begun to move toward the Trotskyist position, though few ever joined a Trotskyist party. But the position of nearly all was anti-Stalinist, and the divisions among left writers became sharper and more definitive. With their departure from *Menorah* the specifically Jewish engagement of most had also lapsed.

The group found in Tess Slesinger an unfriendly fictional chronicler. She had briefly been the wife of Herbert Solow, but the marriage was unhappy. Her husband frustrated her desire to have children, and the marriage broke up, perhaps somewhat as described in her novel, *The Unpossessed* (1934), which satirized the *Menorah* group. The contrast between the radicals of the group and those of Dostoyevsky's *The Possessed* was apparent. Her characters talked interminably without the ability to make unreserved political commitments. Two themes run through the novel: the personal relations of the characters and their failure to make a political commitment. The personal is centered on the husband-and-wife relations of the couple representing the author and her husband, not presented in the novel as Jewish. The second theme revolved around an Elliot Cohen character, called Bruno Leonard, and his futile effort to found a radical magazine. The author's surrogate, Margaret, scornfully tells Leonard, "Oh, Politics...and Magazines; you talk and talk, but I'd like to know what any of you *do*."[14] She contrasts their alleged sterility with the activism of six young Communist students called The Black Sheep, led by a young Jewish student, Firman, for whom Leonard is faculty advisor. The students are the least hypocritical characters in the book and quit a magazine fund-raising affair in disgust at the antics of their elders.

The novel is more personal than political, but it sheds a satirical light on the *Menorah* group. The dazzlingly clever Bruno Leonard is a professor of English, the vocation that Cohen originally wished to follow but was then virtually closed to Jews. This discrimination is satirized when a filing cabinet salesman named Harrison comes to set up a cabinet in Leonard's office. Leonard tells him, "With a name like that I could get you a job in the English department. They're overstocked at the moment on Jews with Harvard accents." Leonard's own failure at commitment is satirized by suggesting the Oblomov character when Leonard tells Harrison that if he were a bright Jew—like Leonard and his colleagues, the reader gathers—he would have "a little streak of madness" and "stay home wondering" about the files "if it were not better to smash them or better to put them together, and after a while you'd stay in bed wondering, unable to get up because you couldn't decide."[15] When Trilling wrote an "Afterword" to a reprint of the novel, he remarked that the author intended to show the group's "inability to surrender themselves to the ideals they profess."[16]

Trilling also observed that the novel primarily concerned personal affairs rather than political ones and portrayed "a group whose tendency was social and moral rather than *political*." But in fact, he comments, the *Menorah* group "was nothing if not political in the particular sense of the radical politics of the time." The author was indeed far off the mark when she charged them, through the self-incriminating words of Leonard, with "sterility."[17] In the impassioned speech of the novel, Leonard said of the group, "We have no parents and we can have no offspring; we have no sex, we are mules—in short, we are bastards, foundlings, phonys, the unpossessed and unpossessing of the world, the real minority."[18]

But subsequent history has shown otherwise. The characterization does have a limited relevance, since some of the central figures did withdraw from radical politics and social activism after some years. But the group did play an important role in the development of American literature, as its activities in those years prepared for the entry of Jews into the center of American literature and culture. With Cohen's editorship of *Menorah* he established a Jewish cultural medium which served as a pattern that matured when he resumed this function, fourteen years later, as founding editor of *Commentary*. For his own part, Lionel Trilling, after breaking the barrier against Jews in Columbia's English Department, became a central influence in the nation's literary criticism and the mentor of following literary generations. (Recently Estelle Gilson recalled [*Commentary*, April, 1986, p. 39] that "Joel Spingarn, a literary critic later instrumental in founding the NAACP, was appointed to the Columbia faculty in 1899 at the age of twenty-two.")

The lines of influence exerted by the *Menorah* group were both literary and political. But its unique contribution was the addition of the Jewish element, and in its sophisticated way it presented a practical demonstration to show that a writer could be Jewish, literary, and radical in one consistent American pattern. Politics was to play an essential role in the development of a core of Jewish writers who became central to American literature. After the end of the *Menorah* phase politics became central, and largely replaced Jewishness for a number of years. Politics absorbed most of the literary activity of the 1930s, whether of the "proletarian" or of a less specifically left party tendency. Since large numbers of young writers were Jewish, they naturally drew on their own experience in the Jewish milieu in their writing. Jewish issues were forcefully brought to general attention by Nazism and the domestic anti-Semitism whose growth it engendered. But whatever the Jewish content, it was usually secondary to the political or literary.

The radical *political* tendency of *Menorah* was taken up by *Paritsan Review*, founded in 1934 as the organ of the pro-Communist John Reed Club of New York. The directing group of the magazine, led by William Phillips and Philip Rahv, were Jewish. By 1937 the literary and political differences between Phillips and Rahv and their colleagues on the one hand and the Communist party on the other had become so great that *Partisan* broke with the party and published independently. While the journal remained radical and even Marxist for a time, it stressed the literary and became a tribune for modernist creativity in line with the work of T. S. Eliot, Ezra Pound, James Joyce, Franz Kafka, and Fyodor Dostoyevsky. Jewishness as such scarcely figures, though many contributors were Jewish; some were assimilationist, unlike those of the *Menorah Journal*. The Jewish element was to be brought back actively into literary creativity with the founding of *Commentary* in 1945 just after World War II. While Elliot Cohen was not involved in *Partisan*, Lionel Trilling was a frequent contributor and formed a literary link between *Menorah* and *Partisan*. The latter magazine proved to be the center for the development of many of the Jewish writers who were to transform American letters by the end of the 1950s. In those days the *Partisan*'s literary position was modernist; its politics were still Marxist, radical, and strenuously anti-Stalinist; and after a time it leaned toward Trotskyism.

The essential work of *Partisan*, later assisted by *Commentary*, was to contribute to the consolidation of the modernist trend in fiction, criticism, and literature in general and to its acceptance in American literary life. When the *Partisan* arrived on the scene, the battle against the so-called Humanist school of criticism had been won after a widespread debate in

practically the entire literary press of the early 1930s. The Humanists, led
by Professor Irving Babbitt and Paul Elmer Moore, were rigid traditionalists
who, in the name of the classic Greek, Christian, and seventeenth-century
French traditions of morality, conduct, and rules of literary decorum and
hatred of Rousseauism and all its works, summarily rejected all realist and
modern trends of emotional and intellectual development since the Enlightenment. Opposed to the Humanists were the several new literary groups
taking shape, rebels against the status quo in social, intellectual, and literary
life, a movement set off by Brooks' *America's Coming-of-Age*, the major
novelists of the 1920s, the formalists of the Southern "agrarian" school,
later to become the New Critics; the social-literary critics led by Edmund
Wilson; and the Marxist literary movement. When the Humanists were no
longer a significant factor, the lines of difference among the various groups
became more clearly marked. The *Partisan*, after its break with the Communist party, became a forum for non-dogmatic literary Marxism, very
soon to be diluted almost out of existence, and a propagator of experimental
modernist writing. It should be emphasized that the *Partisan* was never
formalist or an adherent of the New Criticism, whose earmark was the
"close reading" of texts with a suppressed premise of political reaction.
When *Commentary* arrived in 1946, it immediately shared the field with
*Partisan*. In both journals Jewish writers were prominent, if not
predominant.

A landmark of the entry of Jewish writers into the mainstream of literary
activity was the symposium in 1944, "Under Forty," in the *Contemporary
Jewish Record*, published by the American Jewish Committee. The symposium's editorial preface noted that Jewish participation in American literature in the previous century was "virtually unknown," but that in "recent
decades," some "children of Jewish immigrants" were "taking their place
in the front ranks of American literature ... as poets, novelists, playwrights
and critics." Did their Jewish origin influence their work? Was the Jew as
such more responsive to modern literature than others? What effect did
"the revival of anti-Semitism" have on him as artist or citizen? Eleven
respondents were "under forty," among them Muriel Rukeyser, Alfred Kazin, Ben Field, Delmore Schwartz, Lionel Trilling, Albert Halper, Howard
Fast, and Isaac Rosenfeld. They ranged in acknowledgment of Jewish influence on their work from the central, in Schwartz, to Trilling's declaration
that he would "resent it" if any critic "were to discover" in his work "either
faults or virtues which he called Jewish."[19]

Clearly the fact of such a symposium, with such a lineup of participants,
signified that the Jews in the United States had entered a new era. Many
barriers against full Jewish participation in American higher education and
other areas of business life had fallen. To be sure, latent anti-Semitism
persisted where it was not overt, together with the stubborn survival or
stereotypic conceptions of the Jew. The unprecedented prosperity after

World War II in the rapidly growing middle class and in a large part of the white labor force helped make possible a relaxation of anti-Semitism. Further, as Will Herberg showed, Judaism was accepted by the American people as one mode of an approved way of life—as one of the "three 'communions,' Protestantism, Catholicism, Judaism—considered three diverse but equally legitimate, equally American expressions of an overall American religion, with essentially the same 'moral ideals' and 'spiritual values.' "[20] Although Herberg realized that this was an "idealized" view of the situation, the *tendency* in this direction was sufficiently strong to give his thesis high validity. It was apparent that Jews had never before in American history been so fully accepted into most aspects of American life.

The "Under Forty" symposium in 1944 anticipated this new situation; the founding in November, 1945 of *Commentary* was a decisive step toward its realization. The American Jewish Committee, perceiving the new status of the American Jew, replaced the exclusively Jewish *Contemporary Jewish Record* with *Commentary*, of broader scope socially, politically, and culturally, to develop Jewish participation in national and cultural affairs, as well as internal Jewish matters. The magazine also included material not specifically of Jewish but of general social and national significance. As editor, the committee appointed Elliot Cohen, who had, since leaving *Menorah Journal*, been employed in Jewish fund-raising publicity. By this time, Cohen had abandoned his early radicalism and was obsessively anti-Stalinist. In 1967, his editorial successor, Norman Podhoretz, called it Cohen's "hard anti-Communism."[21] But, as with the *Menorah*, Cohen gathered about *Commentary* a group of talented Jewish scholars and writers, and resumed the lively discussion of Jewish life and its relation to the larger American context begun in the *Menorah*. In the following decades *Commentary*, together with *Partisan Review*, was to exert profound influence through the 1960s not only on Jewish but also on non-Jewish cultural, intellectual, and academic life.

When the *Partisan Review* published a symposium in August and September, 1948, on "The State of American Writing," the responses of six non-Jewish and three Jewish writers were included. And of all these, only Leslie Fiedler introduced the element of Jewishness in recent writing. He wrote that Kafka's

Jewishness is by no means incidental: The real Jew and the imaginary Jew between them give to the current period its special flavor. In *Ulysses*, our prophetic book of the urbanization of art, the Artist and the Jew reach for each other tentatively and fall apart; but in the Surveyor K. [in Kafka's story] a unity is achieved, a mystic prototype proposed: Jewishness as a condition of the Artist.

He named coming Jewish writers then in their thirties—"Delmore Schwartz, Alfred Kazin, Karl Shapiro, Isaac Rosenfeld, Paul Goodman, Saul Bellow."

The American Jewish writer, he added, "helps mediate" for American literature "the conflicting claims of an allegiance to Europe and to the American scene, . . . [and between] writer and intellectual."[22]

Fiedler's keen awareness of the problems entailed in important current
writing by Jews led him, in the next year, to address Jewish writers in a
*Commentary* article (May, 1949) with the question, "What Shall We Do
About Fagin? The Jew-Villain in Western Tradition"—the literary heritage
of the Jewish image in England, from Chaucer to Shakespeare to Eliot and
Pound, down to Graham Greene and D. H. Lawrence. How does this anti-
Semitism, with which the great writings in the English tradition are riddled,
affect the Jewish writer's attitude toward that tradition? The literary anti-
Semitic conception of the Jew, in accordance with the then current position
in literary criticism, he called a "myth." Since we cannot dissociate ourselves
from that literary culture, Fiedler suggests that the writer put forward "rival
myths" of the Jew to replace the anti-Semitic myth, such as that of "the
alienated Jew as artist" and others.[23] Once Fiedler confronted the issue—
and it was a real issue in those days of awareness of the Holocaust—
*Commentary* launched a new symposium, "The Jewish Writer and the English Literary Tradition" (September and October, 1949). "As a Jew and a
writer working within the Anglo-American literary tradition, how do you
confront the presence in that tradition of the mythical or semi-mythical
figure of The Jew?"[24]

A variety of views were expressed in the seventeen replies, most of them
by Jewish writers. Some admitted having been troubled by the phenomenon.
No one suggested anything so absurd as rejection of the tradition because
of occasional anti-Semitism. Stanley Edgar Hyman hotly asked why Fiedler
and others "use 'myth' to mean a damned lie?" He suggested that the Jewish
writer should view such anti-Semitism in historical context, and avoided,
on his own part, "self-pity and parochialism."[25] Irving Howe pointed out
that a distinction should be made between expressions of anti-Semitism in
writers like Chaucer (and we should add, Shakespeare) who lived in a period
of universal acceptance of Jew-hatred, in contrast with Dreiser (and we may
add, Pound and Eliot), who lived in a more enlightened age in this regard.
"The gross caricatures of Jews in English literature," wrote Howe, "make
it impossible for one to be totally at ease with its tradition."[26] Saul Bellow
also noted that "modern Jew-despising writers" are unjustified because
"they know more history" than Chaucer and Shakespeare. "This knowledge
of theirs," he concludes, "makes their dislike of the Jew more terrible if
they are right, stupendously horrible if they are wrong"—and "the gases of
Auschwitz" should help "judge whether they are right or wrong."[27]

Several seemed to disagree with the diagnosis of anti-Semitism in the
English literary tradition, or at least about the works named as anti-Semitic.
Harold Rosenberg advanced the curious aesthetic argument that Shylock is
*acted*, projected as a stage character, and with all his particular qualities,

*as acted*, gives pleasure and hence does no harm. The one who does harm is "the propagandist and the sociological critic" who makes of a "theatrical personification" a "cliche."[28] Would Rosenberg have accepted the implied assumption of his argument that art does not affect our ideas and conduct? Harry Levin argued that it is the complainer who universalizes the invidious image of the Jew in art, not the artist. For he thereby assumes "that the least admirable depictions are the most typical" and thus falls "into a trap which anti-Semitism has baited." It would seem that it has been the artist who has initially influenced the universalization—as witnessed by the fact that anti-Semitic characters in drama or fiction were almost always designated "the Jew" with universal overtness. Levin further argued that Shylock or Bleistein do resemble some Jews and Jewish behavior under certain circumstances, and charges that in such cases "criticism" is written off as "persecution."[29] Again, it is not "criticism" in which the anti-Semitism of some artists consists, but their tone and generalized characterization of such "criticism" as typical of "the Jew," or apply to Jews as an entire people.

In this symposium early in the 1950s, the full impact of Jewish centrality in American letters had not yet become fully explicit. But before the 1950s ended, there could be no doubt of the importance for the national literature of writing by American Jews. The enormous influence of *Partisan Review*, and later of *Commentary*, was fully apparent, and American-Jewish writing was given official recognition and sanction by the appearance of the article in the *Times Literary Supplement* (November 6, 1959), "A Vocal Group: The Jewish Part in American Letters." The central medium for this new development was *Commentary*, which reintroduced the explicit Jewish element into fiction and criticism. In its first few issues it included such younger writers as Alfred Kazin, Saul Bellow, Harold Rosenberg, and Clement Greenberg, as well as some who had written for *Menorah* such as Meyer Levin and Waldo Frank. In addition to articles of general interest *Commentary* published many of the important emerging young sociologists of Jewish life, as well as an increasing number of critical and historical articles on Jews in literature, past and present.

Attraction to the thought of Martin Buber facilitated this awakening sense of Jewishness in some intellectuals. It was apparent that the bestiality of Nazi anti-Semites, climaxed in the Holocaust, challenged younger Jewish writers and intellectuals to assert their Jewish identity as an imperative for self-respect. Added to the social and moral compulsions aroused by Nazism was a related set of events, the fight for the establishment of Israel, which extended beyond provision of a haven for Nazi refugees and persecuted Jews to the felt justification for existence of a national Jewish state. In 1948 *Commentary* noted editorially, "It is no longer news that we are in the midst of something like a revival, if not of religion, then of interest in religion among intellectuals here and abroad, especially of the younger generation." For the Jews this was accompanied by probings into the meaning of, and possibilities for, a Jewish culture. From left to right Jewish intellectuals were deep into discussion of the meaning of Jewish culture.

Even though radical politics had faded among the intellectuals of this "Jewish renaissance," it remained ever present in the negative sense of active disillusionment with earlier dreams of a socialist future. This was manifest in their writing. The disenchantment with the Communist party that came with rejection of its dominance over literary creation gained in intensity with the purge trials of the late 1930s in the Soviet Union and the Soviet-Nazi Pact of 1939. Many who had become anti-Stalinists and turned to the Trotskyist group gradually abandoned even this degree of commitment. In a sense, then, the characterization of some at least of the *Menorah* group as "the uncommitted" or "the unpossessed," as Tess Slesinger had called them, finally proved prophetic. The same was true of many in the *Partisan Review* group, which overlapped the *Commentary* writers. William Phillips, a founding editor of the *Partisan*, wrote in 1976, speaking of those years, that a sincere socialist had to think hard before leaving the Communist party, for, he said, "if one broke with the Communists, one had to retire from effective, radical, organized politics." He went on to suggest that the dilemma confronting a sincere radical at that time was real.

Mostly, the 30's was a period of contradictions. It was a time of sense and nonsense. . . . The trouble starts when we try to figure out the exact relation of sense to nonsense, of right to wrong, both in the radical tradition and in the swing away from it toward the Center and the Right. For this means we must decide whether the radicalism of the 30's was an aberration of a movement in the main line of history, or both, and whether the anti-radical mind that followed was a reaction against being taken in or a reconciliation with things as they are.[30]

The intense revulsion from the Communist party and Stalinism on the part of many young literary people in the late 1930s, reinforced by the recoil from the Nazi-Stalin Pact in 1939, is an essential aspect of the American literary picture of the period. Some central figures in this trend realized that the reaction had sometimes gone too far. Indeed, so deep was hostility to the Soviet Union that it led a number of writers and intellectuals, even those influenced by Trotskyism, to oppose the war against Nazism (despite Trotsky's own position that the Soviet Union should be defended) as an imperialist war on both sides (some were pacifists) or to remain neutral. And as Irving Howe observed, "Later, in the 40's and 50's, most of the New York intellectuals would abandon the effort to find a renewed basis for a socialist politics—to their serious discredit, I believe."[31] In the heyday of McCarthyism some even opposed McCarthy equivocally, or not at all. By the 1950s they joined in the "American celebration" of postwar prosperity. Both *Partisan Review* and *Commentary* failed in their obligations as organs of the intellectual. *Partisan*, writes Howe, "failed to speak out with enough force and persistence," and "*Commentary*, and Elliot Cohen's editorship, was still more inclined to minimize the threat of McCarthyism." Cohen had written, in 1952, that "in the popular mind" McCarthy was just a "blowhard," and "his only support as a great national figure is from the fascinated fears of the intelligentsia."[32] The American Committee for Cultural Freedom, later exposed as a CIA-funded operation, was the dominant organizational influence among them. Indeed, as Philip Rahv observed in 1952, for some, "anti-Stalinism has become almost a professional stance. It has come to mean so much that it excludes nearly all other concerns and ideas." Thus, trying to convert anti-Stalinism into "a total outlook on life," they even found it "easier to put up with a political bum like Senator McCarthy."

At this time the attitudes of the important intellectuals, creative writers and social scientists, most of them Jewish, were indeed exposed in the *Partisan Review* symposium beginning in the May-June, 1952 issue of "Our Country and Our Culture," and continuing for the next two issues. The editorial preface heralded the United States as the "protector of Western Civilization, at least in a military and economic sense" and obviously this was "a new image of America." So deeply were they drawn into an uncritical view of the country that they uttered literary statements soon to be discredited by literary events in the 1960s. "Most writers," the editorial said, "no longer accept alienation as the artist's fate in America.... More and more writers have ceased to think of themselves as rebels and exiles." The only cloud they could see on the horizon was the "enormous and ever-increasing growth of mass culture—... which converts culture into a commodity." Mass culture not only removes the artist from "his natural audience," but also deprives the people of the art for "their human and aesthetic" needs. The editors apparently did not connect this apprehension with their earlier statement that the writers "no longer think of themselves as exiles." Nor did they apply the Marxism of their earlier days when they held that mass culture "converts culture into a commodity" or had perceived that one root of mass culture they deplored was the immense profits to be derived from it.[33] Hence, they abandoned the radicalism of their younger days as an artistic and intellectual imperative. What C. Wright Mills—he did not then regard himself as a Marxist—said in his response to the symposium might have reminded them: the "leveling and the frenzy effects of mass culture" was not owing to " 'democracy' but to capitalist commercialism which manipulates people into standardized tastes and then exploits these tastes and 'personal touches' as marketable brands."[34]

Among the numerous responses from mostly Jewish intellectuals, "a drift which is noticeable," is "toward conformism."[35] *Partisan* editor William Phillips noted that in some of the symposiasts, there was "an overadjustment to reality, marked by an uncritical acceptance of everything American."[36] Editor Philip Rahv remarked on "the rise of a neo-philistine tendency...

growth of the mood of acceptance and of the defensive reaction to Communism, which, if unchecked by the revival of the critical spirit, threatens
to submerge the tradition of dissent in American writing."[37] For instance,
Lionel Trilling, the link of critical continuity between the old *Menorah* group
and the *Partisan* group, commented that the current (1952) cultural situation
was better than that of thirty years earlier. One reason, he went on, was
the tendency has become "apparent," that "wealth shows a tendency to
submit itself to the rule of mind and intellect." In a limited sense, this was
true, with the rise of a growing "new intellectual class" to which the mon-
eyed class turned for standards of taste. What Trilling does not say, and
surely once knew, was that such taste was so far removed from any direct
challenge to the power of wealth over the system, that the affluent consumer
could have his taste and hold onto his money. But Trilling was too sophisticated and world-weary not to remain critical of some aspects of education
and of our cultural life. So he concluded that "a reaffirmation and rediscovery of America can go hand in hand with the tradition of critical non-
conformity."[38] What is apparent throughout Trilling's statement is the
isolation of the "cultural" as a separate, largely autonomous world. Yet,
incredible as it may seem, Trilling uttered not one word about the most
serious contemporary threat to our intellectual, cultural, and political life,
McCarthyism, which was then at a hysterical level.

Some of the symposiasts dissented from the assumptions of the symposium. Norman Mailer expressed "total disagreement" and "dared" to suggest
that the major novelists of the time—he mentioned Dos Passos, Farrell,
Faulkner, Steinbeck, and Hemingway, since the end of World War II when
their work had moved from "alienation to varying degrees of acceptance"—
had been "barren and flatulent."[39] C. Wright Mills, who was one of the
most influential dissenting intellectuals of the period until his death in 1961,
agreed that a change had come over American intellectuals to "a shrinking
deference to the status quo; often to a soft and anxious compliance."[40]
Irving Howe also dissented from the generalized love of "America" in the
magazine's introductory statement, affirming that there are some things
about America he admired while others, like "the drive against civil liberties"
and "the trend toward conformism" disturbed him. He even went so far as
to declare that "Marxism seems to me the best available method for understanding and making history."[41] And Delmore Schwartz, who was to be
the harbinger of a wave of postwar literary creativity by Jewish writers,
strenuously dissented. "The will to conformism which is now the chief
prevailing fashion among intellectuals," he wrote," ... is a flight from the
flux, chaos and uncertainty of the present, or forced and false affirmation
of stability in the face of immense and continually mounting instability."[42]
He stressed the urgency of non-conformism in the face of mass culture.

By 1952, the date of the symposium, the growing importance of Jews in literature had not yet emerged into full awareness. True, Jews like Norman Mailer and Irwin Shaw had written widely read war books; Jews had contributed significantly to the increasingly prestigious *Partisan Review* and *Commentary*. Alfred Kazin's *On Native Grounds* (1942) was a recognized account of American prose in this century. Lionel Trilling was achieving recognition as one of the most influential teachers of English and, to a lesser extent, American literature. Saul Bellow had published two highly regarded novels. Yet it was only as the 1950s wore on, with its parade of best-sellers by Jews and the emergence of widely discussed new novelists like Bernard Malamud and Philip Roth, that a full realization of the new literary importance of Jewish writers moved into the center of public consciousness.

In April, 1961 *Commentary* returned to the symposium form to explore the theme of "Jewishness and the Younger Intellectuals." Norman Podhoretz's editorial introduction recalled the largely unfavorable response to the 1944 symposium of the *Contemporary Jewish Record*, which condemned the contemporary form of Jewishness as middle-class chauvinism and sterility, if not worse. But, said Podhoretz, "ten years later at least half of them had become enthusiasts of Martin Buber." In a sense this marked no change, since Buber himself was an anti-Establishment religious and social radical. What was new was the specifically Jewish interest—in Hasidism, for instance—which this turn to Buber involved. The magazine further noted that "the Jews in America had arrived. Discrimination had declined sharply; anti-Semitism was in great disrepute," and, quoting Benjamin DeMott, the Jew now had "a place in the establishment." Surprisingly Norman Podhoretz concluded from the thirty-one respondents (only four women!), most of them under thirty-five, that they did not share their older fellow Jewish intellectuals' awakened interest in "the Jewish heritage and ... the community which is committed to preserving and extending that heritage." They seem rather a reversion to the attitude expressed in the 1944 symposium, except that their view is indifferent, in contrast to the hostility of their elders. Additionally, they tended to identify "the essence of Judaism" with the "struggle for universal justice and human brotherhood," but they believed "their kind of Jewishness provides little hope for the survival of even those Jewish traditions which they admire."[43]

It did not follow, however, from this lack of Jewish commitment, that the Jews tended to be neglected as the subject of fiction, or that the importance of this in American fiction as a whole slackened. On the contrary, Jewish writers in considerable numbers continued to emerge every few years. Jewish characters and milieu in fiction did not diminish during the 1960s. Writing out of their own experience, such writers naturally drew on the Jewish aspects of that experience and were not inhibited from doing so, as the Jew in fiction was already largely accepted by both the literary and the general community. Another of the growing signs of this new situation was publication of the 1964 anthology, *Breakthrough: A Treasury of Contemporary American-Jewish Literature*, edited by Irving Malin and Irwin Stark, containing fiction, non-fiction, and poetry.

Evidence of the centrality of the Jewish writer was a satirical treatment of the Jewish writer as literary celebrity in John Updike's *Bech* (1970). On a visit to Israel for a lecture in 1978 Updike was asked if there was a "Jewish Mafia" in United States publishing. "Well," he replied, "I don't like the term, but it's true that Jews have penetrated all aspects of publishing from sales and promotion to editing and reviewing. I do think that Jewish critics, of whom there are a multitude, do tend to respond more warmly to Jewish writers.... Well, critics like Fiedler and Trilling I'd hardly call provincial." He then added a pregnant characterization: "Jewish writers do have a facility with the rhythms of urban American life that gentile writers seem to lack." There is enough truth in this statement to give it significance. He was asked why he undertook the series of short stories for the *New Yorker* around the Jewish writer, Henry Bech, later assembled as the novel. Updike admitted that he started doing them after he felt he "was being unfairly treated by *Commentary*."[44]

One might suspect from the terms used in the interview—Jews "penetrated" publishing, that Jewish critics show partiality for Jewish writers, that the stories are a response to what he considered unfair treatment, that there is some anti-Semitic animus in the book. This is not the case. The Jewish writer-celebrity was fair game for Updike's tongue-in-cheek treatment of Bech, but there is no suggestion of hostility toward Jews. Bech is depicted as a *shlemiel*, a writer on tour for the State Department exchange program to the Soviet Union, Rumania, and Bulgaria, at a lecture date at a Virginia woman's college, at a London trip for lionization to publicize the appearance of a novel, and finally at his admittance to the National Academy of Arts and Sciences. At nearly each stop there is some sexual involvement, as well as several at home.

There are numerous small, superficial allusions to Jewishness, as well as some Yiddish phrases in the novel. Bech's own Jewishness cannot rise above the author's superficiality in this respect. Updike recognizes the conflicting attitudes in some Jewish writers when he says Bech was praised for "his own quixotic, excessively tender, strangely anti-Semitic Semitic sensibility." Updike also suggests the idea attributed to Bech, that "the artistic triumph of American Jewry lay ... not in the novels of the fifties but in the movies of the thirties, those gargantuan, crass contraptions whereby Jewish brains projected Gentile stars upon a gentile nation and out of their own immigrant joy gave a formless land dreams and even a kind of conscience." To an interviewer, Bech seems to be speaking for Updike's own view of current Jewish writing when he says that Bech "was sustained, insofar as he was sustained, by the memory of laughter, the specifically Jewish, embattled, religious, sufficiently desperate, not quite belly laughter of his father and his father's brothers, his beloved Brooklyn uncles; that the American Jews had kept the secret of this laughter a generation later than the Gentiles, hence their present domination of the literary world."[45] Updike appends a "Bibliography" of writings by and about Bech, which is a clever, very funny satire on current scholarly bibliographies on every conceivable aspect of the work of contemporary writers. If the novel is not taken too seriously, it can be read as a witty, satirical view of writers of the Jewish literary ascendancy of the 1950s and 1960s.

One final sign. Elizabeth Hardwick looks back on her early days as an aspiring writer in her native Kentucky after World War II: "I do not consider myself a Southern writer," she told an interviewer in 1979. "Even when I was in college 'down home,' I'm afraid my aim was—if it doesn't sound too ridiculous—my aim was to be a New York Jewish intellectual. I say 'Jewish' because of their tradition of rational skepticism; and also a certain deracination appeals to me—and their openness to European culture... [and] the questioning of the arrangements of society called radicalism."[46]

# 2

# The Jewish Decade: The 1950s

The unprecedented unleashing of creative energies by Jewish writers by the 1950s, both quantitatively and qualitatively was so abundant that this outpouring, together with unprecedented receptivity to their writing by the general American public, justifies calling the 1950s the "Jewish Decade." Many of the best-selling novels by Jewish authors were popular fiction. The 1950s opened with *The Wall* by John Hersey, a non-Jew's fictional rendering of the Warsaw Ghetto Uprising. Herman Wouk's *The Caine Mutiny* dominated the best seller lists in 1951 and 1952. Leon Uris initiated his series of commercial successes with *Battle Cry* in 1953. Also in 1953 Saul Bellow forged into general notice with his *The Adventures of Augie March*, which won the National Book Award. In 1955 Herman Wouk repeated his earlier commercial success with *Marjorie Morningstar*. Gerald Green's *The Last Angry Man* in 1956 was widely read. The self-hating Harvardian in Myron S. Kaufmann's *Remember Me to God* in 1957 attracted great attention, as did Meyer Levin's *Compulsion* about the Loeb-Leopold murder in Chicago. In 1958 came the phenomenal success of Leon Uris' *Exodus*, an account of the illegal immigration to Palestine and the creation of the State of Israel. Bernard Malamud won the National Book Award for *The Magic Barrel*, published in 1958. And Philip Roth's *Goodbye Columbus*, published in the next year, also won the National Book Award.

Although appearances of the Jew as author and subject had been growing rapidly in quantity, quality, and importance for some time, beginning in the 1940s, the realization of the significance of this development came slowly. In the summer of 1949 I had noted that "Scant attention has been paid to an interesting development in recent years in American fiction, the increasing appearance of the Jewish character."[1] Even when *Partisan Review* conducted a symposium on "The State of American Writing: 1948" (August,

1948), of the nine respondents only three were Jewish, and of these, only Leslie Fiedler mentioned the Jewish element in current literature. But as the 1950s drew on, this reality became indefeasible, and by 1959 this trend received recognition in the London *Times Literary Supplement*. A special issue on "The American Imagination" included one essay on "A Vocal Group: The Jewish Part in American Letters." "Since about 1950," the article noted, " . . . American Jewish writing [has emerged] as a dominant force in American letters." The most important Jewish figures whose influence was "decisive," the article notes, were the critics Lionel Trilling, Alfred Kazin, Philip Rahv, Leslie Fiedler, and Irving Howe; among fiction writers, Bellow, Malamud, and in drama, Arthur Miller ("our most solid and serious playwright"); the poets Karl Shapiro, Delmore Schwartz, Howard Nemeroff, and Stanley Kunitz; and the *Partisan Review* and *Commentary* exerted an "unquestioned influence." There was also a "growing group of younger poets, fiction writers, and critics who are beginning to rise in prominence." All this happened without any attempt on anyone's part to suppress the Jewish identity or significance of their work. "The sense of Jewishness remains," said the article, "but it is a painless one."[2]

What a radical change in taste and mood this represents can be judged from some observations that fiction writer Yuri Suhl made during the 1940s. In his contribution to a *Congress Weekly* symposium on "Why I Wrote a Jewish Novel," Suhl expressed the belief that "the Jewish theme" was "as integral a part of the broad stream of American literature as the American-Jewish community is of the American scene generally." On seeking a publisher for his novel, *One Foot in America* (1950), he found that "many editors and publishers do not share this view," and they "persist in treating the Jewish theme as a second-class citizen in the community of literature." One publisher, he added, rejected his manuscript "because he had recently published a book on the Jewish theme and did not want to be 'stigmatized' as a Jewish house."[3]

Although the Jewish theme was problematic for publishers until mid-century, anti-Semitism was far less often encountered in fiction after the 1920s. If the Jew had been a sensitive subject before the 1930s, he became more so with the growth of Nazism and its influence even in this country. Pre–World War II agitation of pro-fascist demagogues, which included anti-Semitic incitement, sensitized the subject, and this sensitivity endured not only through the war but afterward. The popular media tended to avoid "controversial" issues in popular entertainment so as not to jeopardize, as they believed, their investments. In 1944 the newly awakened Jewishness of Ben Hecht led him to complain, "the greatest single Jewish phenomenon in the last twenty years has been the almost complete disappearance of the Jew from American fiction, stage, radio, and movies."[4] Hecht was exaggerating, of course, but there was limited validity to his charge, at least as far as popular culture was concerned. The Jew certainly did not "disappear" from literature, as is obvious from our account. But the entrepreneurs of the mass arts were unwilling to risk "controversy" and did at least soft-pedal the Jewish presence in their products.

In a densely documented article in 1952, Henry Popkin commented on this reluctance to introduce Jewish characters into the mass arts. He noted a score of novels and plays which, when transferred to the mass media of paperbacks or the movies, dropped the Jewish names and ambience and changed names and situations to eliminate the Jewishness of the original. Paperback editions of some Jewish gangster novels were either softened or altogether eliminated Jewish-name characters.[5] Businessmen were especially anxious to avoid drawing attention of Jewish defense organizations, especially the Anti-Defamation League (ADL). The ADL had often gone into action against a work that they considered unfavorable to the Jew and thus, they charged, reinforced anti-Semitism, even though many regarded the intervention as unwarranted. Consequently in those years something like a taboo of Jewish characters obtained in the movies, radio, and paperbacks. Both Ben Hecht and Henry Popkin deplored the disappearance of Jewish dialect comedy, but this seems rather an advance in public taste and rejection of the blatant stereotype.

That the sensitivity of the Jew as subject was no idle assumption was evidenced from a statement by Arthur Miller in 1947, a few years after publishing *Focus*.

I think I gave up the Jew as literary material because I was afraid that even an innocent allusion to the individual wrongdoing of an individual Jew would be inflamed by the atmosphere ignited by the hatred I suddenly was aware of, and my love could be twisted into a weapon of persecution against Jews.... No good writing can approach material in that atmosphere.... I turned away from Jews as material for my work.[6]

Not until 1964, with *After the Fall* and *Incident at Vichy*, did Miller again introduce a Jewish character, though some critics saw the Jewish character behind the nominally non-Jews in *All My Sons* (1947) and *Death of a Salesman* (1949).

How then to account for public acceptance of the Jew in literature only a few years later and movement of the Jew into the center of American literature? One reason may have been the opening up in public discussion of the problem of anti-Semitism. During the war itself Arthur Miller had written the novel *Focus* (1945), in which he places a non-Jew with anti-Semitic tendencies into a situation in which he experiences what it means to be himself a target of anti-Semitic prejudice. The genteel, commonplace WASP, Lawrence Newman of Brooklyn, is a personnel manager of an anti-Semitic firm. His poor eyesight causes him to hire a Jew unknowingly. He is reprimanded and ordered to wear glasses. But the glasses give him the "look of a Jew," and, because of this, with his name, he is suspected of being a clandestine Jew. Unable to endure his ambiguous situation, he quits his job. He is now everywhere taken for a Jew. The woman he marries had previously lived with a coordinator of anti-Semitic groups, and she urges Newman to join the Christian Front, an active pro-fascist, anti-Semitic organization. When the Newmans are turned away from a summer resort as Jews, the wife is furious at Newman for not being more militantly anti-Jewish. At a Front meeting in Manhattan he is taken for a Jew and roughed up because he doesn't automatically applaud. At home garbage is spilled on his lawn by anti-Semites. Newman now finds himself in the same situation as the corner newsdealer, Finkelstein, whom he has come to respect as an individual. One night he is set upon by Christian Front thugs in front of Finkelstein's store; the newsdealer emerges swinging a bat and disperses the toughs. Instead of complying with his wife's urging to talk to the Front leader, Newman moves together with Finkelstein to resist the Front and reports the incident to the police, offering to identify his assailants.

The novel contributed to raising the issue of resistance to anti-Semitism at the time, and today it has documentary value as evidence of forms of overt anti-Semitism in the 1930s and 1940s. Newman is a passive, dull, conformist figure, but when the reality of anti-Semitism is brought home to him in intimate personal terms, he shifts toward active resistance.

Far more successful in helping break down the taboo against the Jew in the popular media, however, was the widely read *Gentleman's Agreement* (1947) by Laura Z. Hobson, which was high on the best-seller list for over a year. This popularly written novel and the movie quickly made of it led to a widespread discussion of anti-Semitism in the exclusion of Jews from some residential Connecticut towns. Philip Schuyler Green, a basically unprejudiced non-Jewish journalist, is asked to write a series of articles on "I Was a Jew for Eight Weeks." As in *Focus*, a non-Jew is again put into the position of a Jew. Because he is now specifically sensitized to the issue, he reacts sharply against the response to his supposed Jewishness from his magazine colleagues, from his family, from his upwardly mobile Jewish secretary who has changed her name out of self-hatred, from social clubs, from the taunting of his son, and from the residue of prejudice in girlfriends. Finally he is rebuffed trying to buy a house in Darien. Anti-Semitism in all phases of his life begins to spread like a growing oil slick. He learns, especially through his new relations with his girlfriend, that up to now, despite the absence of prejudice in himself, he had tolerated anti-Semitism because he had felt he could do nothing about it. But now he realizes that he needs to resist it actively wherever it occurs. When his friend David Goldman returns from the army, he tells Dave how he feels repeatedly devastated by the experience. Dave replies, "You're not insulated yet, Phil. It's new every time, so the impact must be quite a business." One doesn't get "indifferent to it," he goes on, but "you aren't as quick and raw. You're concentrating a lifetime thing into a few weeks; You're *making* the thing happen every day.... The facts are no different, but it does telescope it."[7]

The novel is slick and facile, but it does expose varieties of anti-Semitism and is vivid enough to make one angry at the phenomenon. In addition to its exposure of injury to Jews, the novel tries to stress the moral damage done to themselves by the perpetrators of anti-Semitism. It is extremely difficult to gauge the social effects of this novel or of *Focus*. What is clear is that the fact of a wide readership indicated a growing interest in bringing the problem into the open instead of allowing it to fester in a suppressed existence.

Other reasons for Jewish entry to the literary mainstream were many and mutually reinforcing. This outcome was a stage in a long-range trend, the maturation of an acculturated second generation come of age in large numbers. They were free Americans aspiring to achievement in the arts, as well as the professions and business. Despite the discouragement from short-sighted editors and publishers in the late 1940s and early 1950s, they persisted. They overcame not only because of quality of writing, but also because their writing was viable in the marketplace. Out of the large reservoir of talent on which the second generation drew were an impressive number of literary artists. Some Jewish writers quickly became recognized as successful popular commercial writers who made their publishers rich; others gained recognition as serious writers. Obvious public interest finally overcame commercial timidity.

Public interest in the Jews was greatly enhanced after the war by the revelation of the Holocaust and the protracted struggle for the establishment of the State of Israel. These events did a great deal to reduce the exoticism with which the Jew was regarded. Jews could be treated in literature as individuals, rather than a stereotype, to a greater extent than ever before. Nor can one overlook the fact that millions of American participants in the war had been brought into contact with Jews, which contributed to their demystification.

Overt anti-Semitism, so widespread during the war and afterward, gradually diminished. The sociologist Dennis H. Wrong in 1965 could write of "the striking decline in the prevalence of anti-Semitic beliefs and attitudes in the United States."[8] An important study of anti-Semitism in the 1960s, however, induced caution that anti-Semitic beliefs were still widespread but were different from earlier periods because they did not affect behavior significantly. As Gertrude Selznick and Stephen Stember expressed it in their study, "acceptance of negative stereotypes far outruns support of discrimination."[9] In other words, while anti-Semitism in some degree in beliefs and attitudes of perhaps two-thirds of all Americans persisted, they are not used to arrest opportunity for Jews. A remarkable change, for instance, took place after the war with respect to college teaching. Millions of young veterans streamed into the colleges with financing provided under the GI

Bill of Rights, and thousands of college teachers had to be hired to teach them. In this expansion the previous barriers to Jews in college teaching fell away, and thousands of Jews were hired in every branch of learning and in administration.

Other influences bore on the lowering of overt anti-Semitism. The small Jewish immigration under restrictive laws failed to provide obvious "foreigners" who might serve as targets of prejudice. Also, extensive devastation in Europe from World War II and depletion of peacetime inventories afforded American industry an immense market during the postwar decades. The country entered an almost unprecedented period of affluence, thus reducing the need for scapegoats. Dennis H. Wrong reports in his study that there was evidence not only of a decline of anti-Semitism, but also "of a general decline in ethnic and racial prejudice" as well.[10] This does not mean, of course, that discrimination had disappeared altogether. The doors of the executive suite were still closed to Jews in the large utilities, banks, and heavy industry, and elite social clubs as E. Digby Baltzell showed in *The Protestant Establishment*. The literary scene, however, was open to talent, and many Jewish writers qualified and published in considerable numbers.

## ACCULTURATION ADVANCES

Whatever inhibiting influences existed in the 1940s and 1950s, however, novels with Jewish characters and some with acculturation themes continued to appear. A recognized short story writer like Hortense Calisher was not at all reluctant to draw occasionally on her experience as a Jew. She wanted to be herself, "what I was," and "it simply never occurred to me" not to treat her own mode of experience as a Jew in America with her ethnic "mixture." This is borne out in her stories. Unlike most Jewish writers of recent generations who were East European, she came of a second-generation German-Jewish father and a first-generation German-Jewish mother. Her family lived in the South in comfortable circumstances. Calisher asserts that "with some Jews later," she was "compromised"[11] because she "had no recent *shtetl* tradition"; indeed, she had never heard of the *shtetl* until she later read about it and "met its traces in friends."[12] She was even suspected of trying to conceal an awareness of the *shtetl* and a knowledge of Yiddish, so much were such signs of origin taken for granted by many. These stories dealing with Jewish characters are largely limited to the German Jews, whom she knows best. Her stories, written during the 1940s and 1950s, show a particularly lively awareness of anti-Semitism. She had little patience with self-deception concerning Jewishness. Her sequence of stories about Hester Elkin from age ten to marriage contain few allusions, but one of the stories, "The Old Stock," published in the *New Yorker* in 1950, concerned a self-hating Jewish mother. The story evoked a storm of disapproving mail and even newspaper comment. In her autobiography, *Herself* (1974), Calisher writes that the story "touched on the same self-hatred and secret fears; I have dared to imply that Jews are not impeccable."[13]

In the story Hester and her mother go to the South Farm in the Catskills. The mother in the story is obviously based on her own mother as described in her autobiography, a self-hating German Jew who despised East European Jews as endangering her social position and who, in the vivid words of the story, which might also describe her own mother, gave a "prim display of extra constraint...in the presence of other Jews whose grosser features, voices, manners, offended her sense of gentility all the more out of her resentful fears that she might be identified with them." Mother and daughter visit an old local aristocrat, Miss Onderdonk, with whom they were acquainted from other years at the farm. Miss Onderdonk complains, "I told Miss Smith she'd rue the day she ever started taking in Jews." Mrs. Elkins replies, "I thought you knew that we were—Hebrews." " 'Say it,' Hester prayed,...say 'Jew.' " With the self-assurance of the bigot the old lady observes, "...ain't no Jew. Good blood shows any day....Can't say it didn't cross my mind. Thought that the girl does have the look."[14] Back at the farm, Mrs. Elkins' hostile attitude toward her fellow Jewish guests also aroused the epistolary ire of some Jewish readers. Calisher observes in her autobiography that in this story she had excited such vehement defensive responses because she had "expressed some of these tormenting self-doubts of even the most outwardly impregnable Jew—rich, assimilated, cosmopolitan, living an easy life scarcely subject to slurs, much less oppression. ...Are 'we' anything like 'they' say we are?...I had explored what must never be admitted to enemy forces—that there are divisions in our ranks,— ...hierarchies. I had turned up the under side of our snobberies."[15]

Anti-Semitism is explored in other stories, in "Two Colonels" and "The Hollow Boy." Social anti-Semitism at college is treated in "One of the Chosen." At a twenty-year reunion of his college victory crew, for which he was coxswain, David Spanner is reminiscing with Number One oar, Anderson, "effortlessly debonair and assured." After catching up on the past, Anderson tells Spanner,

"Remember the house I used to belong to?...The one that got into the news in the thirties because they hung a swastika over the door. Or maybe somebody hung it on *them*....Could have been either way." Then, more confidentially, "You know, Davy....I wanted to take you in....A few of us together could have pushed it through—but all the others made such a God-damned stink over it, we gave in. I suppose you heard....If we hadn't been so damned unseeing, so sure of ourselves in those days....Ah, well,...That's water over the dam."

He gave Spanner a "brotherly slap on the back, and turned away embarrassed. Standing there, it was as if Spanner felt the flat of it, not between his shoulder blades, but stinging on his suddenly hot cheek—that sharp slap of revelation."[16]

Calisher remarks in her autobiography that, after these short stories, "I could not write of Jews again until [the novel] *The New Yorkers* [1964]."[17] In that novel her Jewish characters accept their Jewishness in a relaxed manner. The central character, Judge Mannix, tells his rabbi, "every martyr's alredy half self-made, don't you think?...We all half chose to be victims—to be the chosen."[18] Because, I suppose, they reject either extreme, defensiveness or intimidation, about their identity. The earlier stories had been written from this conviction. They resisted both hypersensitivity and outright anti-Semitism in others.

In this postwar period the acculturation novel was far from an exhausted genre, but continued to be practiced and even read in great numbers by a popular audience. Sam Ross' *The Sidewalks Are Free* (1950), a typical example, is the story of the boyhood of Hershey Malov between 1910 and 1923 and the weakening of his Jewish ties. "In one generation thousands of years of tradition had been lightly thrown away."[19] The essence of the story is the conflict between the old and new values. The father rejects the new, but not to affirm specifically Jewish values but the more general human values of respect for craft rather than money. "I don't care for a world that makes whores out of people.... Measure a man by what he does, the love he has for his family, his not hurting people, his respect for people."[20] This is a cautionary tale against the negative aspects of acculturation.

The problem of intermarriage was a constant feature of the novel of acculturation from the beginning. So absorbed in this problem is Beatrice Levin's *The Lonely Room* (1950) that, although timed just before and after World War II, it is no different in spirit from novels written years before. Located in Providence, Rhode Island, Beth Brickman's family's "Jewishness ...centered in a set of customs and practices more traditional than religious, more stomach than heart, more superstition than culture."[21] They were nevertheless opposed to a young Italian man's courtship of Beth: "Better you should be dead than married to...this Nick."[22] World War II intervenes and Nick goes overseas while Beth, in the Women's Army Corps, encounters some anti-Semitism. Nick marries a French nurse who dies in childbirth. When he returns home with his child, he and Beth overcome resistance to intermarriage, are reconciled, and marry.

The varieties of acculturation among prosperous, established Jews without any radicalism in their history, unlike the experience of East European Jews, are explored in *The Pedlocks* (1951) by the versatile Stephen Longstreet—painter, playwright, and screen writer, as well as novelist. The story follows a Jewish family from its settlement in the United States in the seventeenth century to the post–World War II world, presenting the Southern Jewish family in some detail from 1860 on. Longstreet himself comes of a Jewish family (his grandfather changed his original name of "Wiener-

Langstrasse" to "Longstreet"), and he writes that the Pedlocks "were once living people" and despite adjustments for fictional reasons, "they are the people I once knew."[23] Joseph Pedlock, a major in the Confederate Army, marries Rebecca Manderscheids, whose three children, each of whom, respectively, marries into a German-Jewish garment manufacturer's family, a Boston Brahmin family, and a Russian working-class family. In the next generation we see a mining magnate, an avant-garde esthete, and a Zionist. Several modes of integration into American life are depicted, from retention of Orthodoxy to a mixed marriage and temporary repudiation of Jewishness. Fifteen years later Longstreet followed this with *Pedlock & Sons* (1966), a slickly told story of the German-Jewish branch of the family that built up a national retail business in the mid-nineteenth century and of their progeny. Also important to the tale is an eighty-five-year-old Pedlock, married to a highly sophisticated sixty-year-old man who strains credulity as a scholar and secret promoter of Hasidism. Both books are entertaining and sold well.

Perhaps the most extensive fiction on the acculturation theme was Charles Angoff's series of nine novels chronicling the life of the Polansky family from its European *shtetl* origins to second-generation integration into American life. We may assume the series to have a full autobiographical element. Like Angoff's own family, the Polanskys settled in Boston about 1904. Angoff wrote the series after serving as editorial aide to Henry L. Mencken from the 1930s on, and later as editor of *The American Mercury*. The first volume, *Journey to the Dawn* (1951), is largely concerned with a persecuted *shtetl* existence in Tsarist Russia and final emigration to Boston. Central to the series is the life and career for the second-generation David Polansky, representing Angoff himself. David's schooling and aspirations occupy the next few volumes. His Harvard years are recorded in *The Sun at Noon* (1955), ending in 1923, with some estrangement from his Old World father and experience of discrimination, but retention of a positive feeling for Jewish ritual and customs. In subsequent volumes, David goes to New York to become a journalist and writer. His experience widens, and the varied careers and futures of friends and other members of his family are pursued. In the fifth volume, *The Bitter Spring* (1961) David works on a national magazine (*The American Mercury*) and gives a revealing sketch of its editor (H. L. Mencken). The sixth volume, *Summer Storm* (1963), deals with the Roosevelt New Deal era and the problem of intermarriage. The three final volumes carry the story forward. The entire series is a leisurely, well-informed, deeply sympathetic account of immigrant life and the problems and trials of a variety of characters of the second generation connected with the life of the central figure. Few novels of American-Jewish life exhibit a similar nostalgic and positive feeling for Jewish tradition even as this is strained and tested by its relations with Zionism, socialism, Hasidism, and national nihilism in their relations to conflicting elements in general American life. Such problems receive as full documentation in this series of novels as almost anywhere else in English-language fiction, presenting a large variety of Jews in whom these problems are exemplified.

One aspect of acculturation that was fairly common was the abandonment of radicalism by revolutionary emigrants from Tsarist Russia after success in this country. One such tale is Sam Astrachan's *An End to Dying* (1956). Before emigration the Kogan family had revolutionaries among them. However, after immigration their radicalism soon disappears. One erstwhile radical becomes prosperous in the United States, and nothing more is heard of his radicalism. The story begins in Russia, where the Jacob Kogan family is one of the wealthiest in the country and the rich Jewish society of St. Petersburg is pictured. They all avoid Yiddish but speak German and French as well as Russian. Kogan's fortune is confiscated by the Revolution, he himself is killed, and the family immigrates to the United States. They become garment manufacturers and ship owners. Kogan's son Larry is employed by his uncle Louis Cohen, but he complains about working conditions. His uncle, he says, "is as bad as the Tsar, as black as blackest Russia. I came to America to be free—very free I am! I've hardly enough to eat.... It is slavery.... In Russia we tried a revolution.... We can revolt in New York City, as in Russia."[24] But Larry becomes a manager of his uncle's business, and we hear no more talk of revolution. The lives of other branches of the family are also pursued, and much of contemporary Jewish life is pictured. Unfortunately, the novel has no focus, but is rather a narrative without specific direction. The only element of coherence is family life and a pervasive, vague cynicism.

A gifted writer who emerged after World War II and wrote extensively about Jewish characters is Herbert Gold. Many of his stories center about adolescence and young manhood in the Cleveland suburb of Lakewood. Jewishness as such figures little in the early part of *Therefore Be Bold* (1960) until the young Dan Berman falls in love in the 1930s with the non-Jewish Eva Masters, whose father is a virulent anti-Semite proponent of the anti-Black, anti-Semitic Black Legion and hates Dan. "The very ground you walk on. You poison the earth. You corrupt our civilization. You brought commerce and money into the West." Masters forbids Dan to see his daughter. "Don't you all act alike?" he tells him. "Haven't I met your kind before? the tribe? in business and every place I go? the law offices?"[25] Although Eva defies her father and continues to go out with Dan, they do not marry. Gold later published a novel based on his own father, *Fathers* (1966), beginning with the family in Europe, the father's immigration at the turn of the century as a boy of twelve, and his buildup of a produce business in Cleveland. In nearby Lakewood, he hires thugs to beat up an anti-Semitic produce merchant in retaliation for an anti-Semitic slur. The son's career is followed through the army during World War II, showing the anti-Semitism he meets and resists there. Through the turbulent 1960s and onward the acculturation novel proves itself a hardy literary genre, with such novels as Barbara Probst Solomon's *The Best of Life* (1960), James Yaffe's *Nobody Does You Any Favors* (1966), Zelda Popkin's *Herman Had Two Daughters* (1968), among others.

As the 1950s and 1960s wore on, anti-Semitism continued to be depicted in fiction by non-Jews. Among the non-Jewish writers, Sloan Wilson exposed the anti-social nature of anti-Semitism in his immensely popular *The Man in the Gray Flannel Suit* (1955). This novel was one of a number that were typical products of the 1950s. It caught the mood of conformism and rendered in fiction what sociologists had been describing in analytical prose. These novels heightened this sense of the decade by depicting characters who resisted the trend, and among those who rebelled were Jews. Dr. Abelson of *The Last Angry Man* was one of them. Judge Saul Bernstein of Sloan Wilson's *The Man in the Gray Flannel Suit* was another, one of the most widely read novels of the decade. Judge Bernstein is a maverick in the midst of the corporate society of the Organization Man, the name given to those who lost their identity in their identification with corporate interests. He is a probate judge, a model of personal integrity and sensitivity to the demands of "justice." He is a lawyer in a Connecticut coastal town, and chose to be a probate judge rather than a lawyer or a judge required to impose sentence because he was reluctant to send men to long prison terms or even to death. In his view, a verdict was valid only when the judge was fully informed about the totality of circumstances, as well as the law. In probate cases he was better able to approximate such knowledge, as was demonstrated in his exposure of fraud in the inheritance of the central character. Despite the high opinion in which Bernstein is held in the community, "he and his wife were rarely asked to cocktail or dinners, but he was almost always appointed moderator at town meetings."[26] Limited acceptance of Bernstein here coexists with social discrimination in a 1950s middle-class community.

At the same time we find anti-Semitism manifested by a few non-Jewish writers during the 1950s, such as James Gould Cozzens and Katherine Anne Porter, but they are exceptions. While I am not aware of anti-Semitism in the work of non-Jewish writers who emerged after the 1930s, it is significant that both Cozzens and Porter are writers of the older generation: Cozzens was born in 1903 and Porter in 1890. Neither ever succeeded in shaking off the widespread WASP prejudice of the pre–World War II period.

In *By Love Possessed* (1957), for instance, Cozzens echoes the Shylock concept. His central character, Arthur Winner, is referring to a sharp Jewish lawyer, Woolf, turned Episcopalian. "Glimpsing Mr. Woolf's face in the mirror again," wrote Cozzens, "Arthur Winner could see his lips form a smile, deprecatory, intentionally ingratiating. Was there something in the patient shrug, something of the bated breath and whispering humbleness? ... Did you forget at your peril the ancient grudge that might be fed if Mr. Woolf could catch you once upon the hip?"[27]

Cozzens' attitude is not blatant and is at times ambivalent. We have seen how, in *Guard of Honor*, he treats Captain Manny Solomon without any overtone of prejudice. On the other hand, he betrays his uneasiness with Jews not only in *By Love Possessed* but also by the hint of sharp practice by the Jewish lawyer in *The Just and the Unjust*. However, his ambivalence does not obviate the anti-Semitic aura in some novels. In Frederick Bracher's study of Cozzens' novels he writes, "Cozzens' treatment of Jews *on the whole* is not unsympathetic, but he shows them to be, in the mind of many Gentiles, outsiders" (emphasis added).[28] Cozzens also exhibited prejudice in his novels against "foreigners," Catholics, and Irish as well as Jews, as one might expect from the traditional WASP. Cozzens' effort to be unprejudiced toward Jews in his fiction is evident but not always successful.

What of Katherine Anne Porter's *Ship of Fools* (1962)? Ostensibly an anti-Nazi novel, it more nearly presents a dark view of humanity as a whole, though it contains a few favorable characters. One might suppose that an unfavorable view of a Jewish character in this general critique of humanity would escape criticism. But the one Jew in the novel turns out to be rather more than just another example of fallible humanity. He is presented in an anti-Semitic portrait of Julius Loewenthal, a salesman of Roman Catholic furnishings and wares. Loewenthal is returning home from South America to Duesseldorf in the early 1930s and naturally is frightened at being the only Jew on the ship. Loewenthal's "natural hostility to the whole alien world of the Goyim was so deep and pervasive that it was like a movement of his blood, flooded his soul." Since "it cost him" nothing, he would be friendly. His German cabin-mate, Rieber, a vulgar, detestable person, ignores him and treats him with contempt. Loewenthal is determined to "endure in silence." Another passenger, Wilhelm Freytag, is returning to Germany to take his Jewish wife and her mother back to Mexico, where he works in the oil fields. In discussion Freytag asserts that his wife is "no longer a Jew, but the wife of a German; our children's blood will flow as pure as mine, your tainted stream will be cleansed in their German veins." But his fellow Germans suspect Freytag may himself be Jewish, and they have him transferred to the dining table where Loewenthal has been sitting alone. When Freytag tells his new table partner that his wife is Jewish, Loewenthal talks rudely and offensively about a Jewish girl marrying a non-Jew. "Any Jewish girl marries out of her religion," he says, "ought to have her head examined," and he reveals himself to be a reverse bigot and insufferable. He believed "all religions except his own were simply a lot of heathens following false gods." He would ignore the Goyim and make what money he could out of his trade with them. He "distrusted all Goyim, but ... most of all those who plagued him, ... [talked] about how they disapproved of all racial prejudice, how they had none themselves, and how they had good Jewish friends, and how everybody knew that some of the most talented people in the world were Jews." His ungracious response to friendly overtures prompts an American girl on board to ask him, "Are you always so stupidly crude, or is this a special occasion?"[29] Condemnation of Nazi anti-Semitism in the novel is apparent, but the author's depiction of the one Jewish character to set off against Nazi anti-Semitism is hardly reassuring as to Porter herself. It is no explanation to assert that such characters as Loewenthal existed and do exist. Why in this context?

The novel was written on and off over a period of twenty-two years and was based on a visit by the author to Germany in 1931, when Porter became friendly with Hermann Goering, who was attracted to her. At that time, Goering was helpful to wealthy Jews, no doubt to gain some advantage. As Porter's biographer Joan Givner reports, Goering "boasted" during a conversation with Porter, "that after Hitler came to power there would not be a Jew left in Germany in any position of power." In 1975 Porter is reported to have said that "the person she talked to most in Germany was Goering." At a party in 1931, she said, she had discussed Germany with him, and he had told her "what they were going to do to the Jews." Her response was to "wonder how you dare to do it because it's never done any good and it doesn't suppress them. It does do great damage to a country." We can only conclude that Porter believed depriving the Jews of any power, however desirable this might be, was not practicable without injuring the country involved. Further, her biographer records how she manifested anti-Semitism in her "criticism of the Kleins,"[30] family of a Jewish correspondent of the *Chicago Tribune* who befriended her when she was in Berlin.

However, the animus that I sense behind the portrait of Loewenthal I later discovered had also been remarked upon by others. Theodore Solotaroff regarded it as a "caricature of Jewish vulgarity." Josephine Herbst wrote a friend that she thought the portrait of Loewenthal a "nasty" thing, "her one Jew a stereotyped Jew." The British writer Sybille Bedford, in the midst of an otherwise enthusiastic review of the book, asked, "Did the only Jew on board have to be such an utter wretch? Did he *have* to trade in rosaries?" In confirmation of such comments we may add, as Givner informs us, that Porter wrote in a copy of Albert Memmi's *Portrait of a Jew*, which she bought in 1962, that Memmi was "completely typically Jewish, nose and mouth especially.... It is a look, an expression, a manner that identifies them.... Everybody except the Jews knows the Jews are not chosen but are a lot of noisy, arrogant, stupid, pretentious people and then what?" Givner concludes that Porter's "virulent anti-Semitism was part of racism," and she cites a 1958 newspaper report in which Porter accused the Supreme Court of acting "recklessly and irresponsibly" in 1954 for outlawing segregation. Porter was then quoted there as saying, "The down-trodden minorities are organized into little cabals to run the country so that we will become the down-trodden majority if we don't look out."[31]

But the unfriendliness intimated in a few authors in the 1950s and 1960s was untypical. It does serve to remind us, however, that even in a time of high Jewish participation on all levels, including the highest in American literature, this does not signify the end of anti-Semitism, even in literature itself. It reminds us of the stubborness of the basic problem.

## THEMES OF THE 1950s

Fictions of the 1950s thus far examined were not all distinctive products of their decade. Others could hardly have been written in any other decade, not only because they deal with events that date them, but also because they are infused with the cast of mind prevalent at the time. One might suppose that the great victory over fascism would have led to a period of refreshment of a humanistic view of people and perhaps even optimism. What in fact happened was depression of the spirit and a retreat into privatism. The dominant United States position in rebuilding the war-ravaged world led to an exacerbated consumerism, what can be called the "commoditization" of life, the reduction of all things and even people to commercial terms of pecuniary worth, lowering the moral value system of the country. The lull in political disillusionment among the prewar Left during American participation in World War II resumed its course by the end of the 1940s. Fear of the Soviet Union and an antagonism to it bordering on hysteria, together with the deliberate creation and exploitation of this fear among the population for political purposes, led to the McCarthyite phenomenon. The nation was gripped by a psychology of political repression and a frightened conformity. In 1952, Irving Howe remarked, the prevailing moods were "bewilderment, fear, skepticism, lassitude, confusion, despair."[32]

The usual brief characterization of the 1950s mood was "apathy." This was the period when sociologists were holding a mirror up to American society with David Riesman's *The Lonely Crowd* (1950), William Whyte's *The Organization Man* (1956), and C. Wright Mills' *White Collar* (1951) in which the contemporary pervasiveness of alienation was in effect concretely illustrated and analyzed. C. Wright Mills was quite accurately called by Morris Dickstein "the quintessential fifties maverick."[33] Mills described the political attitude in that decade as social apathy, "political indifference." "To be politically indifferent," wrote Mills, "is to be a stranger to old political symbols, to be alienated from politics as a sphere of loyalties, demands and hopes."[34]

The clashing of hopes of the 1930s and disillusionment with socialism led many writers to share political indifference at least to the extent of rejecting collective effort and turning inward. In this sense, Gerald Green's widely selling *The Last Angry Man* (1956) was a typical book of the 1950s. The central figure, Dr. Sam Abelman (modeled on an actual Brooklyn doctor who died in 1952) has no faith in the political process. He feels surrounded by fraud and is angry at the pervasive dishonesty, private and corporate. His response was simply to act as an honest individual. He practiced in a poor Brooklyn neighborhood with absolute integrity, with love and respect for all people except the dishonest and cruel. Though freely using ethnic epithets, he is a genuine respecter of persons when it comes to deeds. He is perpetually angry at greed, stupidity, aggrandizement, and false superiority. His response is not social but individual and personal action. A television producer is impressed with Abelman's character and wishes to tape an interview with him, for he regards Abelman as the "last angry man. There aren't enough people left who get mad, plain mad. Not mad for a cause or purpose, but generally mad at all the bitchery and fraud."[35] The meaning of Abelman's character as an intense individualist of integrity is worked out in a Jewish milieu among the Jews of his Brooklyn neighborhood, his family, and his Jewish doctor friends, as well as a group of television technicians.

Near-sociological fidelity to the facts of suburban Jewish life of the 1950s, which paralleled that of non-Jewish corporate executive and sub-executive life in Jewish suburbs, is achieved in Ernst Pawel's *From the Dark Tower* (1957). At the core of the novel is distrust of collective action bred of post–World War II disillusionment with radicalism and retreat into reliance on the individual and striving for personal "authenticity." This case study of Jewish suburban life adumbrates many themes of the 1950s—apathy and conformism, the McCarthyite atmosphere, disillusionment with radicalism, anti-Jewish discrimination in the executive suite. The novel finally espouses an existential "authenticity" of the self. Abe Rogoff is the unique Jewish executive at the Tower Insurance Company. He regards himself as "a Jew in the sense of being an outsider." When his close friend and immediate superior with "an immaculate Protestant genealogy" but yet a "Jew" in Abe's sense of outsider, commits suicide, it would be logical for Abe to succeed him, but he is passed over because "Tower was a pure Anglo-Saxon firm." Even though a few Blacks had been employed as clerks in token compliance with FEPC (Federal Employment Practices Commission) regulations, "a Jew as Vice-President was something else again." Abe is under no illusions about his condition. In suburban "Samaria Beach" he was "an underground man" who conformed on the surface to the code of the Organization Man.[36]

I was a community leader, a PTA member, a likely candidate for the Board of Ed, active in the Temple and the AVC [American Veterans Committee] and marginal participant in the ADA as well as a half dozen interlocking Jewish organizations. Quite a record for a nonjoiner.... Most of these activities amounted to nothing more than paying one's dues and attending a couple of meetings a year; they were mere formal responses to the kind of pressures that a parent and homeowner enjoying the blessings of suburban fellowship can hardly afford to resist. [They were] an extension [of] the indispensable process of making a living.[37]

But beneath these surface compliances there was "an authentic self." In other words, his community participation was a mode of conformism. Abe had a dual conception of the Jew. There was the "authentic" self, the "outsider," and also "the sum and substance of Jewishness" in "bellyaching about discrimination . . . and collecting money."[38]

Another aspect of 1950s suburban life was "the ostentatious and highly publicized absence of prejudice. Jew and Gentile lived in an atmosphere of idyllic harmony," and even a few Blacks were "allowed to settle along the fringes of the village," and conveniently, too, for they were the domestic workers. But in social life the different groups—Catholic, Protestant, Jews, Blacks—"kept pretty much to themselves, with remarkably little crossing of lines." The vaunted tolerance of the village was easily penetrated. At a village meeting to promote Civil Defense, Abe cannot contain his opposition and calls the whole matter "unadulterated nonsense. . . . I resent being nagged, bullied, and lied to." The village is scandalized by this non-conformity. At his business office a former Communist is threatened with dismissal, and Abe averts it. Both at home and at work he is suspected of subversion. At work he is shunted off to a small cubicle. His wife is harassed; his son has adopted the community attitude and is alienated from him. He and his wife had actually been followers of Trotsky in their student days, and they now condemn that attitude as conformist for that time. The rabbi of the temple and its leaders fear Abe's presence in the town is "bad for the Jews." Rabbi Kahn had been characterized as the typical 1950s rabbi of an affluent congregation: he was "youthful, handsome, . . . an accomplished actor, the Jewish answer to revivalists and television bishops, . . . a leader in civic affairs, a spellbinding orator, and an amateur psychiatrist." Fearful that Abe's heterodoxy—"subversion"?—would damage the amicable intergroup relations he had built up, the rabbi and a wealthy member of the temple offer Abe $50,000 if he will move out of town. Abe then asserts his "authentic" self: he quits his job, sells the house, and moves his family to a small Rocky Mountain town, where he gets a job with a wartime friend on the town paper. The story ends with the typical declaration of a dissenter from the 1950s: "There is a frontier, all right, . . . the ultimate boundary: ourselves. . . . The reign of the clock in all its variations, from the Tower on the Square to the Superstate on the Volga, is dedicated to the extinction of man's awareness of himself."[39]

A highly individual, sophisticated note was sounded in the short stories of Grace Paley, well known as a peace activist, in *The Little Disturbances of Man* (1959) and later in several stories in *Enormous Changes at the Last Minute* (1974). The style is peculiarly "modern" in its mood and economy, compact, and replete with unexpected and whimsical turns of meaning. Many of her stories convey a bittersweet attitude to the life of everyday Jews in the sense that she combines a hard realism with a sensitive appreciation of human fallibility. The Jewishness of her characters is social rather than religious and sharply outlines a person, child, or adult. A wry preoccupation with human weakness rather than Jewishness is her primary interest.

Eleven years later she published a third volume of stories, *Later the Same Day* (1985), in a more somber mood that reflected the disappointment of many hopes, aftermath of the 1960s counterculture, especially in its effect upon activists and their young, too-soon adult children. The prose is far more compact than the earlier stories; they have lost their pervasively light touch. It is elliptical and at times fragmentary. Many of the characters are Jewish in a Jewish milieu.

The drastic development of international and national events effected changes in attitudes and morals in the 1950s, which were variously reflected in the fiction of the time. Perhaps no greater contrast of response can be adduced than the works of the contemporaries J. D. Salinger and Herman Wouk: the first rejected prevailing values and the second embraced them. J. D. Salinger was half-Jewish, with an Irish mother. Only one of his short stories, except for the Glass family stories to be considered later, is at all directly concerned with Jewishness. In "Down at the Dinghy," Boo Boo Tenenbaum's son Lionel, about four, often threatens to run away from home when insulted or hassled. He is presently anchored in the family's dinghy and refuses to come ashore. Boo Boo tries to entice him back on land in a charming conversation—Salinger has a special talent for depicting children and their relation to sympathetic grownups—and finally succeeds in getting Lionel on her lap. Why did he want to run away, she asks him. He replies that he overheard one of their domestic workers tell the other that "Daddy's a big—sloppy—kike." She asks him if he knows what a kike is. "It's one of those things that go up in the air. . . . With *string* you hold."[40] Nothing further is said about it. Lionel has shown us that anti-Semitism is conveyed not only by words, but also by tone and inflection.

*The Catcher in the Rye* (1951) is Salinger's only full-length novel and has no Jewish aspect. Leslie Fiedler has erroneously, I believe, identified Salinger's sixteen-year-old hero, Holden Caulfield, as coming from a "world of comfortably assimilated and well-heeled Jews (though his name cagily conceals his ethnic origin)."[41] I find nothing specifically Jewish about Holden. His revulsion from the philistine, consumeristic, the "phony," society in whose midst he lives, though shared by many Jews, signalized the distress of many sensitive persons at its superficialities and hypocrisies. And the novel was in fact adopted by an entire high school generation of the early 1950s as their thematic lament. The young people of this decade were generally acknowledged to be "apathetic"—either they wished to withdraw from social concern like Holden, reserving their complaints to the privacy of their individual lives, or they simply adopted the supine consumeristic attitude of their parents and the commercial society around them. What both those who conformed and those who personally rebelled had in com-

mon was the "privatization" of their lives, since, as C. Wright Mills put it
in the 1950s, "The distance between the individual and the centers of power
has become greater, and the individual has come to feel powerless."[42] Holden can find consolation in the affection and understanding he expects and
receives from his younger sister, "old Phoebe," a charming child beautifully
drawn by Salinger. Holden had not yet succumbed to the aspirations of
Oriental religion with which Salinger imbued the children of the Glass
family.

No greater contrast to the rebellious mood of *Catcher* can be imagined
than the Jewish version of the totally conforming acceptance of current
values in Herman Wouk's *Marjorie Morningstar* (1955). Where Holden is
the dissenter from contemporary values, Marjorie finally embraces them as
the most comfortable and convenient code. We have already seen how Wouk
smugly proclaimed his anti-intellectualism and conformism in *The Caine
Mutiny*. *Marjorie* was also an extremely lucrative commercial success, not
only as a book but as a movie. Wouk has immense skill in popular narrative,
which brought him a series of commercial successes from *Caine* onward.
How limited the outlook of the novel is can be gauged from the fact that,
although much of its action is set during the Great Depression of the 1930s
at a time when anti-Semitism in the United States was in high gear, these
important aspects of the life of that decade hardly receive mention. Marjorie's family lived a comfortable existence on Central Park West untouched
by these exigencies. Her mother Rose "had been a Yiddish-speaking immigrant girl toiling in a dirty Brooklyn sweatshop, dressed in rags. As she
watched her daughter burst into bloom on Central Park West, her own
lonely, miserable adolescence came back to her, and by contrast it seemed
to her that Marjorie was living the life of a fairy-tale princess."[43] *Bar-
Mitzvahs*, *Seders*, and weddings occur in the affluent mode of the new-rich
Jewish middle class. After a luxurious childhood and adolescence, Marjorie
is off to college hoping to become an actress. Marjorie Morgenstern becomes
Marjorie Morningstar, a more suitable stage name. She persuades her parents to allow her a summer vacation as an actress at the summer camp
South Wind.

There she meets the play director, Noel Airman (né Saul Ehrman), signifying *Luftmensch*, Yiddish for the man without visible means of support.
Noel is a pseudo-intellectual, a composer with small talent, a womanizer,
and the target of Wouk's suspicious, antagonistic attitude toward the free
intellectual. In order to facilitate his conquest of Marjorie, who falls in love
with him, Noel encourages her in her yearning for a bohemian life and for
the stage. The rest of the novel plots the course of their love affair. The
heart of the novel is, in the terms set by Wouk, is or is not Marjorie a
"Shirley," conceived by Noel as the daughter of rich Jewish parents, "the
respectable girl, the mother of the next generation, all tricked out to appear
gay and girlish and carefree, but with a terrible threatening dullness jutting

through."[44] Clearly, Wouk approves of "Shirley," in contrast to Noel's disdain. Noel goes on to describe her—the archetypal middle-class Jewish woman of the decade. What Shirley

wants is what a woman should want, always has and always will—big diamond engagement ring, house in a good neighborhood, furniture, children, well made clothes, furs—but she'll never say so. Because in our time those things are supposed to be stuffy and dull. She knows that. She reads novels. So, half believing what she says, she'll tell you the hell with that domestic dullness, never for her. She's going to paint...or be a social worker, or a psychiatrist, or an interior decorator, or an actress....Not just a wife....She talks Lady Brett and acts Shirley.[45]

Noel has in fact been describing Marjorie, past and future, as the unfolding novel reveals.

Wouk describes the desired end toward which this 620-page travail has striven. "She's a regular synagogue goer, active in Jewish organizations of the town....Her husband is active too. They seem to be rather strictly observant." She argues that "religion still worked for a hell of a lot of people. She said her parents would never have survived the death of [her brother] Seth without it, and she didn't know whether she and Milton could have stayed in one piece after the baby died if they hadn't had their religion." For Wouk Judaism is a great convenience. Its ritual makes you feel "at home in the world, warm, safe, good, while you were observing your laws."[46]

Joining *Marjorie* a few years later in this "Jewish Decade" with enormous commercial success was Leon Uris' *Exodus* (1958). One may say without exaggeration that this novel exploits the ultimate horror of the Holocaust and the establishment of Israel. Its central theme is the struggle for the creation of the Jewish state. It attempted to put this struggle in historical perspective by linking it with the persecution of the Jews through history and most particularly with the Nazi onslaught on the Jewish people. It opens with the voyage of the ship *Exodus*, crowded with refugee Jews from Nazism, illegal immigrants to Palestine. It movingly depicts their effort to be allowed to land there after a journey from a refugee camp in Cyprus. In the course of the story the author recalls the first modern settlements in Palestine in the 1880s, follows the lives of several pioneer families there, and gives a not wholly accurate account of the Warsaw Ghetto Uprising as well as the Arab-Israeli war that finally secured the State of Israel. Unfortunately the literary value of the book is low: its language is commonplace, the characters synthetic and incredible. The narrative often summons up typical scenes of Hollywood hokum, and indeed the story was made into an elaborate and highly successful movie.

But the social significance of the novel cannot be dismissed. Rarely has a book had such a specific, calculable social effect. It reinforced a lively awareness of the depth of Nazi criminality among both Jews and non-Jews. It helped arouse in the younger generation, which had not lived through the Nazi period, a lively sense of the bestiality of Nazism. It also told, however inaccurately, some of the history of the Warsaw Ghetto Uprising, and, above all, the extraordinary heroism of the struggle to realize the existence of Israel. It gave both Jews and non-Jews an awareness of and interest in Israel which had scarcely existed before, and it awakened in many Jews a sense of pride in their Jewish identity. Yet, to some extent, the nationalistic and chauvinistic mood of the novel may have contaminated the soundness of these valid achievements. But the novel did stimulate among Jews a new level of interest in Israel.

Most disturbing is the treatment in the novel of the Jews as superhuman and of the Arabs as subhuman. As to the Jews, this characterization is Uris' own. There is no ordinary person among the Jewish characters. For instance: "Yakov's fertile brain in Jossi's powerful body could well have created a superman." The hero, Ari, "comes from a breed of supermen"; Israel "has created a race of Jewish amazons"; the army of Israel, indeed, "is no army of mortals." Such characterizations were protested by some Israelis. A survivor of the real-life ship *Exodus*, Yehudi Lev, said of the novel that the wars of liberation were fought and won not by supermen, not "with Gary Coopers and Ari Ben Canaans to lead us...but with just plain Yankeles and Moshes and Itzhaks who started life as merchants and intellectuals and middle men." The Jews, even Israeli Jews, are ordinary people who rise to defend their rights and whose heroism is called forth by circumstances. Uris does not raise the dignity of the Jews by his assertion that "no people, anywhere, have fought for their freedom as have our people." This is misleading as history and arrogant and runs the danger of distorting the conception of Jews among non-Jews and promoting chauvinism among Jews.

Uris' conception of Arabs as an inferior people is no less distorting than his notions of Jewish superiority. Nearly every reference to the Arabs is contemptuous. This Arab is "fat," another "looks stupid." They are dirty, their villages stink, they have always built on other civilizations. They "quaked in terror" at Jewish revenge, they are cowed by the bull-whip of Jossi and later of his son Ari. The impression left is that Arabs are an inferior breed. Uris betrays no understanding whatever of the historical situation of the Arabs, nor does he credit them with a range of character like that of any people. Indeed, the *muktar* of the Arab village near Ari's *kibbutz* and his son are, up to a point, treated sympathetically because they have the good sense, in Uris' terms, to grasp that "the Jews are the only salvation for the Arab people." The nature of the "friendship" that grew up between the family of the *muktar* and Ari's father's family is shown in an incident reminiscent of the paternalistic "friendship" of Southern whites for Blacks. During the Arab-Israeli war in 1947, Ari visits the *muktar*'s son Taha, who had been his boyhood friend, to rally his village against cooperation with the attacking Arabs. Taha is in love with Ari's sister Jordana. "Are you going to tell me I am your brother?" asks Taha. "You always have been," Ari answers. "If I am your brother, then give me Jordana." Ari's reply to this—"Ari's fist shot out and crashed against Taha's jaw." Ari regrets the act. Taha draws his conclusions: "You have told me everything that I need to know. Get out of my house, Jew." In American minds, visions of an unreconstructed South are evoked by this scene.[47] Yet in spite of the inferior literary and social values of *Exodus*, its extraordinary social impact in its day cannot be ignored.

The literature of our country and of the Jews within it suffered a grievous loss with the premature death of Edward Lewis Wallant in 1962 at the age of thirty-six. In the two years before he died, his first two novels were published: *The Human Season* (1960) and *The Pawnbroker* (1961). At his death he left two more novels, which were published posthumously: *The Tenants of Moonbloom* (1963), written last; and *The Children at the Gate* (1964), the third novel. His literary quality was quickly recognized. *The Human Season* was given the Jewish Book Council Award in 1961, and *The Pawnbroker* was nominated for the National Book Award for 1962. Wallant was born and brought up in New Haven, served in World War II, and after college became art director of a New York advertising agency. The first two novels were written after work, and only in 1960 could he devote himself to writing full time.

All four novels convey one coherent view of life which in each novel is developed in four stages: at first, spiritual desolation of the central character and his detachment from other people; a series of encounters with a variety of suffering, unhappy people; a violent, traumatic experience which shocks him out of his sense of distance from others; the final expression of an awakened outgoing feeling for other people. Though the structure of each novel is roughly similar to the others, the main ideas are developed in entirely different contexts, and are thus amplified and enriched as one reads through the novels. The style is concise and taut, that of a verbal athlete. Jewish characters are central to all the novels, and this entails a more or less Jewish milieu. While I believe it likely that the devastating post-Holocaust disillusionment about God and man had an influence on Wallant's setting of the problem of initial unfeeling detachment of his central characters from other people, the total viewpoint of the novels does not seem to me specifically Jewish.

His second, and generally accounted his best novel, *The Pawnbroker* (1961) was made into a successful movie and is on the whole faithful to the original. The central character, Sol Nazerman, is a survivor of the Holocaust and an especially poignant instance of the survivor anesthetized against admitting any emotional relation with others. In Sol's case, the death camp experience and the loss of his wife and children there have drained him of any feeling for others: he tolerates all others without responding to any emotional demands. As manager of a Harlem pawnshop, which he knowingly operates to provide a cover for a gangster's funds, he helps support in Queens the philistine family of his sister, brother-in-law, niece, and unhappy, artistic misfit nephew. They aspire to become totally assimilated "Americans." Sol's sister looks at her husband and children and thinks, proudly, "You wouldn't even guess they were Jews." Sol craves only peace and quiet and the absence of emotional demands on him. He has a mechanical sexual relation with the surviving widow of a friend killed in the Nazi camps. As in all the novels, a variety of pathetic characters, both Black and white, are part of Sol's experience. His treatment of those he meets in the pawnshop is not unkind but tolerant, taciturn, and indifferent. He chooses to be unaffected by the troubles which they try to make him share. His assistant, the young Black man Jesus Ortiz, wonders at Sol's cynicism and discusses it with him. Sol says, "I do not trust God or politics or newspapers or music or art. I do not trust smiles or clothes or buildings or scenery or smells.... But most of all, I do not trust people and their talk, for they have created hell with that talk, for they have proved they do not deserve to exist for what they are." Ortiz then asks, "Ain't there nothin' you trust?" Sol replies, "Money.... Next to the speed of light, which Einstein tells us is the only absolute in the universe, second only to that I would rank money."[48]

But it turns out that his relationship to Ortiz is pivotal and the agency of his return to humanity. Ortiz is bright and observant and senses that he can learn much from Sol, who agrees to teach him the trade. Sol is a reluctant teacher because he wishes to avoid the human closeness which might be generated if he let down his emotional defenses in the course of instructing Ortiz. For his part, Ortiz is eager to learn, though he occasionally slips into conventional anti-Semitism. He reassures his mother about Sol, who works him hard. "You know Jews," he tells his mother, "they get full value." But he senses that Sol will not exploit him. "But it, like I feel.... I don't know ...*easy*. I got the feelin' he ain't gonna do me no evil like," he tells his mother.[49] Nevertheless, after a peremptory rebuff from Sol he succumbs to the temptation to participate in robbing Sol. The friends who involve him in their plot have guns, but promise not to use them. When the attempt is made and one of the thieves threatens Sol with a gun, Ortiz, seeing that it will be used, throws himself between it and Sol, and is killed. This sacrifice is the electrifying shock that reawakens Sol to a feeling for others. For the first time in many years he breaks down and weeps unrestrainedly. The floodgates of feeling are reopened: "...He realized he was crying for all his dead now, that all the damned-up weeping had been released by the loss of one irreplaceable Negro who had been his assistant and who tried to kill him but who ended up saving him.... What had impelled Ortiz to throw himself like a shield before him?... Rest in peace, Ortiz," and he names to himself his close friends and relatives who have died.[50] He has experienced a rebirth of feeling and a reaffirmation of life.

The novel is written in a condensed style, without a wasted word. It penetrates the depths of ordinary people, not only Sol and his family, but the pathetic parade of clients of the pawnbroker. Why is Sol, formerly an art historian, a pawnbroker? This is quite a deliberate enhancement of Wallant's theme because this stereotypical Jewish occupation accentuates the Holocaust aspect of his story and signifies a part of what has been imposed on the Jews by history. In the store, writes Wallant, Sol "found a pair of mother-of-pearl opera glasses and looking in the wrong end, scanned the store so that the place looked vast and ancient, like a museum dedicated to an old history. And all the while, half consciously, he got a perverse pleasure from the sense of kinship, of community with all the centuries of hand-rubbing Shylocks. Yes, he, Sol Nazerman, practiced the ancient, despised profession, and he survived."[51] Wallant's Jewish self-awareness is keen and is implicit in all the novels, in terms of both his Jewish characters and their relations with non-Jews. His basic theme is passage from a traumatized anesthetic relation with fellow human beings to the opening up of the possibilities of love for others. The theme is placed within a Jewish context in all his stories.

In the few years in which he conceived his novels he rang variations—by no means monotonous—on the single theme of the necessity of "entering into others," a synonym for comprehending love of fellow human beings. How might he have developed if he had survived past thirty-six? Would he have grown into a major American novelist?

## ISAAC BASHEVIS SINGER

Confirmation of the 1950s as the Jewish Decade can be drawn from the fact that Isaac Bashevis Singer forged into general public attention at that time. He had been writing in Yiddish since his first story was published in Warsaw in 1925, and in the United States since his arrival here at the age of thirty in 1935. From that moment his stories and journalistic pieces were published in the *Jewish Daily Forward* (*Forverts*). But his introduction to the English-speaking audience did not occur until 1950 with the appearance of his novel *The Family Moskat* in English translation, originally published serially in Yiddish in the *Forward* in the 1940s. This Warsaw Jewish family chronicle was favorably received, but the public did not come to know the essential Singer until 1953 when the *Partisan Review* published an English translation by Saul Bellow of the story "Gimpel the Fool." Thenceforth, translations of his stories poured out in a range of English periodicals from the *Saturday Evening Post* to *The New Yorker*. His first short story collection, *Gimpel the Fool and Other Stories*, appeared in 1957, and additional volumes of his short stories followed every few years amid great acclaim. For his work he received the National Book Award in 1970 and 1974, and in 1978 his career was climaxed with award of the Nobel Prize.

But can we identify Singer as an "American" writer? His first novel, *Satan in Goray*, which some (including me) believe his best, was originally published in Yiddish in Warsaw in 1935 and was reprinted serially in the *Forward* in 1945 and in an English translation by Jacob Sloan in 1955. All his work is first written and most even first published in Yiddish; until the mid–1960s all his stories were set in the *shtetl* or the Polish city, steeped in the minutiae of that life and in its superstitions and its folklore. When Singer felt secure in his knowledge of English and of American life, he ventured to write about New York, but even in these stories he did not cut himself off from the Yiddish milieu. "I have developed roots here too," he wrote in 1973. "Just the same," he added, "my American stories deal with the Yiddish-speaking immigrants from Poland so as to ensure that I know not only their present way of life but *their* roots—their history, their ways of thinking and expressing themselves."[52] While these "American" stories are entertaining, there probably would be no dispute over the judgment that they are not his best work. So far as his content is concerned, one cannot regard him as a full-fledged "American" writer.

But other considerations are relevant. He has controlled translations of his work by close cooperation with the translator, so that the English is ultimately his own. Stylistically his work then becomes a story in American English. Indeed, the Yiddish poet Jacob Glatstein found it "puzzling" that a Singer story "reads better and pleasanter in English than the original Yiddish."[53] And in fact Singer's stories have entered the stream of American writings as one expression of its multiethnic character, as part of the folk memory of one of its constituent ethnic components. As an acculturated American who became a citizen in 1943 Singer is entitled to be regarded as an American writer. If an Irish-American were to write short stories based on Irish folklore, or if a citizen of Vietnamese origin were to write fiction based on Vietnamese folklore, would it not be considered American fiction?

In recent decades the concept of the American has undergone broadening under pressure of events that have added complexity to the concept by the infusion of immigrants of Asian and African origin as well as renewed Jewish immigration from the Soviet Union and from Israel. Within this context of the broadening and acceptance of cultural pluralism, one must grant greater flexibility to the nature of American-ness. Under this dispensation Singer's work may be considered American. While labels as such are trivial, the meaning behind the label, as in Singer's case, has significance. The past half-century has witnessed a widening and more diversified set of traditions on which Americans draw as Americans. The old New England, Anglo-Saxon tradition is no longer the sole cultural source for the American imagination.

Singer's relation to Yiddish literature is dubiously regarded by some within the Yiddish-speaking literary community. They deplore what they regard as his departure from the tradition of the trio of Yiddish classical writers, Mendele Mocher Seforim, I. L. Peretz, and Sholem Aleichem. For Singer abandoned their concern for the welfare of the Jewish community nor is he interested in pursuing themes of social amelioration and social justice, which were essential to that tradition. He understands, Singer has written, why "Yiddish writers and critics complain that I didn't behave like a Yiddish writer" because "I didn't worry so much about the community as I worry about the character whom I describe." He charged current Yiddish writing with avoidance of sex, which he regards as central to life and hence to literature, and claims that they have not paid attention to the great upheavals of the Jewish past like "the False Messiahs, the expulsions, the forcible conversions, the Emancipation, and the assimilations, to the Jewish underworld, the gossips, prostitutes, and even white slavers."[54] In short, he considers the tradition "primitive and naive, and even its radicalism was provincial." Further, it was "sentimental."[55] Singer draws an important distinction between the Yiddish tradition and the Jewish tradition. While he is not in the former, he is in the latter tradition. For he writes about Jews, past and present, drawing deeply from the well of Jewish life, lore, and custom, but his point of view differs from that of the Yiddish writers. He summed up his attitude in an interview with Irving Howe in 1973. "The Yiddish tradition is a tradition of sentimentality and social justice.... This ... is not in my character.... It is not in my nature to fight for social justice, although I am for social justice. But since I am a pessimist, I believe that no matter what people do, it will be wrong and there will never be justice in the world."[56]

Since the Yiddish-speaking world is almost hermetically sealed off from the English-speaking one, the attitude of his fellow Yiddish writers to Singer was not generally known until he was acclaimed for his writings in English. The situation was brilliantly satirized in a novella by Cynthia Ozick, "Envy; or, Yiddish in America," first published in *Commentary* in November, 1969. The attitude of Yiddish writers is shown as compounded of envy at Ostrover's (Singer's) phenomenal success in English translation and bitter, pathetic despair over the shrinking audience for Yiddish and the opacity of Yiddish literary achievement to the English-speaking public. The late Jacob Glatstein, discussing Singer's "fame" in 1965, wrote that Singer "enjoys today a much more important place where he has more friends and is read with greater interest, than in Yiddish literature." The reason, thought Glatstein, was unflattering to the English-speaking audience. The stories, with their "distasteful blend of superstition and shoddy mysticism" are "more attuned" to the "non-Jewish" reader. The stories lack the "humaneness" characteristic of Yiddish literature, which does not "drag" its characters through "spiritual and physical depravity." Glatstein also charged that Singer lacked "a sense of style," and his "drab stylelessness" makes him "easy to translate."[57] But others disagree. Singer's translator Jacob Sloan writes that he "rejoiced in the felicities of style" of *Satan in Goray* as he worked on it. While Sloan does not believe that Singer is as great a writer as Sholem Aleichem, he holds that Singer has the artist's right to "distort reality and reassemble it in structures often quite unrecognizable." But Sloan warns Singer that, although "his preoccupation with the demonic is genuine," he is wrong to limit his creation to "fantasies." Nor does Sloan believe that Singer is merely "exploiting a current fad." Rather, Sloan believes Singer is "the lucky writer whose interests coincide with movements of public taste in literature."[58]

Indeed Singer's modernism accounts for his popularity in the English-speaking world and beyond. He was a child of the post–World War I disillusionment. The classic Yiddish writers were all dead before the war ended, and when Singer began publishing in the 1920s, the world had changed from the one these masters had known, and literature had changed with it. In Yiddish literature Singer is roughly analogous with the "lost generation" of American writers of the 1920s who struck off into modernism. Singer did not feel bound by the sexual inhibitions and taboos of the masters, and indeed of most prewar literature. He was unaffected by the deep concern of the masters for the Jewish community welfare. As a child, Singer has reported, his pious father was disturbed by the threat of the enlightenment and he sought to minimize secular contamination of his family by feeding his younger children, Isaac and his younger sister, with "tales of transmigrated spirits, dybbuks, and miracles performed by wonder rabbis and saints."[59] And young Isaac imbibed the superstitions and folklore of *shtetl* life during a four-year residence with his mother's family in Belgoray, which gave him a treasure of lore on which to draw for his stories. By the time he began to write, Singer was exploring the "dark depths and strange undercurrents of Jewishness."[60]

Endowed with an original and independent spirit, Singer came to maturity when literary modernism was on the rise. In his case freedom from conventional restraints found sanction in the Kabbalah, in Sabbatianism, and in Frankism. The sexual revolution was gaining ground, with the publication of *Ulysses* (1922), for instance. Although I am not aware that Singer was directly influenced by Freudianism, he did adopt from his study of the Kabbalah and Frankism the centrality of sex. Although Zolaesque naturalism had barely touched serious Yiddish writing, except perhaps for Sholem Asch, it could be found in badly written, sensational, lurid ephemeral stories in the popular Yiddish press, and Singer had written for that press. But he complains about classical Yiddish literature.

Yiddish literature ignored the Jewish underworld, the thousands and tens of thousands of thieves, pimps, prostitutes and even white slavers in Buenos Aires, Rio de Janeiro, and even in Warsaw. Yiddish literature reminded me of my father's [rabbinical] courtroom where almost everything was forbidden. True, Sholem Asch had in a sense created a minor revolution and taken up themes that till then had been considered taboo, but he was and remained a rustic.... His stories personified the pathos of the provincial who has been shown the big world and describes it when he goes back to the town where he came from.[61]

Interestingly enough, it was Sholem Asch who, in the 1940s, was the first writer whose original Yiddish works translated into English gained the best-seller lists.

Although World War I hardly figures in Singer's writing (it is touched upon in *The Family Moskat*), he seems somehow to have broken with the world destroyed by that war and given voice to a "modern"—that is, a sophisticated, detached—approach to literature devoid of that former world's inhibitions, as he broke the link between the social and artistic consciousness that pervaded Yiddish literature. From his very first stories he deliberately violated all taboos and populated his stories with all sorts of extra-human beings. He was especially attracted to the fantastic phenomenon of Sabbatai Zevi and his disciple, Jacob Frank. Quite early he steeped himself in books about these figures and "many books that described the punishments imposed upon witches in Europe and America, the Crusades and their mob hysterias, as well as various accounts of dybbuks, both Jewish and gentile. In these works I found everything I had been pondering—hysteria, sex, fanaticism, superstition." To this was added the lore of "Hasidism, the Cabala, miracles, and all kinds of occult beliefs and fantasies" which he had absorbed as a child.[62] His rabbinical studies rounded out his equipment as a story-teller of Jewish fantasy and the supernatural. It was in this sense that he partook of the "Jewish tradition." Since these sources flow from pre-Emancipation, indeed, medieval Jewish life, he was not in that Yiddish tradition that was founded on the Haskalah, that is, Enlightenment. His most distinctive and best works were in this vein—novels like *Satan in Goray* and short stories like "The Gentleman from Cracow" and "The Mirror."

His scope was not restricted to the fantastic, however. Even if we exclude his ephemeral journalism, he was also a practitioner of realism in both the novel and the short story. Most important of these is his *The Family Moskat*. Spanning the years 1912 to 1939 in the lives of various members of the wealthy Warsaw Moskat family, it is packed with realistic detail of affluent Jewish life in the city. Three characters stand out: Abram Shapiro, tolerant, generous, pleasure-loving, self-indulgent son-in-law of the patriarch Moskat; Asa Heschel Bannet, the ineffectual, sensitive intellectual lover and later husband of Moskat's granddaughter Hadassah; and Hadassah, a sickly, attractive, unhappy woman. In contrast to his fantastic tales, Singer's realism, in this novel, achieves characterization. In contrast, the fantastic stories convey symbols rather than individual human reality. A few years after *Moskat* Singer completed an even longer family novel, which later appeared in English in two parts, *The Mansion* (1967) and *The Estate* (1969). They dealt with the Jacoby family from the time of the Polish insurrection in 1863 to the end of the century.

Singer is at his best and most significant as the artist of the mystical, neo-medieval tale. Out of the "adventurous" Jewish past, which he charges the Yiddish tradition with neglecting, how can we account for his choice of material from Sabbatianism, and especially the Frankist heresy? The false Messiah Sabbatai Zevi emerged in 1664 but, writes Gershom Scholem, Sabbatai "represents the Messianic tradition in a conservative sense." For Scholem writes that he was a manic-depressive who "in moments of religious exaltation . . . tended to commit bizarre acts which violated the law."[63] When Sabbatai converted to Islam as the alternative to martyrdom, the doctrine of "redemption through sin" was developed, which held that the depths of sin and apostasy had to be undergone before redemption would occur.

Among the Sabbatians in the next century was Jacob Frank (1726–1791) who carried the doctrine of "redemption through sin" to its ultimate conclusion. The age-old Judaic laws, Frank maintained, were no longer binding, since the advent of the Messiah (Sabbatai) had already raised the world to a new level, rendering the law obsolete and no longer applicable. Scholem calls the Sabbatian and Frankist views "nihilistic," so that "violation of the Torah becomes its true fulfillment."[64] Singer himself characterized these teachings succinctly in "The Destruction of Kreshev": "an excess of degradation made greater sanctity and . . . the more heinous the wickedness the closer the day of redemption."[65]

Singer has written that as a beginning writer he was drawn to a study of Frankism, which he found to touch the problems he had been pondering, "hysteria, sex, fanaticism, superstition." He was also attracted to the Kabbalists, he said, who "attributed sex to God"; to them sex was "synonymous with creativity," for God is "eternally in Genesis."[66] Much of Singer's work, his demonology and treatment of sex, lends credence to the assertion of Rabbi Samuel H. Dresner that "Sabbatianism has become the ground for his thinking and believing."[67] When Irving Howe asked Singer if he was a "secret follower" of Sabbatai, Howe reports that Singer was "delighted at the idea."[68] The ubiquity of plural eroticism in Singer's stories and his preoccupation with the Frankist episode in Jewish history support this view. *Satan in Goray* gives a brilliantly imaginative picture of Sabbatianism, and particularly its Frankist form, through its intense focus on the advent and progress of the movement in the *shtetl* of Goray, and Gedaliya seems to stand for Jacob Frank himself, with his imputed magical powers and sexual irresponsibility and persistence in Sabbatian precepts after the apostasy. The story ends with the apostasy of Gedaliya and his condemnation as recounted in a presumed later chronicle. This latter Orthodox chronicle asserts that the Messiah will come in his own time and "Satan die abjured, abhorred."[69]

By attributing the condemnation to an author other than himself, was Singer distancing himself from it, and thereby leaving open his own attitude?

But Singer can not be tied down to one viewpoint. The evidence from his novels, *The Slave* and *The Magician of Lublin*, contradicts the Frankist approach. The action of *The Slave* is contemporary with *Satan in Goray*, but its central character is a devotee of the Law even while enslaved by the Poles. After marriage to his Polish master's daughter Wanda and her conversion to Judaism, Jacob's fidelity to the Law remains unwavering. Jacob and Wanda flee to Palestine where Jacob is caught up in the Sabbatian movement and "had almost put on the fez," but finally renounced the movement. Singer concludes: "Heaven decreed that Jacob should not perish a heretic." Later, "at the mention of Sabbatai Zevi's name, Jacob spat and cried loudly, 'Let his name and memory be blotted out.' "[70] It is apparent that Jacob is deeply revered by Singer himself—hardly a model for a Frankist or Sabbatian of any kind. And in *The Magician of Lublin* a life of antinomianism by the central character, Yasha, is finally arrested by a return to the Law.

The short story "Gimpel the Fool" leads to a similar conclusion. Gimpel is incredibly credulous, is teased and tortured by others, is everywhere and always taken advantage of for his naiveté, but unfailingly remains gentle and humane to everyone. He has totally curbed his aggressiveness toward others under all circumstances—quite the opposite of a release from all inhibitions under the Sabbatian code. Gimpel is, as has often been noted, the ultimate *shlemiel*, put upon by everyone—a saint, in other words. The rabbi tells Gimpel, "It is written, better to be a fool all our days than for one hour to be evil. You are not a fool. They are the fools. For he who causes his neighbor to feel shame loses Paradise himself."[71] Gimpel's reward, according to the rabbi, will come in the hereafter.

Singer never totally liberated himself from his earliest *shtetl* experiences and from his immersion in folklore. There is a certain imaginative momentum from these early impressions, which were too strong for Singer ever to have completely shaken off. He is quite aware of the strength of these early experiences when he says, as in 1964, that "the truth is that I am still living [in Poland]. . . . You know that your experiences in childhood are the most important for the writer."[72] The same, for instance, is true of James Joyce in *Ulysses*, which is penetrated with Irish Catholic imagination, for Joyce used Catholic imagery for artistic purposes while discarding the beliefs. But Singer never wholly gave up the beliefs of his childhood. Thus he is in part a modern and in part a premodern. It is not his personal belief in God but rather in the demons of more credulous days that sets him to some extent apart from the modern.

Paradoxically, Singer's immersion in the demonology and folklore of Jewish life in effect places him in a pre-Enlightenment frame, the very element that contributes to his modernism. He uses demonism and all sorts of supernatural intervention into the affairs of living men and women. The function of this primitivism in his writing is roughly equivalent to that of African and pre-Western art and figuration in modernist fine art. Singer's resort to primitivism is not purely formal like that of the fine artists, but it does place him in a post-Enlightenment situation like that of the modernists. Singer is also modern in his detachment from his literary materials, neither believing nor disbelieving demonism and necromancy even though he has often expressed a belief in demons. His writing conveys the impression of his being essentially uninvolved in the being of unnatural creatures.

This detachment differentiates him also from the classical Yiddish tradition. This can be illustrated from the important difference of "Gimpel the Fool" from Peretz' "Bontshe Shweig," stories which have often been compared. They are both presented as delineations of the *shlemiel*, which they are. But the differences lead to the heart of Singer's divergence from the Yiddish tradition. For Singer, Gimpel is an eternal type, timeless and spaceless, the ultimate *shlemiel*. But for Peretz, Bontshe is a victim of social conditions which impoverished him in body and spirit, until he finally became the passive sufferer of abject deprivation. While alive, Bontshe's back was "breaking under its load." No one paid any attention to him. While alive he "dreamed he was picking money off the floor—heaps of it—only to awaken poorer than before. [But] he never complained to anyone; neither of God nor of man; his eyes never flashed with a spark of hatred.... He never raised it with a claim of heaven." After death he is given a hearing before God and admiring angels and praised for his forbearance. The Divine Court offers anything he wishes. "Really?" he answers incredulously. He is finally convinced of the genuineness of this offer and utters his wish— "What I really want is a hot roll and fresh butter every morning"—to the shame and consternation of the assembled angels. The fable is Peretz' whimsical method of conveying the deprivation of elementary humanity an oppressing society inflicted upon its most deprived members. For the Presiding Officer tells Bontshe, "On earth there was no understanding. Perhaps you yourself did not know that you might have cried out and that your cries could have shaken and toppled the walls of Jericho! You yourself did not know of your slumbering self."[73] The allusion is clearly to the strength of organized poor workers.

Peretz' story is finally political, the kind of writing which Singer cannot tolerate. Gimpel's reward will come in the hereafter; Bontshe could have become fully human by toppling the walls of Jericho here on earth. Peretz' social intent is clear from the fact that he was arrested by the Tsarist police in 1899 while he was reading this story to a meeting of workers in Warsaw. Singer for his part has no interest in politics and is in practice a conservative.

Singer's demonism is cast into relief by comparing his "The Gentleman from Cracow" with Mark Twain's "The Man Who Corrupted Hadleyburg." In both stories the respective towns, the *shtetl* and the Western town, are disgraced by their inability to resist the blandishments of money or luxury obtained through immoral means. Frampol is corrupted through the wiles of the chief devil Keter Mriri in the guise of a newcomer to town; the people yield to the temptations he puts in their way and finally lose everything in the devastating fire, which climaxes the story. "Hadleyburg," it will be recalled, exposes hypocrisy and corruption by insinuating the bait of $40,000 among the "Nineteen Incorruptible" elite of the town by a visitor wreaking vengeance for ill-treatment suffered on an earlier visit. Singer's is a "moral fable"; Mark Twain's is a short story. The difference is that the corrupting agent for Singer is extra-natural, while that for Twain is a natural human being with the motivation of revenge. The difference between Mark Twain and Singer hinges on the fact that temptations are put in their way by natural and supernatural agencies, respectively.

Singer is a superb storyteller whose resources in the Jewish past have helped to deepen general American interest in the literary expression of Jews. By his freedom from parochial feeling, by the detachment with which he depicts his characters and events, his work, for decades sealed off from the English-reading public by sequestration in Yiddish media, reached that audience precisely at the time when it had been made receptive to the Jewish milieu and character by talented second-generation American-Jewish writers. It is no matter to this audience that Singer's philosophy and his art are "eclectic" or ambiguous. Side by side we find in him an attraction toward Frankism and exaltation of the saintly, rejection of religious dogma, doctrine and ritual and acceptance of an extremely personal God. And, beyond all this, his deepest belief, that by which he actually lives, is, as he said in his Nobel Prize acceptance speech: "There must be a way for a man to attain all possible pleasures, all the powers and knowledge that nature can grant him, and still serve God."[74] He is simultaneously a theist and a hedonist—which sounds like having one's cake and eating it too.

# 3

# The Critics: Trilling, Rahv, Kazin, Fiedler, Howe

Non-Jewish literary influences were among the main generative forces on the work of Jewish writers during the efflorescence of Jewish creativity in the 1940s and 1950s. The sterilizing gentility of the late nineteenth century had been swept away by the works of such critics as Van Wyck Brooks, Randolph Bourne, and Henry L. Mencken, and by Marxism for a time, and by the modernist mentalities of writers like Ezra Pound and T. S. Eliot. During this early period the only Jewish critical voice with any influence was Ludwig Lewisohn, but by the 1930s he had lost his general relevancy by his extreme Jewishness. On the side of creative literary influence, the derivation was almost exclusively from the European and American modernists.

During these years of incubation of those writers who were to emerge by the late 1930s and later, the *Partisan Review* and the fledgling Jewish critics entered the mainstream. Unlike the earlier critical group of Ezra Pound and T. S. Eliot, whose contributions as poets was as great as that as critics, the Jewish writers exerted their influence almost exclusively on the critical side, helping to fertilize the ground of creativity for the writers who forged to the center of attention after World War II. Of these critics, the most important for the Jewish entry into the heart of literary America were Lionel Trilling, Philip Rahv, Alfred Kazin, Leslie Fiedler, and Irving Howe.

When second-generation Jews grew to maturity, they belied the widespread belief held by many academic literary figures that the "Jewish mind" was incapable of grasping the essential nature of the American experience, which had hitherto been shaped by the Anglo-Saxon mentality. With the *Partisan Review* as the main medium, edited by Philip Rahv and William Phillips with several others, the group of young American writers and exponents of modernism around the journal were exerting deep influence on both the creation of American literature and the interpretation of the American past. Lionel Trilling was one of these. After a permanent appointment to the English Department at Columbia in 1939, he trained generations of English teachers for universities all over the country and published his *Matthew Arnold* (1939) and *E. M. Forster* (1942). The twenty-seven-year-old Alfred Kazin in 1942 published his *On Native Grounds*, an analysis of the development of prose and literary realism in the United States in the current century, a book that has remained a standard work ever since. Irving Howe published critical biographies of William Faulkner and Sherwood Anderson as well as a flood of critical essays. And Leslie Fiedler surveyed in his excessive manner the history of American fiction in *Love and Death in the American Novel* (1960). In the decades since the 1940s the *Partisan Review* and a number of Jewish writers championed the cause of modernism in the modes of T. S. Eliot, Ezra Pound, W. B. Yeats, Franz Kafka, and others. In short, Howells' prophetic insight of 1915 was fulfilled. Jewish writers and critics born in American ghettos were now among the leading arbiters of taste in American literature.

That influence, however, was not purely aesthetic, but more broadly "cultural" and even in an undoctrinal way "historicist." The point can be brought out by contrasting the influence of the "New York Intellectuals," as they came to be known, with that of the contemporaneous and competing "New Critics." The leading figures of the "New Criticism" were mostly traditionalist, conservative, non-Jewish writers and professors, mainly from the South, writers like John Crowe Ransom, Cleanth Brooks, Allen Tate, W. K. Wimsett, R. P. Blackmur, Yvor Winters, and others. They were formalists who maintained that one need not go beyond a "close reading" of a text to grasp its full meaning. Indeed, they objected to the introduction of historical or any other than aesthetic considerations in either the analysis or meaning of a literary text. The Trilling–*Partisan Review* approach insisted on viewing a work in a historical and cultural context. This perspective was an outgrowth of the earlier flirtation with Marxism by the group's leaders. The New York Intellectuals early threw off Marxist dogmatism, and as time went on, the Marxist connection became ever more attenuated. What survived was an opposition to aestheticism, for instance, as practiced by the New Critics (although the values of close textual criticism was not denied, despite its inadequacy for a full grasp of the art work) and they tenaciously asserted the relationship of an art work with the culture from which it sprang and the history of which it was necessarily a part. The contrast between the New Criticism of mostly non-Jewish critics and the cultural-historical criticism of the largely Jewish writers was itself to be explained by their respective places and situations in American life: the one belonging to the dominant culture, the other newcomers to that culture; the one from a Southern conservative, even reactionary sector of the culture, the other from an alienated, Left-oriented immigrant origin.

## LIONEL TRILLING

The emergence of the Jewish writer into the mainstream of American literature is in one respect exemplified by the career of Lionel Trilling (1905–1975). He is the axial figure in the sense that he was an active presence from the origins of the "Jewish Renaissance" in the *Menorah Journal* group around Elliot Cohen, in both the literary and political movements of the mid–1930s, which issued in formation of the *Partisan Review*. Although personal estrangement from Cohen prevented Trilling from direct participation in *Commentary* until Cohen died, his influence was nevertheless felt by writers for *Commentary* and by his student, Norman Podhoretz, who succeeded Cohen as editor of the magazine. From 1936 on, Trilling's teaching at Columbia influenced oncoming Jewish writers and English teachers all over the country. There is symbolic significance in the fact that Trilling wrote the introduction to the first anthology of writing from the *Partisan*, published in 1946. The magazine, he wrote, "is a representative of some of the tendencies that are producing the best" in current American writing. "For more than a decade," he wrote, *Partisan* has been committed to the "work" of organizing "a new union between our political ideas and our imagination," despite the fact that "in recent years the political intensity of *Partisan Review* has somewhat diminished."[1] Trilling did not allude to the significance of Jewish participation.

Trilling was primarily a cultural critic. In the 1940s, however, he published short stories and in 1947 a novel, *The Middle of the Journey*. The novel is a psychopolitical analysis of the mind of a character modeled on Whittaker Chambers after he left the Communist party and espionage work for the Soviet Union. In a preface to the 1967 edition of the novel, Trilling says his intention was to expose "the clandestine negation of the polemical life which Stalinist Communism had fostered" among Western intellectuals, by which I suppose he means suppression of the critical attitude. Trilling did not regard Chambers as a friend, for he couldn't "stomach Chambers' religiosity," but believed him "a man of honor" in his connection with the Alger Hiss affair.[2] Trilling used the travail of Chambers in his recoil from the dogmatism and anti-humanism of Stalinism and from its pursuit of an end without regard to the means. There are no Jewish allusions in the novel, and the narrator, John Laskell, representing the author, might or might not be Jewish.

Trilling was born in a New York suburb in 1905 to a middle-class family. His father emigrated from Bialystok and was a prosperous businessman. Although English was spoken at home, his mother kept a kosher house and observed the Friday twilight candle-lighting ceremony. His wife, Diana Trilling, reports that Lionel's mother was "among the best-read people I have known." For six years following Trilling's graduation from Columbia in 1925 he wrote regularly for *Menorah Journal* as we have seen, on topics relating to both literature and Jewishness. In August, 1978 *Commentary* posthumously published an essay of his, "The Changing Myth of the Jew," which had been accepted for publication by *Menorah* in 1931 but never published. Trilling had, his wife reports, called this essay "inferior and dullish," but Mrs. Trilling has included it in her edition of her late husband's fugitive essays. It rapidly surveyed the treatment of the Jew in English literature, an area far more fully and deeply researched since then. It is interesting, however, in that it advances the theory that the stereotype in literature is a "myth." "The Jew in fiction," he wrote, "was never treated in a way that demanded realism or truth—he was never treated as more than a type.... The Jew in fiction was ... a racial stereotype created by men whose chief concern was obviously much less to tell the truth about the character of the Jew than it was to serve their own emotional needs." To assert so categorically that the image of the Jew was not believed by the writer, was intended to be other than the truth, seems unwarranted. This image served its authors and readers precisely *because* it was deemed the truth. The fact that we know that the authors' interests and needs were involved does not mean that both authors and readers did not intend to be believed. The objectively observed function of this, to me misnamed, "myth" was to reinforce in the reader the falsehood that all Jews are similar to the stereotype, and that its authors believed their characterization to be true to life. Our conclusion therefore conflicts with Trilling's: "it became relatively unimportant," he says, if one accepts his theory, "to discuss the truth or untruth of the portraits of Jews in literature."[3] This ignores the damage done by the stereotype through its general acceptance as a true description.

Trilling was for a time the victim of anti-Semitic discrimination in college teaching. "When I decided to go into academic life my friends thought me naive to the point of absurdity," he remembers. "Nor were they wholly wrong—my appointment to an instructorship in [Columbia] College was pretty openly regarded as an experiment, and for some time my career in the College was complicated by my being Jewish."[4] After serving as an instructor in the English Department for four years, he was informed in 1936 that he would not be reappointed. His being a Jew was only one reason for this, for he was known "as a Freudian, a Marxist, and a Jew," a compound of ineligibilities in academia of that day.[5] Trilling himself later wrote in unpublished notes, "Upon my life in criticism, upon my intellectual life in general, the systems of Marx and Freud had, I have never doubted, a decisive influence." Diana Trilling comments that by 1936 "he had moved away from his earlier Marxist commitment."[6] On being denied reappointment, for once in his life Trilling made a noisy scene, confronting his colleagues with their prejudice, and he was given a reprieve. In 1939, when he published his distinguished doctoral dissertation, *Matthew Arnold*, Columbia President Nicholas Murray Butler invited him to dinner and followed this up by appointing Trilling an assistant professor of English, the first Jew in Columbia's English department.

In these years, it was not only "Marxism" from which Trilling was retreating, but Jewishness itself, not that he would ever attempt to conceal the identification. "It is never possible," he wrote in 1944, "for a Jew of my generation to 'escape' his Jewishness." But preoccupation with defining a secular, cultural Jewishness which had so deeply engaged him and his colleagues in the *Menorah* in the 1920s, was now past. He had had a Jewish upbringing and granted that "my existence as a Jew is one of the shaping conditions of my temperament, and therefore I suppose it must have its effect on my intellect." But he did not consider himself a "Jewish writer" because he could "not discover anything in my professional intellectual life which I can specifically trace back to my Jewish birth and rearing." He would even "resent" having a critic find "either faults or virtues which he called Jewish."[7] He now believed all Jewish cultural movements he knew of, including *Menorah*, were "sterile at best." While he knew writers who used Jewish experience in their writing to good effect, he did not know of any writer who "added a micromillimetre to his stature by 'realizing his Jewishness,' " while some had "curtailed their promise" by trying to increase their Jewish awareness.[8] The date was 1944. Would he have reaffirmed this view twenty years later?

Does Trilling too much protest his freedom from parochialism and illusions about Jews? We have already seen what seems to be his confusion of the stereotype as "myth" and not an intended truth. Again, in his response to the 1949 *Commentary* symposium on "The Jewish Writer and the English Literary Tradition," there seems to me a resort to a "literary" excuse to mitigate the anti-Semitic import of some writing. He makes the important observation that anti-Semitism is not *essential* to the literary tradition. It is true that anti-Semitism is well nigh ubiquitous in that tradition, but this does not mean that it is a *necessary* part of it. Its anti-Semitic aspect can be rejected without substantial damage to it. It is also true, Trilling observes, that although "I naturally meet hostile statements about Jews with hostility," this does "not necessarily destroy my relation with the writer who makes them." The truth is, I myself believe, that such total rejection would mindlessly impoverish the entire European literary tradition to almost nothing. But Trilling then goes on to absolve from anti-Semitism "Eliot's symbolic use of the Jew in his poetry," little as he is attracted to it.[9] This he regards as different from the outright anti-Semitism of Eliot's prose allusions to Jews. We have already seen how this "symbolic use of Jews" in Eliot is grounded in anti-Semitism in that it ascribed to Jews the traits about which anti-Semitism in prose is entirely explicit. Another instance of such "literary" insensitivity occurs in Trilling's essay on Keats (1950). In discussing Keats' mother, Trilling recalls that she left her second husband, Rawlings, and "formed a liaison with a Jew named Abraham."[10] The phrase, "a Jew named Abraham" is a prejudiced locution of the time and obviously is repeated from Trilling's sources. Why, then, did he not use quotation marks, if only to dissociate himself from this prejudiced form of allusion to a Jewish man? Robert Gittings, in his biography, *John Keats*, uses the same phrase, but encloses it in quotation marks.[11]

However, the totality of Trilling's attitude toward Jewishness is mixed. In his *Matthew Arnold* (1939) he does not mitigate the anti-Semitism of Arnold's distinguished father Thomas when he encountered it in Thomas Arnold's rigid "Christian" principles, "betokening," wrote Trilling, that "Jews should be banned from universities and from citizenship." Trilling must have thought of his own experience as a Jew at Columbia in the early days when he had to break through the barriers to academia when he wrote of Thomas Arnold that "he dreaded the possibility of examining a Jew in history at the University of London (of which he was a Trustee)."[12] After the revelations of the Holocaust in World War II, Trilling was driven to the conclusion, in an essay, "Art and Fortune" (1948), that the Holocaust definitely proved Jonathan Swift's conviction that humanity is incurably depraved and thereby refuted the liberal presupposition that humanity can be humane. Trilling wrote: "The simple eye of the camera shows us, at Belsen and Buchenwald, horrors that quite surpass Swift's powers" and that "the great psychological fact of our time which we all observe with baffled wonder and shame is that there is no possible way of responding to Belsen and Buchenwald."[13] (The Jewish victims of the Holocaust *did* enjoin us to a response—"Never forget!"—and never again permit such an obscenity.)

Jewishness also enters Trilling's mature work, in addition to his "Afterward" to Tess Slesinger's *The Unpossessed*, discussed earlier. In 1950 he delivered an address, which he later published as "Wordsworth and the Rabbis." Why, Trilling asked, is Wordsworth "unacceptable" to us? Trilling's answer, because of "a Judaic quality." The implication, of course—which Trilling does not draw—is that Judaism is "unacceptable" to moderns, and no doubt many would dispute this. To support his view, Trilling suggests parallels between Wordsworth's poetry and the *Pirke Aboth*, Sayings of the Fathers, compiled between the third century before and the third century after Christ, and the last of the tractates of the *Mishnah*, the rabbinical opinions and decisions on the Law. Trilling argues that there are similarities between the rabbis' conception of the Law and Wordsworth's attitude toward Nature. What the Torah was for the rabbis, says Trilling, Nature was for Wordsworth, in both cases "surrogates" of God, with which one can have an "intimate passionate relationship." Hillel's famous saying, "If I am not for myself, who, then, is for me? And if I am only for myself, what then am I?" is said by Trilling to be an interplay between "individualism and the sense of community," which is also to be found in Wordsworth. Among other parallels, Trilling regards as especially important the fact that the maxims of heroes like Akiba "never speak of courage" but of "heroic joy." This, Trilling asserts, is similar to the basic quietism of Wordsworth. This does not imply lack of courage but "calm submission to the law of things." This quietism, adds Trilling, does not negate life but is "an affirmation of life so complete that it needed no saying." What makes both Wordsworth and *Aboth* "quaint and oppressive" to the "modern reader," Trilling says, is that both quietistic viewpoints deny sexuality, whose affirmation is an essential mark of modernism.[14]

Trilling's second important essay relating to Jewishness is his fine analysis of Isaac Babel's short stories. In "Isaac Babel" (1955), he confronts that great writer's "more than an anomaly, it was a joke," of "a Jew in a Cossack regiment" during the war with Poland in 1920, a position in which Babel found himself as supply officer for such a battle unit. To Babel, the Jew and the Cossack were in "polar opposition," and Babel's stories explore this opposition within himself. To Babel, the Jew ideally was "intellectual, pacific, humane," while the Cossack was "physical, violent, without mind or manners." In the Cossack environment Babel felt most deeply challenged by his need to prove himself equal to the violent aspect of the Cossack, testing "whether he could endure killing." It was not the violence itself that appealed to Babel, says Trilling, but the spirit behind it of "the boldness, the passionateness, the simplicity and directness—and the grace." This feeling in Babel was not a late development in him, Trilling points out, but rather in continuity with Babel's boyhood fascination, which never left him, with the Jewish gangs in Odessa about which Babel wrote in the Benya Krik stories. Moreover, Babel was determined to compensate for the subservience his father showed to the Cossacks, Trilling suggests. It was not only the Cossacks who impressed him on that expedition, but also the Jews of Poland, who seemed to him different from his own acculturated Odessa Jews. Trilling quotes Babel: the Polish Jews "move jerkily, in an uncontrolled and uncouth way; but their capacity for suffering is full of a sombre greatness, and their unvoiced contempt for the Polish gentry unbounded."[15] But, like Cossack life, says Trilling, this spiritual quality of Polish Jews, which attracted him, was in the end alien to him personally. Trilling concludes that in such opposition within Babel was the stuff of his art. Altogether, it was Babel's quite remarkable talent for expressing conflicting tropisms within himself that especially appealed to Trilling.

Significant as these essays involving Jewishness may be, this theme is distinctly minor in Trilling's work. Once the *Menorah Journal* and its Jewish interest were behind him, this theme retreated to the distant background and came to the fore only in these few essays. In his maturity he was primarily a cultural critic whose medium of criticism was largely literary and cultural, like that of his admired master Matthew Arnold. His first task was to shed his early radicalism, and this he did with his *Matthew Arnold* (1939) and *E. M. Forster* (1943). Most influential, however, was *The Liberal Imagi-*

*nation* (1950), his first collection of essays, which spanned the 1940s. There he subjected the radicalism and "liberalism" of the preceding decades to analysis that offered elements of a program for the radicals and liberals disillusioned by the events of the late 1930s and the 1940s. It should be noted that Trilling's critique, though projected in terms of "liberalism" alone, also applied to radicalism, which somehow Trilling refrained from designating as such. He first noted that liberalism tended to be a self-limiting vision as "to what it can deal with" and "to develop theories and principles ... that justify its limitations." The imagination he regards as a victim of this limitation, especially as to "the nature of the mind." Hence liberalism tends to "simplify," and in this connection Trilling uttered what was to be a key word in his critical vocabulary: the "complexity" of the world is thereby scanted. "The job of criticism," he concludes, "[is] to recall liberalism to its first essential imagination of variousness and possibility, which implies the awareness of complexity and difficulty," and this is best achieved in literature, he concludes.[16]

In his opening essay, "Reality in America," he applies the critique of liberalism to Vernon L. Parrington's *Main Currents in American Thought* (1927, 1930). By the time Trilling wrote this essay (1940), it was clear to many that this important, highly influential work was seriously deficient in its perception of literature as art and analyzed the literary tradition almost exclusively in terms of ideas. Ideas were quite narrowly construed when Parrington came to treat literary figures. Trilling also quite correctly notes that Parrington's ubiquitous use of the term "romantic" is "scandalously vague."[17] Thus far, Trilling performed an important service to American letters.

But in 1946, Trilling added a second part to this essay by charging "liberal criticism" with "indiscriminate" acceptance of Theodore Dreiser as a "significant expression" of the liberal spirit: Trilling tries to show that Dreiser has been treated with "sympathetic indulgence." He believes Dreiser to have been grossly overrated as an example of the political skewing of literary judgment. To support his view, Trilling adduces Dreiser's weakest qualities, which everyone indeed recognizes, his "doctrinaire," crude cast of mind, his anti-Semitism, and "intellectual vulgarity." He disputes the widespread view that Dreiser's awkward prose is transcended by the depth of his observation. Trilling replies that "the great novelists have usually written very good prose."[18] While one would agree that this is "usually" the case, Trilling does not see that Dreiser is an exception in this respect. It was unfortunate that publication of *The Bulwark* (1946), one of Dreiser's weakest works, appears to have been the occasion for this essay. It is fair to say that the literary community as a whole has not supported Trilling's wholly negative judgment of Dreiser. The weakness of Trilling's assault on liberalism is thereby revealed: in the guise of a critique of liberalism he tended to throw doubt on the validity of liberalism—and radicalism—altogether.

I say "tended" because at this point the process is subtle. His real target was the radicalism that he had himself rejected. No sensible person would dispute that both liberalism and radicalism were wide open to severe criticism, then and now. The effect of Trilling's critique, however, was to contribute to the minimizing of liberalism and rejection of radicalism. As Alfred Kazin was to remark in 1978, "Trilling, with his strong sense of history and his exquisite sense of accommodation, was the most successful leader of deradicalization—which was conducted in the name of the liberal 'imagination' against those who lacked it or had the wrong kind."[19]

This "deradicalization" can not be better illustrated than in Trilling's response to the 1952 *Partisan Review* symposium in "Our Country and Our Culture." What is remarkable about his contribution was that Trilling's movement away from his earlier radicalism and liberalism had come so far that he makes no mention of the Cold War or McCarthyism, which were then debilitating the moral and political integrity of large sections of American intellectuals by the failure of most to resist a mindless imperative to political and intellectual conformity.

Trilling even went so far as to assert without qualification that "there is an unmistakable improvement in the present American cultural situation over that of thirty years ago"—this at a time when many people refused to sign their names to a copy of the Bill of Rights for fear of being charged with "subversion." In the face of this repressive atmosphere, Trilling could write that "for the first time in his life" one could "wag his tongue as he pleases." He held that "liberal ideas," though not "dominant," were by then "strongly established." What *might* be a hint of a blemish is that he would not deny that "resistance" to liberal ideas "often takes an ugly and mindless form." At the end, however, he joins to this "reaffirmation and rediscovery of America" the need to continue "the tradition of critical non-conformism."[20]

Trilling did indeed sustain this "critical non-conformism" to the end of his life, but his criticism did not extend to the social and political. It was confined to the strictly "cultural" and to the conflict within the individual, the "self" as exemplified, for instance, in Freudianism. For several decades he made this clear in the titles of his next two books: *The Opposing Self* (1953) and *Beyond Culture* (1965). He modernized Arnold's view of literature as a "criticism of life" by interpreting "life" to include essentially the cultural and psychological. He was explicit: "I speak of the realization of self to *culture* rather than *society*" (emphasis in original), and always he emphasized the "complexity" of the relation of society to culture.[21] The concept of *Beyond Culture* is another way of saying the same thing: the critic stands above and beyond culture in order to criticize it. He has the "adversary intention, the actually subversive intention" of modernism in literature, gaining "a vantage point" from which to grasp and criticize and "perhaps revise" his culture.[22] The presupposition of this approach would appear the conviction that there is an inevitable tension between the individual and his culture to which the critic must be sensitive and which he must articulate.

This type of criticism is entirely compatible with the "deradicalizing" influence of Trilling, since it limited its critical scope to "culture" and assumed anti-radical and even sometimes anti-liberal sociopolitical positions. The "adversary culture" which he advocated was indeed limited to culture. His influence tended to lose some of its strength as the 1950s wore on, and by the 1960s many of his students took their stand with the "New Left." By the 1970s, however, a curious change took place. His former student Norman Podhoretz diverted *Commentary* from the Left course it had taken after Podhoretz became editor in 1960 and launched the magazine on a systematic, unrelenting attack on every aspect of current liberal and radical tendency. *Commentary* took the neo-conservative course that a number of Jewish New York intellectuals had adopted in extreme reaction against the excesses of the New Left. Trilling was also in some manner part of this tendency, though he refused to join the shrill campaign after Podhoretz asked for and received consent for cooperation from Trilling. But apparently Trilling drew back and did not join the crusade after all. Podhoretz later wrote that Trilling had "accused" him of "overreacting to the excesses of the new radicalism and of going too far in celebrating the virtues of American society and the values of the middle class spirit."[23] A number of Trilling's pupils were now turning on the master's notion of "adversary culture," which they now regarded as "the ruling spirit of an entire 'new class.' " It became the target of the neo-conservative attack, as Peter Steinfels observed.[24] Trilling's caution and care for "modulation" of approach arising from the "complexity" of ideas and culture had left him behind in a period calling for incisive thought and firm action. His final stance was passivity: he did not articulate in public his distaste for the course of Podhoretz and his allies.

Although the active influence of Trilling fell off after the 1950s, he probably holds a secure place in the history of American literary criticism. Shortly after his death in 1975 all his important work was republished in a uniform edition of twelve volumes under the editorship of his wife, Diana Trilling. His call in the 1940s for a recognition of greater "complexity" in the approach to literary and cultural—and, it should be added, social—problems was salutary, if not used as an excuse for passivity. While a call for "complexity" sometimes turned out to be a cover for the simplistic, especially in sociopolitical debate during the Cold War and McCarthyite periods, Trilling's *caveat* has enduring value, despite the limitations on his thought of his basic timidity, both in the scope of his "criticism" and the inadequacies of his realization of his Jewishness.

## PHILIP RAHV

Among the many critics brought forth by the "Jewish Renaissance," one of the most important was Philip Rahv. But he scarcely touched on the Jewish aspect of contemporary writing except when it could not be avoided. One can only suppose that this feature of literature did not interest him deeply. It is significant, for instance, that the editors of the first anthology of current writing by Jews, *Breakthrough* (1964), included an essay by Rahv, which was the only prose piece in the volume that had no connection with Jews as such. Rahv also wrote an essay introducing a collection of Kafka's stories, very briefly and inadequately in a single paragraph noting Kafka's attitude toward the Jews and Jewishness.[25] In a 1967 essay on Bernard Malamud, however, he does make important observations on current American Jewish writing. He warns against the "homogenization" of such writing, noting that these writers do not form a "school," but vary widely in their "literary process," as well as in the "Jewishness" of their "sensibility and feeling."[26] In some cases, Jewishness is remote from their creative process. He is right, I believe, in judging that Norman Mailer's "consciousness of himself as a Jew is, I would say, quite unimportant to him as a writer"— though I would add, only after *The Naked and the Dead*. In some Jewish writers, Rahv says, "it is only in their bent for convictions that they call to mind some vestigial qualities of their ethnic background." And most, he holds, are "ambivalent" about their Jewishness. Malamud is distinctive in that he "fills his 'Jewishness' with a positive content." Malamud identifies this with the comic potentialities in tragedy and suffering (Rahv quotes from one of the stories, "*Leid macht auch lachen*," which he translates as, "suffering also makes for laughter"). To Malamud, Rahv says, literature is not a compartmentalized aesthetic category, but "a mode of truth-saying."[27] Rahv also finds Malamud adapting his English style to the emotional intensities of his Jewish characters, while permitting errors in grammar and syntax so that the result sounds like "apt imitations of Yiddish."[28] The Jewish in Malamud is also his sensitivity to suffering and refusal to assent to the fashionable current nihilism.

The minimal attention to the Jew in literature in the body of Philip Rahv's criticism should not be taken as a rejection of his Jewish identity. The reason must have been that other literary-cultural problems held far greater interest for him. He was surely no sycophant of the non-Jewish moderns like T. S. Eliot and Ezra Pound, much as he admired their work. His response in 1949 to *Commentary*'s symposium on "The Jewish Writer and the English Literary Tradition" vigorously condemns the "neo-Christian revival in literature" that Leslie Fiedler had charged as responsible for a recent increase of literary anti-Semitism. He agrees with those who hold that anti-Semitism is "integral to the Christian epic," which is in turn "integral to the kind of religiosity professed by writers like T. S. Eliot." He calls on all intellectuals to "struggle against the new religiosity" but on "wholly non-sectarian grounds, such as that the new religiosity is hostile to the best interests of the mind" and facilitates evasion of "truly urgent problems." He argues against the trend of some Jewish writers to "accommodate themselves to the current literary enthusiasm for myth and tradition," and asks that they devote themselves to a "radical secularizing and internationalizing of culture."[29]

This response reveals his categorical rejection of any compromise with the reactionary aspects of the modernist masters, and particularly their anti-Semitism. His international intellectual outlook further requires condemnation of "neo-Christian" religious anti-Semitism. This form of anti-Semitism was in fact only one phase of a broader problem, which was continuous with the pre–World War II upsurge and had been widespread during the war. While Rahv confines himself to the "religiosity" of T. S. Eliot, he does not consider the breadth of the problem as manifested in the secular form it took, for instance, in Ezra Pound. Pound's anti-Semitism was not itself influential in the literary community, but it is symptomatic of the broader scope of the problem in literature, which Rahv ignores. Rahv was obviously little interested in responding as a Jew, but responded mainly as a literary internationalist devoted to the development of basically American contributions to this internationalist culture.

He must be reckoned a leading influence on the course of American literature from the late 1930s through his participation in the foundation and editing of the *Partisan Review* and especially his work on Henry James and Fyodor Dostoyevsky, both in editing editions of their fiction and in his essays on them. A number of his miscellaneous essays have continuing interest for students of American literature, such as that in "Palefaces and Redskins," which signalizes a "polarization" and "fragmentation" of our literature between the types of Henry James ("Paleface") and Walt Whitman ("Redskin"). It is the division which "has produced a dichotomy between experience and consciousness—a dissociation between energy and sensibility, between conduct and theories of conduct, between life conceived as an opportunity and life conceived as a discipline."[30]

Rahv was also one of the few New York Jewish writers and intellectuals who kept his head during McCarthyism and did not compromise his integrity. He derided his fellow anti-Stalinist intellectuals for their equivocal response to McCarthyism and for attempting to make anti-Stalinism a total outlook on life and culture, thus grossly distorting their political and cultural judgment. These views are openly expressed in his personal contribution to the *Partisan* symposium on "Our Country and Our Culture," which criticized not only the "petrified anti-Stalinism" of many of his colleagues, but also that of some who are "parvenu conservatives, for instance, who, having discovered the pleasures of conformity, are now aggressively bent on combating all dissent from the bourgeois outlook and devaluating the critical traditions of modern thought."[31] During the turbulent 1960s Rahv found this atmosphere at *Partisan Review* stifling and broke away after three decades as an editor.

## ALFRED KAZIN

Each Jewish critic related his work to Jewishness in his own way. Trilling (after his *Menorah Journal* period) virtually ignored Jewishness in his writing, except for a few occasions. And although Philip Rahv took his Jewish identity for granted in less problematic fashion than Trilling, he introduced it even less in his writing. Alfred Kazin is far more overt and assertive about his Jewishness. But this emerged only after *On Native Grounds* appeared in 1942. Despite the mature modernism of this account, subtitled "An Interpretation of Modern American Prose Literature" from 1890 on, Kazin was still a prisoner of the Anglo-Saxon bias that prevailed in American literary history until the post–World War II period. There is in his book no mention, let alone discussion, of important Jewish writers within this period who wrote about the Jewish milieu. Among the absent are Abraham Cahan, Daniel Fuchs, Meyer Levin, Clifford Odets, and Henry Roth (by 1965 Kazin was calling attention to *Call It Sleep* as the most neglected masterpiece of the past quarter century!). Mike Gold's *Jews Without Money* is mentioned only in passing while his leading role in "proletarian" criticism gets more attention. On the other hand, Ludwig Lewisohn receives about ten pages of discussion as critic of the drama and literature generally. There is no mention of *The Island Within*, but discrimination against Lewisohn as a Jew in academic life is noted. The reason for the extended treatment was, of course, that Lewisohn was Kazin's predecessor in the history of American literature—and a Jewish one. Lewisohn's *Expression in American Literature* (1932) was a predecessor—only chronologically—of Kazin's *On Native Grounds*. Lewisohn's critical works during the 1910s and 1920s, with all their faults in being overshadowed by the author's emotional personality, were important. Lewisohn's "worst qualities," wrote Kazin, "represented the exaggerations of a mind which was itself indispensable to the growth of a mature criticism in America." Kazin recognized in Lewisohn an earlier colleague who, with all his faults as a critic, was "a force for progress."[32]

Lewisohn's work in criticism and literary history has not been durable; it is now of mainly historical interest. Kazin's *On Native Grounds*, however, differed from the earlier Jewish critic's work both in its superior viability and in the fact that it was only one manifestation, if one of the most important, of the emergence of a multitude of Jewish talents in criticism, creative literature, and literary scholarship. Lewisohn had few Jewish peers in his time; Kazin had a number. Most stemmed from an immigrant generation and were only a few decades away from the East European ghettos.

They gave the lie to the obtuse belief, which persisted into the 1930s, that Jews were incapable of grasping Western philosophy and literature. (A Jewish recipient of this myopic Anglo-Saxon vision told me in the 1930s at Harvard that the eminent professor of philosophy, Ernest M. Hocking, had told him that Jewish students could not understand Western philosophy.) As Rahv observed, these Jewish writers did not form a "school," but were varied. They did have several features in common, however. They were nearly all "modernists," that is, emulated the new sensibility exemplified in the works of Henry James, James Joyce, Marcel Proust, T. S. Eliot, Ezra Pound, Franz Kafka, and Fyodor Dostoyevsky. They did not follow the hermetic esthetic of the New Critics, but rather saw literature as a social and historical expression, and located it in a cultural context, while they rejected the constricted, politically dominated approach to literature of mechanical Marxism. While abandoning the Marxism from which they had emerged, they did not altogether forsake the historical approach that was a residue of that Marxism.

Thus, when at the age of twenty-seven Kazin published *On Native Grounds*, a son of immigrant parents and still living in the Brownsville Jewish quarter, he became an authoritative critic of American literature. His book was a peak of historical American criticism, preceded by the works of Van Wyck Brooks and the social criticism of American ideas by Parrington. Alfred Kazin in the "Under Forty" symposium was among those who responded to define his relationship to the Jewish heritage. His omission of leading works set in the Jewish milieu did not signify rejection of the Jewish heritage but was only a sign of the more general neglect of the ethnic element in American cultural life at the time. In his response, Kazin affirms that there is much in the Jewish heritage that he admired—the Yiddish writers Sholem Aleichem and I. L. Peretz, the heroic Jews of the Jewish Socialist Bund, Rosa Luxembourg, builders of a Hebrew culture in then Palestine, contemporary writers and artists like Hayim Nachman Bialik, and artists like Marc Chagall and Ernest Bloch. He admires in the Jew the "texture of a genuine and received Hebrew culture; an indestructable belief in the spiritual foundations of a human life; the feeling for the book; ... universal curiosity." What he did reject were attempts by Jewish writers toward an American-Jewish culture, which he believed had no real ground on which to grow. "The experience of being an immigrant, or an immigrant's son," he thought, was confused with "the experience of being Jewish." The "confusion" is in some degree his. True, immigrant life, whatever the nationality, had much in common in its poverty, slum living conditions, oppressive labor, and exploitation. But the life of each immigrant nationality group had its own ethnic character, which it brought with it from the country of origin. Thus the life of immigrant Jews for many years bore the marks of an East European ghetto origin and a Western European sense of difference from the dominant ethnic group. Perhaps Kazin's failure to comment in his first book on the existence of an ethnic American-Jewish fiction may be rooted in his confusion about fiction set in the American-Jewish milieu. However, it is true, as he remarks—and is true of so many other Jewish writers—he was "Jewish without being a part of any meaningful Jewish life or culture."[33] This is very different from his erroneous denial of any Jewish element in Jewish immigrant life. He was, for the most part, a full and conscious participant in American cultural life without interest in or significant participation in Jewish ethnic life, whether religious or secular.

But the consequences of being a Jew could not be ignored. The writers around *Commentary*, sensitized by their knowledge of the Holocaust and the struggle to establish a Jewish state, were troubled that those writers of our time they most admired, not to speak of many of the greatest English writers through the centuries, were anti-Semitic and expressed their anti-Semitism in their creative work. In his response to *Commentary*'s symposium on "The Jewish Writer and the English Literary Tradition," Alfred Kazin angrily remarked about modernist masters—Eliot, Pound, Henry James, Dostoyevsky, and others—"How we love them, though they love us not!" Like the Jews, he says, they are alienated from the majority, yet "they are always stupid about us, and insult us." Even more, the irony is that "some of us would be indistinguishable from them, if we are not that already." In the face of this situation, "to exile us from them" would be "stupid." "Forgiveness," he says, is irrelevant: "We must read them and endure—angrily so, of course; without toadying, not afraid to call ignorance and heartlessness by their right names even if they do come from our literary dictators."[34]

During the postwar years, in the midst of his incessant university teaching, book reviewing, and critical writing, Kazin turned to recording reminiscences of his life with his parents in Brownsville. The first volume, *The Walker in the City* (1951), recreates the atmosphere of his boyhood to age sixteen and is drenched in nostalgia. He described his self-enclosed Jewish milieu with its strong sense of the "beyond" of the non-Jewish community totally alien to him. He loved to wander the streets of New York, looking at the city about him with a suffusion of warmth, but circumscribed by his then only partial adaptation to non-Jewish life. Indeed, this book is a significant document in the literature of the transition to acculturation. It is subjective and emotionally wrought with the sensibility of a highly sensitive boy who vaguely gropes toward a broader life than that afforded by his poverty-stricken immigrant milieu. "Why," the boy asks himself, "did they live *there* and we always in 'Brunzvil'? . . . Why was it always *them* and *us*? . . . Beyond was the strange world of Gentiles, all of them with flaxen hair, who hated Jews, especially poor Jews, had ugly names for us I could never read or hear without seeing Pilsudski's knife against our throats. To be a Jew meant that one's very existence was always brought into question."[35] But this sense of alienation did not inhibit the absorbed use of the public

library, which played so important a role in the acculturation process for
so many Jews in those years.

Kazin's home life is relived in a haze of tenderness, of lyric nostalgia. His
parents observed the Jewish rituals, though they were hardly religious. Inevitably he describes what was without doubt one of the loveliest recollections
of any second-generation youth: the mother's ritual lighting of the candles
at sundown on Friday to usher in the Sabbath. Socialism was the family
creed, and Kazin describes the discussions around the kitchen table. He
describes in moving terms the selfless, unremitting labors of his mother,
both in keeping the family properly fed and in her home dress-making
occupation. When the boy learns that his father, a house painter, while on
a job in the West had been offered a homestead in Omaha and had refused
it because all his friends and his "people" were back home, the boy learns
that "we were a people; I was one of those people. Unthinkable to go one's
own way, to doubt or to escape the fact that I was a Jew."[36] This conviction
was no doubt later heightened by the Holocaust.

Kazin did not attempt to write fiction, but these reminiscences about his
boyhood and young manhood in the immigrant Jewish milieu were the
equivalent of the almost inevitable novel of acculturation among so many
second-generation Jewish writers of fiction. Communication of this vanishing experience seemed almost obligatory for these writers. And Kazin fulfills
this perhaps unconscious obligation with distinction. The memoir is tender
and, like so much of his writing, emotion-laden and lyrical, though not
excessively so. Kazin took up the story in *Starting Out in the Thirties* (1965),
recounting his opening to the larger world and growth into the life of
literature and the radical politics of the decade. During this period of dis-
covery, he writes how in 1935, "Sitting in the Belasco and watching my
mother and father and uncles and aunts occupying the stage in *Awake and
Sing* by as much right as if they were Hamlet and Lear, I understood at
last. It was all one, as I had always known. Art and truth and hope could
come together—if a real writer was their meeting place, Odets convinced
me."[37]

When Kazin resumed his story in 1978, the title was a manifesto of ethnic
assertion and defiance—*New York Jew*. It was by implication a demon-
strative statement that a son of immigrant Jews was a standard-bearer of
American literature, living in an intellectual and literary ambience in which
other sons of immigrant Jews were also leaders of the mode of literature in
which they were engaged, whether fiction, poetry, criticism, or scholarship.
Opening with publication of *On Native Grounds*, Kazin recounts aspects
of his experience in World War II and personal life for the next few decades.
Most interesting, however, are the vignettes of leading contemporary American men of letters, from Edmund Wilson and Lionel Trilling to Saul Bellow,
and of leading figures around the *Partisan Review* and *Commentary*. His
comments are not always complimentary. However, despite assertion of his

Jewish identity and respectful treatment of his Yiddish-speaking early environment, he alludes very little to Yiddish literary culture; he is wholly steeped in American culture in English. He criticizes the ambiguous attitude toward McCarthyism of many of his colleagues, but, judging from his allusions to Communists, his own attitude toward them was one of mass, collective, undifferentiated contempt and hostility.

Just as Trilling's leadership of modernist American literature and culture was recognized in his introduction to the *Partisan Review* in 1946, so Kazin's status was implicit in his introduction to the anthology of two decades of writing in *The Commentary Reader* in 1966. His essay, itself much anthologized, discussed "The Jew As Modern Writer," a most appropriate subject for a retrospective look at the magazine. He advances the interesting idea that the American public was prepared to receive the Jew as a modern American writer "in the first years of this century . . . not in the universities, not even in journalism, but in the vaudeville theaters, music halls, and burlesque houses" by such figures as "The Marx Brothers, Eddie Cantor, Al Jolson, Fannie Brice, George Gershwin, Jewish clowns, minstrels, songwriters." The "ease" with which they fitted into American life and their welcome by the mass public conveyed (contrary to the popular stereotype, I might add) "the Jew's averageness and typicality that were to make possible the Jew-as-writer in this country." Emerging from a milieu not too far from persecution and enlightenment in their East European homelands, the Jewish writer "lived at the crossroads between the cultures and on the threshold between life and death." Such people, Kazin goes on, "naturally see existence as tension, issue and drama." This situation bore fruit in the 1930s, he holds, when numbers of Jewish writers appeared, and some even wrote memorable fiction and drama—named here by Kazin, but not mentioned in *On Native Grounds*. The next phase, which Kazin believes "saved Jewish writing from its innate provincialism," was dominated by intellectuals of the post–World War II around *Partisan* and *Commentary* who rejected Marxism and created a body of writing that exercised great influence on American culture. "There were now," wrote Kazin, "Jewish novelists who, as writers, had mastered the complex resources of the modern novel, who wrote English lovingly, possessively, masterfully, for whom the language and the form, the intelligence of art, had become as natural a way of living as the Law had been to their grandfathers."[38]

## LESLIE FIEDLER

Though not on a level qualitatively with Trilling, Rahv, and Kazin, Leslie Fiedler does have importance in bringing to awareness and widespread discussion the emergence of Jews in the literary mainstream. Of all the well-known writers of the century, he has probably published more, with the exception of Irving Howe, on the Jew and literature. When he published his *Collected Essays* in two volumes in 1971, about one-third of the space of one volume was given over to the Jewish theme. He was born in Newark, New Jersey (as was Philip Roth) in 1917 and became a fervent Communist in his teen years. Disillusionment set in by the late 1930s with the Moscow purge trials and the Soviet-Nazi pact in 1939. As in so much else, his anti-Communism was a swing to an anti-Communism to outdo the anti-Communists. When Alfred Kazin reviewed Fiedler's first book, *An End to Innocence* (1955), he commented indignantly on Fiedler's "outrageous calculation that *we* murdered only two Rosenbergs whereas *they* can shoot millions without arousing the same indignation."[39]

Writing in the *Congress Weekly* after the war, Fiedler suggests that he considers the difficulties of the intellectual who tries to reach " 'back' toward Judaism." Fiedler rejects much in contemporary Judaism—what is "moribund" in Orthodoxy and its stifling *pilpul* and the glibness of the middle-class American stylishness of Reform. He complains that "in general American Judaism has made everything its center in God." To "the returning Jew,... the heart of Jewish belief seems to be in the phrase, the Messiah *will* come!... This sense of the endless futurity of redemption strikes me as the essential beauty and truth of Judaism.... Our aspirations point the way out of time."[40] However, he did attach himself to institutional Judaism sufficiently to contribute to *American Judaism* in the 1960s. For about two years he wrote a bi-monthly article of comments on current American writing by Jewish writers.

His frequent writing on the Jew in American literature no doubt stimulated thought and discussion of the matter in literary circles. We have seen how, in 1948, his contribution to the *Partisan Review* symposium on "The State of American Writing" was the only one which thought Jewish participation should be mentioned, triggered by notice of the central importance of the Jew Kafka in that writing. Kafka's "Jewishness," wrote Fiedler, "is by no means incidental; the real Jew and the imaginary Jew [that is, as he appears in literature, as for example, in Joyce's *Ulysses*] between them give to the current period its special flavor." He points to a "generation of writers and critics" in their thirties—Delmore Schwartz, Alfred Kazin, Isaac Rosenfeld, Paul Goodman, Saul Bellow—who exemplify that in our time "Jewishness" is "a condition of the Artist."[41] We also saw how, in the next year, Fiedler's challenging *Commentary* article, "What Can We Do About Fagin?" bringing into the open the anti-Semitism in the English literary tradition, and even among the revered modernist masters, like T. S. Eliot and Ezra Pound, precipitated, as the editors noted, the *Commentary* symposium on "The Jewish Writer and the English Literary Tradition."

During this period Fiedler applied this wide vogue for literary interpretation via "myth" to the problem in his article on Fagin. Fiedler was notoriously ridden by one passing fashion after another. In the early post–World War II years, as Irving Howe writes, some avant-garde intellectuals underwent "that series of gyrations in opinion, interest and outlook.... Some intellectuals turned to a week-end of religion, some to a semester of existentialism, some to a holiday of Jewishness without faith or knowledge, some to a season of genteel conservatism. Leslie Fiedler, no doubt by design, seemed to go through more of such episodes than anyone else: even his admirers could not always be certain whether he was *davening* [praying] or doing a rain dance."[42] At this time his work was ridden with "myth" to which he resorted as a kind of panacea of explanation. Thus in his *Commentary* article he offered an answer to the anti-Semitic "myth" of the Jew in English literature: create "rival myths..., other images of the Jew to dispossess the ancient imagery of terror," that is, in plain language, the anti-Semitic stereotype of the Satanic Jew. He observes that some of these already exist—"the alienated Jew as artist (Kafka's K),...or citizen (Joyce's Bloom)," and Saul Bellow's characters.[43] Are these "myths"? Is it not more accurate to think of them as *symbolic concepts* with a substantial element of reality and rooted in that reality? For the relation of "myth" to reality is ambiguous—the connotation of myth is predominantly that of fantasy—while what is needed is not still more fantasy but an approximation of the truth about Jews. Stanley Edgar Hyman was properly indignant, in his contribution to the symposium, at Fiedler, "like so many others, [who] use 'myth' to mean a damned lie."[44] Hyman explains that the "*reality* of myth," for instance of the anti-Semitic ritual murder story in Chaucer, lies in its origins, in ancient ritual sacrifice—*this is the* mythical aspect of the story. The literal anti-Semitic aspect of the story is not a "myth" but a "damned lie." The correction, so far as literature is concerned, is not a "counter-myth," which is just as false as the myth, but in the symbolic figures—for instance, as Fiedler notes, Joyce's Bloom or Kafka's figures, or Bellow's Jewish characters. Such is the Jewish character in so much fiction of the post–World War II period—an alienated person recognized as the symbol of the prevailing general mood of alienation.

Associated with Fiedler's modish notion of "myth" is his use of the idea of archetype, the recurrent character type throughout history—and in consequence ahistorical—and he applies these concepts to his major work, *Love and Death in the American Novel* (1960). The literary historian and critic Robert Alter, who has delved deeply into the Jew in literature, remarks that Fiedler in his use of archetypes "clearly shares with the medieval Midrash an indifference to historical perspectives,"[45] and this leads him into misinterpretation and even anachronism, which in turn lead him erroneously to regard the biblical Joseph as an archetypal figure represented in modern times by Freud and Kafka. Fiedler's thesis in his history of the American novel is not only that its characters are archetypal, but that the novel is throughout deformed by its genteel avoidance of sex and an attachment to death. Fiedler thereby applies to the novel the two cardinal precepts of Freudianism, eros and thanatos. A by-product of this large project was

Fiedler's pamphlet, *The Jew in the American Novel* (1959), which is one of his most influential pieces of writing on the Jew in literature. The pamphlet is to some extent informative and often commonsensical, but the imposition of the archetype and love-death pattern often ignores facts that weaken his thesis. So, for instance, Fiedler says of the half-Jewish characters, the Ruth of Melville's *Clarel* and the Miriam of Hawthorne's *The Marble Faun* that they are "prototypes" of "dark projections of sexual experience or allure, foils to the pale, Anglo-Saxon maiden...being death-driven."[46] But there is no "pale, Anglo-Saxon maiden" in *Clarel,* and while Ruth does die, Miriam survives. However, for the most part, Fiedler rides his hobby horses only occasionally through his swift summary of some highlights of the Jew in fiction, and most of it, when it deals with fact and generally recognized judgments of writers and movements, is helpful, especially as an introduction to the whole subject.

Fiedler continued to write about Jews in both criticism and fiction. In his criticism he projected a universal aspect of human existence into a special Jewish feature. In 1963, together with David Boroff, Max Lerner, and Philip Roth, he participated in an Israeli-American dialogue in Israel, sponsored by the American Jewish Congress, on the meaning of Jewish identity as it relates to Jewish intellectuals and writers in the United States and Israel. Fiedler offered his conception of the Jew: "quite simply," he said—and we should be wary of any suggestion that anything about the Jews is "simple"!—"*not to belong,* but to belong; to be an exile; to be alienated; to know at every moment that wherever one finds himself he is alienated." In the course of the discussion of this concept, Fiedler acquiesced in Philip Roth's interpretation of its meaning as that a Jew's essence is to be a dissenter or, as Fiedler preferred, "the duty of the Jew is to bear witness." In any case, as a loose thinker Fiedler tends to be carried away by an idea and to slip into exaggeration and sometimes misstatement. What this conception does is to ignore altogether the ethnicity of the Jew and to define the Jew by one historical fact about this people, because this is what happens to interest him most. The essence of the Jewish tradition, he believes, is to dissent, to "bear witness" against "ignorance and sloth and discrimination and failure to live up to ideals and bribery and corruption," which are "always" with us, wherever we may be.[47]

But Fiedler is saying both too little and too much. Too little, because the Jewish ethnic character is not simply, up to now, a sense of not belonging owing to historical conditions that have not yet been completely removed anywhere. If Fiedler were to apply this measure to the Jewish community throughout its existence, there would have been precious few Jews in all history. As an ethnic group the Jews have developed certain psychological and social characteristics that, *as Jews,* have differentiated them from other ethnic or national entities. They are Jews by virtue of these ethnic characteristics, of which a tendency to dissent is only one feature because of their peculiar history. Their ethnic character includes a complex of customs and cultural features. Fiedler is here confusing one ethnic feature of the Jewish tradition with the whole ethnic character. Whether Fiedler is aware of it or not, he is defining the Jews in religio-ethical, rather than ethnic terms. Conformist Jews are no less Jews in objective fact than non-conformist. Indeed, there is a conformist as well as a prophetic dissenting tradition among Jews. All are Jews in some sense though they have conflicting social and ethical judgments as to their mode of life.

And Fiedler is saying too much because he arrogates to Jews the human essence of "bearing witness," of being the heroic dissenter. He accepts the traditional view of Jews as the "Chosen People" but gives it his peculiar interpretation: "If you are chosen," he says, "*you cannot choose!*" That is, if you would be a Jew, then you *must* dissent, you *must* "bear witness"; otherwise you are not one of the Chosen People. It is true that, because the Jew has been victimized throughout so much of history, he should be and is, in fact, out of proportion to his numbers, a resister of victimization of any kind. His history, one might say, obliges him to "bear witness." But this is one ethnic characteristic and not the whole of the ethnic character. Under pressure of criticism Fiedler later restated his view: "I meant to say that it is the duty of the Jew, at any moment to 'bear witness.' "[48] One might agree with this statement without asserting that this is all of Jewishness.

Furthermore, all ethnic and national groups have a tradition of dissent. Dissent is a *human* rather than a unique trait of any one people. Could not one say with equal validity of the American as of the Jew that it is his duty to dissent against injustice of any kind? That it is the duty of every human being to do so? The fact that his history and condition renders the Jew more susceptible to dissent does not make this the beginning and the end of his Jewishness. Fiedler says that it is the duty of every American Jew to bear witness with the Black against the latter's second-class citizenship. The fact that history has made the Jew especially responsive to this obligation does not mitigate the duty of every non-Jewish American to bear witness against deprivation of the rights of Blacks. In this sense it is equally the duty of non-Jewish Americans to do so.

Fiedler's exaggeration in this case is one aspect of a phenomenon that tended to occur in the era of Jewish emergence into the center of the mainstream. This is described by Robert Alter in his comment on Fiedler. "There has been a tacit conspiracy afoot in recent years," wrote Alter in 1968, "to foist on the American public as peculiarly Jewish various admired characteristics which in fact belong to the common humanity of us all." Alter cites as an instance Fiedler's attempt in an essay on the biblical Joseph story to have us "believe that the Jews all along exercised a privileged control over the cultural market in dreams. . . . [Fiedler] is describing not a distinctively Jewish imaginative mode but the central tradition of the novel."[49] On this, as on most subjects, Fiedler lacks judgment and vitiates much of what he writes by allowing an idea to cavort on a hobby horse, as he did, for instance, in his application of Freudianism to American fiction in his *Love and Death in the American Novel*. His voluminous writing on the Jew in literature is written with brilliance. He tosses off dubious generalizations and sometimes inaccurate observations. One senses at the root a quick articulateness which attempts to cover up the vulnerability of a hypersensitive temperament. Through the 1960s he continued to discuss the Jew in literature and publish short stories and novels in which his extravagant notions are embodied.

When the 1960s were over, his interests had shifted again and he announced in the preface to his *Collected Essays* that the section on Jewish themes was his "valedictory, my farewell to the subject... which seems at the moment exhausted, both in terms of my own interests and that of the young audiences who no longer find in Jewish experience viable images of their own characteristics and fate."[50] By this time, however problematic one may consider his contribution to an understanding of the Jew in literature, the stimulus of his writing to interest in the subject was considerable.


## IRVING HOWE

But more than any other critic of the post–World War II period, Irving Howe has been influential and deeply involved in the effort to understand the functioning of the Jew in current American literature and to heighten awareness in the country as a whole of Jewish social and cultural traditions. Perhaps one can, in part, find the reason in the fact that he is the youngest of the critics discussed here, and hence the assimilationist trend among the second generation affected him less strongly than the others. He was born in the Bronx of poor immigrant parents in 1920—fifteen years after Trilling, five years after Kazin, and three years after Fiedler. In addition, Howe's body of writing is evidence that he was differently, perhaps more profoundly, touched by the Holocaust and the renewal of Jewish statehood than the others. For he was moved not only to probe the significance of the cultural expression of his Jewish literary contemporaries, but also to make available to the entire American public something of the cultural heritage of the Yiddish-speaking culture, the greatest part of whose living community was obliterated in the Holocaust. This he did by editing, in conjunction with the Yiddish poet Eliezer Greenberg, one volume after another in English translation of Yiddish stories, poetry, essays, memoirs, diaries, and other anthologies. And the climax of all this devotion to the Yiddish past came, as everyone knows, with the enormously popular *The World of Our Fathers* in 1976.

Howe's resolve to widen the knowledge of Yiddish culture among all English-speaking people, non-Jews as well as Jews, was only one substantial response to the Holocaust. Another—not pursued by Howe—was to study and disseminate awareness of Hebrew literature as the legacy and fortune of the Jewish people, the path generally taken by those touched by Zionism. This path was followed, for instance, by Robert Alter, who is younger than Howe, and hence is more likely to have been affected by Zionism and the creation of Israel. For Howe is a product of the Jewish Left and has never been a Zionist, though a staunch defender of the existence of Israel. As a teenager Howe became a member of the Young People's Socialist League and was for a time a Trotskyist. Like most of the Jewish Left, whether Stalinist, Trotskyist, Bundist, or any other variety (except for Socialist-Zionist), Howe was critical of Zionism and did not at any time ally himself with that movement, much of which tended to denigrate Yiddish as part of its rejection of the bi-millennial "diaspora." But Howe felt a keen identification with the Yiddish-speaking past of his forebears, and felt an affinity with it as the language of the pioneer Jewish labor movement, which was Yiddish-speaking, both in Tsarist Russia and in this country.

Unlike the other critics of the period, Howe sustained his political interest by writing and editing. Indeed, the variety of his published writings is extraordinary, ranging from a history of the United States Communist party (co-authored with Lewis Coser) and editorship of anthologies on sociological themes and socialist theories, to literary biography. Since 1954, when he founded *Dissent*, a journal of loosely liberal and Left tendency, he has been involved in sociopolitical journalism. Throughout he has poured forth a stream of articles and reviews on literary and socioliterary topics. Interspersed among all this writing activity and editing were critical literary biographies of Sherwood Anderson (1951), William Faulkner (1952), and Thomas Hardy (1967), as well as a short life of Leon Trotsky (1978).

While still a graduate student at Brooklyn College, Howe was already interested in diagnosing the mentality of his Jewish intellectual contemporaries. An article, "The Lost Young Intellectual: A Marginal Man, Twice Alienated" (*Commentary*, September, 1947) tells much in the title: the subject of this analysis is estranged from both the general American and the Jewish community from which he sprang. He is beset by multiple tensions: "*It is difficult to be a Jew and just as difficult not to be one*"; "*He has lost the sense of continuity which was such sustenance to his forefathers.*" He is in conflict with his immigrant father's ambition that he become a successful "professional" man because he is an anti-bourgeois radical, and their cultural interests are far apart and they find it hard to communicate. And finally, the respective statuses of parents and children are reversed: By the time the second generation has emerged from adolescence, his parents have become more or less integrated into American society, while the children are the new outsiders. Howe rejects several proposed solutions—Zionism, "return to traditional Judaism," "Jewish education," "reconstruction of a Jewish community and a Jewish culture." None of these is "realistic" to Howe. The only solution is socialism—though he doesn't use the term—

"an American society in which both the Jewish intellectual and his people, along with everyone else, can find integration, security, and acceptance."[51] Would Howe make the same analysis three decades later? Probably not. Too much had intervened, and the situation of the Jew had become even more complex, in view of his successful entry into numerous areas of American life which had been closed to him in the immediate postwar period, and many erstwhile, now disillusioned, radicals had made their peace with the Establishment.

Howe himself remained a socialist, and indeed never swerved from commitment to some form of socialism, differing in this respect from most of his colleagues among the "New York intellectuals," that is, writers and critics orbiting around the *Partisan Review* and *Commentary*. He was a contributor to both journals. Evidence of his deepening interest in the Jew in literature was another *Commentary* article, "The Stranger and the Victim: The Two Stereotypes of American Fiction" (August, 1949). The piece discusses the Jewish character in modern American novels by Jewish writers from Abraham Cahan to Henry Roth, and the major non-Jewish authors of the 1920s. Most American authors, he notes, deny the Jew in fiction "the one right the Jew needs most: existence as a unique human being, with an individuality of his own."[52] Then in the October, 1949 issue, Howe contributed his response to the challenge in the symposium on "The Jewish Writer and the English Literary Tradition." He leaves no doubt that he does not condone anti-Semitism, whatever the source. But he makes an important distinction between the anti-Semitism in the ritual murder story in Geoffrey Chaucer and the anti-Semitism of modern writers like Ezra Pound and T. S. Eliot. Chaucer was "expressing a point of view universally accepted in the Christian world of his lifetime," but such mitigation is not available to Dreiser, Eliot, and Pound. Yet one cannot be "totally at ease" with a tradition of Jewish caricatures. "Far more reprehensible," however, is anti-Semitism, "occasional, unsystematic, even unmalicious," in modern writers because they should know better in a more enlightened age in this respect. We must not, Howe concludes, "let any notions about the inviolability of literature or the sacredness of art sway us from expressing our spontaneous passionate feelings about those contemporary writers who succumb, willingly or not, to anti-Semitism."[53]

Howe was one of the minority of New York intellectuals, many Jewish, who did not succumb to what has been called "the American celebration" of the 1950s, a largely uncritical acceptance of the postwar affluence and complacent assent to the Cold War policies of the government. The *Partisan–Commentary* group were perhaps at the height of their prestige and influence at this time. They were so bitterly anti-Stalinist that among a number it became an obsession and the center of their thinking. Most of them abandoned the socialism of their earlier years and some even became conservative. Howe was not among these. He had shed his Trotskyism, and his own socialist conceptions became less precise and indeed, vague. But he never renounced the necessity for socialism in some sense. During the McCarthy period he was critical of the weak, ambivalent opposition to the primitive anti-Communist demagogy of Joe McCarthy among his fellow New York intellectuals. He was consequently one of the dissenters from the Cold War Americanism in the 1952 *Partisan Review* symposium, "Our Country and Our Culture." Almost the entire critical energy of the now conforming intellectuals in this symposium was taken up with concern over the danger of a commercial mass culture—a real danger, to be sure, to standards, social, ethical, and esthetic. But Howe did not share the social complacency of many of his colleagues. He complained that they were more concerned to be anti-Stalinist than alert to the danger of war. He disputed the dismissal of Marxism, asserting that "Marxism seems to me the best available method for making and understanding history." I am not sure he would reassert this so categorically several decades later. He pointed out that despite the "peace" or "truce with the status quo" by certain intellectuals, their writing remained "profoundly withdrawn from official American life" and negativistic. The mood of current writing, Howe agrees with John Aldridge, is full of "bewilderment, fear, skepticism, lassitude, confusion, despair." Further, Howe fails to see "the 'acceptance' of America" among younger writers among established intellectuals around the *Partisan*. Howe is one of the few symposiasts who even mentioned the danger posed by McCarthyism, alluding to "the drive against civil liberties."[54] A few years later he launched a full-scale attack in *Partisan Review* (January-February, 1954) against the uncritical stance of many intellectuals toward American society in his article, "The Age of Conformity." More substantially, in light of this "conformity" in the journals of the intellectuals like *Partisan*, Howe struck out to establish in the quarterly *Dissent* a journal that would try keeping alive the strivings toward socialism, however loosely construed.

In the decades to follow Howe continued to pour out essays, books, and some books co-edited on literary criticism, sociopolitical topics, and the Jew in modern life, mainly the Jew in American literature. He was largely untouched by the school of "close reading" of texts of the New Criticism; he continued to scrutinize literary works within a social and historical context, though his work could hardly be called "Marxist," which requires a more intimate examination than he made of the socioeconomic sources, however indirect, of the literary expression. His *Politics and the Novel* (1957) is perhaps his most substantial contribution to criticism. During the 1960s his feelings toward the New Left, the revolt of the college generations against middle-class affluence and complacency, were mixed. In the May, 1965 issue of the *New Republic* he wrote with sympathy of the "positive" aspects of youthful radicalism. But later in the year he published a very long article in *Dissent*, "New Styles in 'Leftism',"which made a greater impact than the "positive" one. That there was much to criticize in the New Left, even severely, no sensible, mature person of the Left could deny. There was excess, extremism, sometimes even criminality. Criticism is essential, but it can be constructive or destructive of the basic cause with which the critic is presumably in sympathy. Howe's criticism leaves a strongly negative impression of the movement as a whole. It is interesting to note the impression left on a detached observer, the Left British social and cultural critic, Raymond Williams, in a review of Howe's *Steady Work* subtitled "Essays on the Politics of Democratic Radicalism, 1953–1966," in which the essay is reprinted. Williams says he had expected to find in this book a fellow fighter for democratic socialism. Instead, he found it necessary to report that the "steady work" of the book was "not a sustained socialist or radical criticism of those elements of United States life and policy that are profoundly dangerous to the world and to its own people." While he found some of this "occasionally present," the "dominant theme" was "sustained criticism of groups on the left." Criticism of others on the Left, he added, is necessary "as an aspect" of constructive criticism, but Howe's critiques "came through as something else."[55]

Howe's accumulated impressive competence in both social and literary disciplines was applied to the Jews in *The World of Our Fathers* (1976), which was his tribute to his forebears and to the American-Jewish community from which he came. He felt the obligation the more acutely because he believes that the Yiddish language and community have no future. He was overhasty in prematurely announcing its demise as many did before him. The mass immigrant community of the first few decades of the century that he lovingly, yet candidly and nostalgically describes is largely past, but many in the third and fourth generations are seized with an interest in Yiddish, and the language is by no means dead, as one might gather from Howe's book. Written with help of Kenneth Libo and thirteen research assistants, this 700-page book enjoyed astonishing success, gaining the Pulitzer Prize for History and becoming a best-seller. Many of the major phases in the life history of the Yiddish-speaking immigrant subculture in the United States and more specifically New York City, are treated, from their "Old Country" sources to the ebbing of its vitality owing to adaptation to the dominant culture and the shift upward in class composition. The writing, like all of Howe's work, is sprightly and readable. As might be expected from a socialist, secularist writer, the labor and socialist, as well as cultural, aspects of immigrant life are extensively treated. This is not a work of original historical research but a well-written assemblage and organization of materials gathered by innumerable researchers and presented as one coherent, comprehensive account of American-Jewish life, especially of the Yiddish-speaking immigration. However, some historians have criticized the adequacy of aspects of his labor history.

But is it true, as Robert Alter has observed in a review, that "nothing touched on is treated unfairly?"[56] Unfortunately this is not true. For despite

Howe's criticism that the anti-Stalinism of some of his literary colleagues blunted their critical social sense and led to "conformity," Howe's own anti-Stalinism on occasion led him to be careless with facts. Howe flatly asserts that after 1971, "The [*Jewish Daily*] *Forward* was now the only remaining Yiddish daily."[57] But Howe knew that the *Morning Freiheit*, the erstwhile Communist Yiddish daily, was still publishing, since he interviewed its editor. When a *Freiheit* reader challenged Howe's statement, he unceremoniously replied that "it would be hard to do it an injustice" because of its past "record as an apologist" for "Russian totalitarianism."[58] He repeats his denial that the paper is a daily—on what grounds he does not say. The fact that for at least the past two decades the *Freiheit* has severely criticized Soviet policy on the Jewish and other issues and that its editor Paul Novick was expelled from the Communist party seem to leave Howe untouched. True, financial stringency forced the *Freiheit* to publish five days a week. But the *Forward* itself has been reduced to six days a week. In the end all this argument is beside the point—the *Freiheit* was a daily when Howe wrote, and Howe obstinately denies the fact because he refused to forgive its politics of some decades ago. (More recently, *both* the *Forward* and the *Freiheit* have become weeklies.) There are other anti-historical aspects of his treatment of the Jewish labor movement where the Communist-influenced Jewish unions are concerned. While every error diminishes the value of the book, it remains an extremely valuable popular introduction to the Yiddish-speaking American subculture.

In treating more briefly the second and third generations, Howe in one section discusses "The American Jewish Novelists" and there advances the suggestive thesis that the fiction by Jewish writers that emerged since the 1930s was a "regional" literature, just as the Southern writing of that period was a "regional" literature. These two comprise the main forms of regionalism in this century, he notes. Howe further shows that, just as the Southern regionalism emerged "exactly at the moment" when the Southern subculture "approaches disintegration," the same is true of the Jewish writing. For the Jewish subculture was breaking down as the Jews became increasingly integrated in American life, just as the Southern subculture was breaking down with the growing industrialization of that region. Howe emphasized what is obvious enough, namely that the two regionalisms vary drastically in content. The Jewish development, Howe goes on to say, has enriched the English language by the stylistic influence of Yiddish. The novelists, wrote Howe, by their "Englished Yiddish and Yiddished English," have created "a new and astonishing American prose style."[59]

This observation is given extended treatment in an essay, "Strangers," which introduces his *Celebrations and Attacks: Thirty Years of Literary and Cultural Commentary* (1979), a compilation of Howe's short essays from the 1940s through the 1970s. Howe suggests that to recent Jewish writers the Russian masters like Leo Tolstoy, Ivan Turgenev, and Anton

Chekhov were closer than the individualistic American tradition of Ralph
Waldo Emerson and Walt Whitman. Howe further observes that, at the
same time, "American Jewish writers turned inevitably and compulsively
to their own past...[which] was the one area of American life they knew
closely and could handle authoritatively." But the fact was that most of
them knew little of Jewish culture and traditions and even their hold on
Yiddish was often tenuous. Their literary and cultural strivings were out-
ward toward the general American milieu. What they did know was American urban life together with the intimate social circumstances of their life
in a Jewish milieu, the daily customs and mores of their immigrant parents.
What they did with their literary talent, in consequence, was to bring "to
the language of fiction turnings of voice, feats of irony, and tempos of
delivery that helped create a new American style,...a grating mixture of
the sardonic and sentimental, a mish-mash of gutter wisdom and graduate
school learning." Howe finally maintains that, since the stylistic innovations
of Hemingway and Faulkner, "the one major innovation in American fine
style has been the yoking of street raciness and high culture mandarin which
we associate with American Jewish writers."[60] The most important exponent
of this new American style was Saul Bellow.

# 4

# A Literature of Alienation: Schwartz and Rosenfeld

### DELMORE SCHWARTZ

If the launching of the *Partisan Review* in December, 1937 severed from the Communist party, can be regarded as the symbolic opening of the post–1930s literary era, the publication of the first item in that issue of the magazine, the story "In Dreams Begin Responsibilities," by Delmore Schwartz, marks the symbolic beginning of its creative aspect in fiction and poetry. Schwartz was among the first to articulate in artistic form the mood and outlook that was instantly recognized by the most advanced figures in the literary community. Virtually overnight Schwartz became the standard-bearer of the new mentality. In him were fused political disillusionment and an existentialist modernism heightened by the tensions of the second-generation Jew teetering on the margins of the semi-acculturated worlds of his Jewish family and the native American cultural milieu. In certain respects, Schwartz' entire career was of the most excruciating marginality because it was the most advanced and subtlest form of the acculturation process. His career marks the opening of the period of American creative writing in which the Jew became a central influence. While only a small volume of his writing may endure, his significance as the herald of this period must be recognized.

Schwartz was born in Brooklyn in 1913 of a middle-class Jewish family. His parents' marriage was unhappy—his father, a successful businessman, was a cynic and philanderer who lived apart from the family after he deposited them in Washington Heights in New York City when Delmore was about eight. Domestic discord and abrasive relations between his parents affected the impressionable boy so deeply that his entire life was scarred by them, as his finest story, "In Dreams," attests. This story, which established his reputation at the very start of his career, is an extraordinarily imagined fantasy about his intense suffering over parental discord. Their quarreling courtship is unrolled before him as if in a movie theater. The tension aroused in him by their conflicts mounts until he can endure it no longer, and he rises in his seat, shouting to the figures on the screen, "Don't do it. It's not too late to change your minds, both of you. Nothing will come of it, only remorse, hatred, scandal, and two children whose characters are monstrous." After later quarrels evoke his further shouting, a movie usher drags him out of the theater, reminding him that he "can't do everything you want to do. . . . you will be sorry if you do not do what you should do," as the narrator awakens in his bed to his twenty-first birthday.[1]

The technical virtuosity of the story is impressive, but it is the mood of despair over an inexorable personal prospect that informs the story. The intensely personal character of the mood is in polar contrast to the social tone of the prevailing 1930s fiction. Although at this time the *Partisan* group were anti-Stalinist radicals, their embrace of modernism implied a distancing of their politics from their art. On the surface that art transcended politics, but in its deepest layers that art was a reflex of the basic socioeconomic human state in industrialist capitalist society. The great modernists were the heirs to a century-old European tradition of sensitive artists, artists who were emblems of the victimization to which a burgeoning industrialization was subjecting the members of that society. Robert M. Adams, in his *Nil: Episodes in the Literary Conquest of Void in the Nineteenth Century* (1966), traces what we may identify as an existentialist tradition in terms of its conception of the Void, Nothingness—the meaninglessness and ultimate hopelessness of human life. As Adams expresses it: "In art, in literature, in science, in our culture as a whole, we are a void-haunted, void-fascinated age." He follows this complex of ideas and feelings in nineteenth-century writers, among many others, Novalis, DeQuincey, Flaubert, Baudelaire, Mallarmé, and the American precursors of modernism, Edgar Allen Poe and Herman Melville. His analysis could be extended to the central figures of twentieth-century modernism, Kafka, Yeats, Eliot, Pound, and Valery. Adams' analysis of individual writers is sensitive and acute, but he deliberately eschews any "diagnostic approach" to the phenomenon, and rejects any attempt at "the stock Darwin-Marx-Freud-World War I answer." His interest is in the "process" rather than the "causes."[2]

But when we confront the problem in post–World War II creative literature, as it first appeared before the eyes of an astonished avant-garde in 1937 with Schwartz's story, "In Dreams," we cannot evade the question of how it happened. Schwartz was prepared not only by his talent and by the kind of personal history that made him peculiarly susceptible to such ideas and feelings (much as Poe's early years prepared him a century earlier). The personal fused with an immediate social past: his unease at being a Jew in a society unfriendly to Jews; his association with a group of brilliant young

Jewish intellectuals radically critical of the social order during the Great Depression; and finally, disenchantment with the high expectations aroused by a Soviet socialist society after its lapse into Stalinism. But this is not to say that he was not affected by the pervasive sociopolitical and cultural atmosphere generated by it. It is fair, I think, to say that modernism reached him mainly through the poetry of T. S. Eliot, who was himself the most recent exponent of "The Nil" in terms of "The Waste Land." In short, Schwartz was the prophet of the post–World War II literary era of "alienation."

The concept of alienation was borne in upon the *Partisan Review* group, of which Schwartz was a member, as a concomitant of its embrace of modernism, for its modernist masters were the literary spokesmen of the twentieth century. The association of the Jews with alienation was not accidental. Franz Kafka, one of its crucial exponents, was a Jew, as was the modern master Proust, and as was Bloom, a pivotal character in Joyce's *Ulysses* (1922). Schwartz was quite explicit on this point. Already in 1941 in his short play, *Shenendoah*, he condensed in one passage the intimate relation of the Jew and alienation. The play is the dramatization of events around the *bris* (circumcision ritual) of Shenendoah Fish (Shwartz). This ceremony, Schwartz wrote, forever stigmatized its subject as one of a "chosen" people, "chosen for wandering and alienation."[3]

The poet also expressed the idea in prose in 1944 in his contribution to the "Under Forty" symposium. By then he was indeed a leading spirit of American modernism. His story "In Dreams" had been followed in 1938 by the collection of stories and poetry, *In Dreams Begin Responsibilities*, which was widely hailed. Of this book, F. O. Matthiessen wrote in 1943 that it "was greeted with more critical acclaim than has come to any other poet of his generation, the generation since Auden." But *Shenendoah* appeared in 1941 to disappointing notices. Then, in 1943, his long autobiographical poem *Genesis* received a mixed reception, although to Matthiessen it was "a marked advance over all his previous work."[4] While Schwartz was teaching English at Harvard in 1944, he decisively linked his Jewishness with the alienation he sensed as the mood of the period. In his contribution to the 1944 symposium, he wrote, "the fact of being a Jew became available to me as a central symbol of alienation, bias, point of view, and certain other characteristics which are the peculiar marks of modern life and, as I think now, the essential ones."[5] In him, and it turned out, for a whole postwar generation, the alienation which is an "essential" trait of modernism, was indissolubly linked with the situation of the Jew as its most available expression.

What does this mean? Alienation means essentially loss of connection—with one's own inner being, with others, and in the case of the workers in mass production, at that time the decisive segment of the work force, with the product of their labors. The existential hero in literature is alienated, bedeviled by the question of human identity, the individual in a universe in which he is a meaningless cipher and in a society in which corruption and deception of self and others is pervasive. How to justify continued existence? All accepted values have become trivial to the artist in the face of this realization. Redemption, justification of continued existence, lies only in the gaining of absolute freedom of individual choice and rejection of contamination by the corrupt values pressing on social relations. If vital connections with one's inwardness and with others, a measure of rest in self-identity can not be achieved, at least one can cling to one's freedom of choice even if connections are weak or lost.

But why is the Jew a "symbol" of this alienation? It is an elementary historical fact that the Jew has been an "exile," an "alien," wherever he has lived for two thousand years (until Israel was founded), set apart from the non-Jewish world by Christian tradition of the Jews as a deicide people and successive varieties of anti-Semitism over the millennia. Since emancipation a new element has entered into the character of the Jew's alienation, paradoxically produced by his liberation from the ghetto. Prejudices rooted deeply in the non-Jewish consciousness over centuries and imbibed with mother's milk cannot easily be obliterated. The Jew remains more or less strange and "different" to most non-Jews. The Jew himself is poised between two worlds, his traditional Jewish world and the non-Jewish world into which he is becoming increasingly—but seldom totally—integrated. He is, as the sociologists have named him, a "marginal" man. His connections with both his worlds are only at their margins. He is alienated to some extent from both. In 1944 Schwartz wrote about feeling "left out." "It was the revival of political anti-Semitism," he wrote, "which illuminated for me the difference between being left out by Christians and by Jews." Could not Kafka also have spoken of being "left out by Christians and Jews"?[6] The sense of being "left out"—unconnected—experienced so acutely by the Jew had become a general social condition in the course of socioeconomic development. The malaise was the experience of nullity that Adams traced among sensitive artists over the past century. By virtue of their special experience as Jews and as writers in the margin of modern United States society, Jewish writers were peculiarly suited to articulate the prevailing condition of alienation. The philosophical counterpart of this experience— existentialism, as expounded by Jean-Paul Sartre and others—was gaining favor in postwar society, as shown by the widespread interest in Kierkegaard, nineteenth-century prophet of existentialism. A number of elements were thus converging in the post–World War II period—one of these, the literary maturation of the Jewish second generation—to produce the centrality of the Jewish creative writer for a few decades after the 1940s. Of these Delmore Schwartz was the first recognized exemplar.

The fact of his being Jewish was an ever-present reality to Schwartz, from beginning to end. While he lived in his youth in New York City, he knew anti-Semitism only as a name: for himself, he wrote, the fact of Jewishness "was a matter of naive and innocent pride, untouched by any sense of fear,"[7] although in *Genesis* he relates that he was Jew-baited as a boy. But he became sensitive to it as an actuality after he left New York to go to school, and especially during his years at Harvard. First as a graduate student in the mid–1930s and later as a teacher, he felt alien in the predominantly WASP atmosphere of the place at that time. He did become friends with the awesomely erudite Professor Harry Wolfson, who was a bachelor and easily formed friendships with Jewish students, especially of philosophy. When Schwartz returned to Harvard in 1939 to teach English, he was repelled by the anti-Semitism, real and imagined, that he sensed. It must be recalled that there were relatively few Jews on the Harvard faculty at that time, and Schwartz never got over his feeling of estrangement. "He continued to recall," wrote his biographer, James Atlas, "how much he had 'suffered in being a Jew at Harvard.' "[8]

Despite his awed admiration of T. S. Eliot as a poet, he was profoundly incensed at the anti-Semitism in Eliot's poetry, which he declared an "abomination." His biographer reports that Schwartz was "increasingly obsessed by Eliot's anti-Semitism" and made a strong case against it in his unpublished book on Eliot. So little was he *over*-awed by Eliot that he turned the tables on Eliot in his journal by substitution of "Anglo-Catholics" for "Jews" in Eliot's notorious statement in *After Strange Gods*, "In the good society reason and religion contrive to say that free-thinking Jews in large numbers would be an anomalous and undesirable element."[9] He was disturbed by Edith Wharton's stereotypic Jew, Rosedale, in *House of Mirth* and Henry James' pejorative picture of the East Side Jews in *The American Scene*. Schwartz took this as a personal insult to his parents, who were living in the East Side at about the time James wrote this. So incensed was he at the anti-Semitic allusions he read in Ezra Pound's *Guide to Kulcher* (1938) that on March 5, 1939, he wrote Pound that he "resigned" from Pound's admirers "without ceasing to distinguish between past activity and present irrationality." He wrote, "I want to resign as one of your most studious and faithful admirers."[10] Schwartz never allowed his condemnation of anti-Semitism in an artist to interfere with his aesthetic judgment of the person's work. He used anti-Semitism as the theme of a story only once, in "A Bitter Farce," retailing the egregious anti-Semitism of some of his students in English composition at Harvard during World War II.

But Jewishness was an essential underlying element in his stories and poetry as he was well aware. He reiterated in his writing that the situation of the Jew made him a ready symbol of the alienated of modern society. In an essay, "The Vocation of the Poet in the Modern World," published in *Poetry* in July, 1951, Schwartz acknowledged the influence of his contemporary and friend, the noted art historian and critic, Meyer Schapiro, on his conception of poetry. Schapiro said that James Joyce had introduced as crucial characters the Jews Bloom in *Ulysses* and Shem in *Finnegan's Wake* because, wrote Schwartz, "the Jew is at once alienated and indestructible, he is an exile from his own country and an exile even from himself, yet he survives the annihilating fury of history. In the unpredictable and fearful future that awaits civilization, the poet must be prepared to be alienated and indestructible."[11] He was already aware of this bleak future in 1938, the time of his short story, "New Year's Eve," a satirical account of a party of a *Partisan Review* group celebrating the coming of 1938. "No one knew," wrote Schwartz, "that this was to be the year of the infamous Munich Pact, but everyone knew that soon there would be a new world war because only a few unimportant and powerless people believed in God or in the necessity of a just society sufficiently to be willing to give anything dear for it." As they "parted in emptiness and depression, Shenendoah [Schwartz] was already locked in what was soon to be a post-Munich mentality: complete hopelessness of perception and feeling."[12] This passage compressed the dual source of alienation of Schwartz' generation—world-destroying international relations and disillusionment with the Soviet Union as the socialist solution to the future.

How did Schwartz' ever-present sense of Jewish identity affect his writing beyond the mutual reinforcement of his identity with the current mood of alienation? What was the specific nature of this Jewishness? Like so many second-generation Jews, perhaps the overwhelming majority, his Jewishness was largely limited to acquaintance with the imperfectly acculturated social life of a Jewish milieu with no commitment to or depth of interest in or knowledge of the Jewish religion or Jewish history in its many aspects. He was a Jew because he was born of Jewish parents, lived willy-nilly in their cultural ambience, and was determined not to renounce the ethnic group to which he belonged. Although his father, not a religious Jew, saw to it that Delmore went through with his Bar Mitzvah, there is no evidence that the boy and the man explored Jewishness beyond what was at hand in the course of his life, what he could learn from the surface of that life. For instance, his attention to Jewish custom or culture was not even deep enough to realize that the greeting for long life was "Till a hundred and twenty" and not "a hundred and ten" as he has one of his characters in *Shenendoah* say.

In those aspects of American-Jewish life in which his interest was keen, in its use of language, he was most apt, as demonstrated in "America, America." In this story of the history of an upwardly mobile Jewish family he italicizes their characteristic turns of English usage: "bringing [someone] into the house"; being in business "for himself"; the son is sent away "on his own"; and endures "hard knocks"; and many others.[13] As Shenendoah (Schwartz) listens to his mother tell the story, he "reflected on his separation from these people" because they had absolutely no interest in the kind of writing he produced. But when the narration ended, he "felt for the first time how closely bound he was to these people. His separation was actual enough, but there existed also an unbreakable unity," for "the life he breathed was full of their lives and the age in which they had acted and suffered."[14] He was rooted in two cultures, one, by choice, his adopted high culture of modernism; the other, by inheritance, the middle-class Jewish milieu of the 1930s and 1940s, from which he felt at the same time separated and yet felt inexorably a part of himself. The difference between his attitude toward the two cultures was that he actively acquired and deepened his involvement in the first and passively accepted his place in the second. Beyond the rote Hebrew training his father required him to receive in preparation for his Bar Mitzvah, there is no evidence that he ever took steps to deepen his Jewish cultural self.

In what, then, does the Jewishness of his story consist? In his penetrating rendering of the specific life-styles of two phases of Jewish middle-class life: both the semi-acculturated middle-class milieu in which his family lived and that of the rootless intellectual second-generation young Jews of the Depression period whose emblem was alienation. Most of his best stories were transparent interpretations of his personal experience as a young man who had not yet found himself. But by 1935, when he wrote "In Dreams Begin Responsibilities," he manifested the alienated mentality in his ruthless realism respecting his parents and their mode of life. "America, America" conveys the ambivalence of the second-generation intellectual to his Jewish middle-class associations. "The Child Is the Meaning of This Life" gives unsparing portraits of members of his own family, especially of his Uncle Irving, and is a concrete candid overview of the constricted philistine milieu of three generations of his immediate and collateral family; this story includes that rare occurrence in Schwartz' writing, a beloved character, his grandmother "Ruth." What is Schwartz to make of the meaning of "this life"? As he leaves the hospital where his grandmother is convalescing, a stranger asks him, "Do you have a light?" Jasper (Schwartz) replies, "No, I have no light."[15] In the end, family relations are an enigma to Schwartz. But his stories do convey some notion of such relations.

The second aspect of his Jewishness, his portrait of the early years of the Jewish New York intellectuals as alienated, is exhibited in "The World Is a Wedding" and "New Year's Eve." Not all the characters in "The World" are Jewish, but the mood is predominantly that of the young Jewish intellectuals. It is a satire on the circle of the self-consciously sophisticated, brilliant youth with pretensions to worldly intellectuality orbiting around Paul Goodman during the mid–1930s, who personify the alienated attitude. Schwartz' rendering of his generation was so perceptive that it is no wonder they adopted him as their literary spokesman. "New Year's Eve" has the same import. It is a satire of some of the *Partisan Review* group, not exclusively Jewish. Schwartz ends his account of the party which mirrors the mood of the new year, 1938: he leaves the party with his friend Nicholas

(William Barrett) and Wilhelmina (his bride-to-be Gertrude Buckman) in "emptiness and depression."[16]

There was an element of intellectual and spiritual valetudinarianism in Schwartz' writing, not to mention his personal life. He was greatly preoccupied with others' view of him and of his effect on others. Hence so much of his writing is commentary on his relation to those around him and to the state of the world. One persistent theme is implied in much of his work, his distress at the anomalous combination in his name—"Delmore," an Anglo-Saxon name, and the Jewish "Schwartz." In *Shenendoah*, the playlet centering on the circumcision ritual when he is named, Schwartz sets forth his mother's deliberation over a name. She cannot name the boy Jacob, after her dead father, because her husband's father, still alive, was also named Jacob, and a child may not be named after a living person. She then settles on "Shenendoah" (Delmore), a name she got from the newspaper society page, after much acrimonious discussion within the family. Schwartz resented his first name all his life and in his writing endowed the characters representing himself with the names of Shenendoah, Cornelius, Jasper, Hershey, and others. His importance for his generation, however, lay in the fact that delineations of his personal history of necessity placed him in his social and intellectual environment, and it was in the course of setting forth this social ambience that he conveyed the first intimations of a literary generation which was in large measure Jewish in personnel and characterized by a marginality which most sharply exemplified the alienated Jew.

We have thus far dealt almost wholly with Schwartz as a prose writer, but he was better known as a poet. Indeed, he was the first Jewish American poet who was generally regarded, for a time at least, as being of leading national literary importance. While he first created a stir in 1937 with his short story "In Dreams" in *Partisan Review*, his collection of poetry and prose published in a volume also named *In Dreams Begin Responsibilities* the next year, when he was twenty-five, immediately placed him in the forefront of American poets. The date must be kept in mind, for the wave of post–World War II poets, from Robert Lowell onward, had not yet emerged. Would Schwartz fulfill the promise of this early brilliance? His next publication, *Shenendoah* in 1941, the short play in verse and prose, is today, except for a few passages, of minor interest. Then, two years later, in the midst of World War II, *Genesis: Book One*, again in both poetry and prose, appeared. The work dealt with Schwartz' own genesis, from his grandfather's life in Russia to his own first few years in elementary school in this country. Later books carrying the poem further into his life never appeared. Only an excerpt was included among Schwartz' selected poems in *Summer Knowledge* (1959). One reason is no doubt its intensely personal character—"narcissistic," James Atlas has written—and flawed by "megalomania." Although Atlas found as well "flights of rhetoric that vivified the poem," he concludes that "it belabors private themes which lack even the semblance of universality needed to give them dramatic interest."[17]

This largely autobiographical poem of two hundred pages, which stops when the boy is in his second year in school, is Schwartz' version of the acculturation novel of the Jewish writer. Already in an early poem, "The Repetitive Heart" (1938), he called on Jewish as well as Greek sources of inspiration in the refrain, "Abraham and Orpheus be with me now."[18] We have seen how he repeatedly declared his Jewishness to be a central element in his creation. In *Genesis*, however, the acculturation theme—explicit presentation of accommodation of Jew as Jew to the American milieu—is already diluted. Schwartz' poem begins with his grandfather in Tsarist Russia, his escape from the Tsarist army, and immigration to America. It takes up the story of his father's and mother's lives in Russia, immigration to this country, their courtship and marriage, and their son Hershey's (Schwartz') first years until he is about seven. Once his father and mother are in America, however, explicit Jewish references are few, for the concentration on conflicts in personal and family life is then too intense. Actually, explicit Jewish allusions are few altogether. The circumcision ritual (*bris*), which is the entire theme of *Shenendoah*, is once more recounted in *Genesis*. While still in kindergarten Hershey's non-Jewish schoolmates train a hose on him, crying "You are a Jew! a Jew!" The chorus expresses pity for the "poor boy" who suffers as he learns what it means to be a Jew and be "born...to alienation." Later, at a summer resort with his father and mother, Hershey hears a rabbi urge his father to give the child a Jewish education, and the father agrees. After leaving the rabbi, his mother expresses pleasure at the prospect, but his father, thinking that to be cynical was to be intelligent, replies that "he had not meant a word of what he had said about the child's education."[19]

Nevertheless, the work can be said to be an acculturation poem in that it is a narrative of a third-generation Jewish boy growing up in a milieu of first- and second-generation Jews. But it can also be seen as a transition between the acculturation and modern narrative. Since a third-generation Jew is at the center, the Jewish element has been considerably diluted, as the immediate family had no substantial Jewish interests. But the awareness of ethnic difference and of the presence of anti-Semitism was keenly felt in these early years of the century. This awareness was to become more lively as Schwartz grew to manhood and to be abetted by such other social influences as fascism, war, and disillusionment with socialism. These influences contributed to making Schwartz a precursor of a literature of alienation.

The poem alternates between blank verse and short prose paragraphs reminiscent of the biblical line. The prose carries the narrative while the verse is spoken by a chorus of "ghosts" who comment on the action. This device suggests (as Schwartz notes) the choral device in Hardy's *The Dynasts* as well as Greek drama. Schwartz gave his prose a "deliberate flatness," he

said, "to declare the miraculous character of daily life and ordinary speech."
His success was dubious. In one of the more successful passages, the boy
is listening to phonograph records, and noted how Al Jolson sang songs as
he thought Blacks did as "metaphors" for the Jewish people.[20]

Of the choral device, F. O. Matthiessen, who wrote in his review that the
poem was a "marked advance," doubted its success. "The chorus," he wrote,
"a shadowy group of the dead," aims at "full knowledge" of what has
transpired. But Schwartz' chorus, unlike that of Hardy, does not, as Hardy's
choruses do, have a "dramatic point of view." Schwartz' choruses are a
"succession of views [that] have no clear identity and often lose themselves
in mere fluidity." And Schwartz' use of the choral form "seems frequently
too relaxed for effectiveness."[21] The collective literary judgment of *Genesis*
as a whole, in the perspective of several decades, seems unfavorable.
Schwartz was, for whatever psychological reasons, unable to fulfill his earlier
promise. His creative energies would seem to have been sapped by his
excessive self-absorption.

The Jewishness of the poem, like most such accounts by second- and
third-generation Jews, has no Jewish cultural depth but is a passive reflection
of life in the Jewish immigrant and semi-assimilated milieu. The same can
be said for his poems, despite his early invocation to "Abraham and Orpheus" for inspiration. Except for *Shenendoah* and *Genesis*, there are only
occasional Jewish allusions in his poetry. However, in his last volume of
poetry, *Summer Knowledge* (1959), which was a selection from all his work,
he added several late poems on biblical themes, "Abraham," "Jacob," and
"Sarah," which turn the familiar Bible stories to his own purposes. Abraham's story concludes with the current preoccupation with "alienation."
To the Jewish people the poet attributes the traits of an alienated people.
In "Jacob," however, the story of Jacob's apology for his "usurpation" of
Esau's birthright and contemplation of his son Joseph's "gift" is turned to
Schwartz' comtemplation of his own "gift," which carried "guilt" with it,
and asks tragically why this need be so.[22]

Delmore Schwartz' "gift" was problematic. For whatever reason—his
personal pathology, a crippling self-absorption, limited talent or whatever—
he left only a small body of lasting work, a few stories and poems. His
biographer, who had access to all his papers, informs us that he also left a
mass of unpublished manuscripts, which are chaotic and unfinished. How
much of the collapse of his early promise can be explained by the mental
instability that overtook him severely in the 1950s and rendered him cre-
atively sterile until his death at fifty-three in 1966? But he was the first of
the postwar literary artists to be recognized as such by his peers. His career
ushered in both the "Jewish Renaissance," the replacement of the reigning
Southern school by an urban Jewish literary development which places itself
in the center of the nation's literary scene. An editorial note in an article
on Schwartz in *Commentary* written in 1950 at the height of his fame states

the matter succinctly: "Delmore Schwartz has come to be considered the most representative literary man of the Jewish intellectual generation of the '30s, certainly in its own view.... No other poet or novelist is felt to have come nearer to reflecting that generation's inner struggles with America and with itself."[23]

## ISAAC ROSENFELD

Although Delmore Schwartz is far more generally known than Isaac Rosenfeld, he must share his status as precursor of the coming American literature, and especially its Jewish cast, with Rosenfeld. The fact that Rosenfeld was born in Chicago and did not come to the literary mecca of New York until 1941, when he was twenty-three, indicates the national and urban character of the mentality that gave rise to American post–World War II modernism. There was also a certain fitness in the fact that a representative of the second literary city and center of midwestern literary life should participate in the genesis of this modernism. What Rosenfeld's final achievement would have been, had he not died at the age of thirty-eight, is a matter of speculation. Once in New York, however, he was quickly acknowledged to be the leading spirit of a group of young New York Jewish intellectuals, and he seemed to exercise magical attraction on those around him. Saul Bellow, a "close friend for twenty-five years," wrote, "He swayed his friends with an unknown power."[24] From the brevity with which he held various teaching and editorial jobs one would guess that he chafed at not being able to devote himself completely to his vocation as writer about the human predicament. He came to New York to take up a fellowship in philosophy at New York University, and after a year became an editor at the *New Republic*, a position he held only for a year. Then, until he left New York in 1952, he lived in Greenwich Village, writing short stories and reviews, as well as his novel, *Passage from Home* (1946). After two more years of teaching at the University of Minnesota, he returned to Chicago, where he died in 1956. After his death, a selection of his essays and reviews, *An Age of Enormity* (1962), and of his stories, *Alpha and Omega* (1966), were published.

All his work, in whatever genre, was informed by a probing analysis of inner intellectual, emotional, and moral activity—not without irony and humor. He was profoundly Jewish in his awareness even if he had no resort to the Jewish religion. He had a Kafka-like sensibility, as is apparent in his short stories—Schwartz called him "The American Kafka"—and, like Kafka, he gave voice to the human predicament in the modern era, especially in its mature industrial phase. Like Schwartz, he was not a political person. Bellow recalls, "Of politics—I use the term in its minor sense—he had no understanding."[25] In the 1930s, like so many sensitive Jewish youth who turned to politics during the Great Depression, he became a Trotskyist, but his membership in that party was brief, and his writings show little direct political character. But their implications in politics in the broad sense of organized human association are great. The two-thousand-year stigmatization of the Jew, even in America, the Depression, the rise of Nazism, and finally World War II with its special catastrophe for the Jews deeply convinced Rosenfeld that modern man was "alienated," driven by a fragmented inner self and separation from fellow beings, especially as a Jew.

Like Schwartz, Rosenfeld articulated the sense of alienation in the 1944 symposium, "Under Forty." He begins with the general observation that a "conscious" Jew is "overconscious" because of "distress" over differences in "race and religion" which would be considered "healthful" in a "healthy society." This is especially onerous for the artist, since he "may at any time be called to account not for his art, not even for his life, but for his Jewishness." This condition of the Jew as artist has its advantages. Because of his marginal condition, he can observe "much that is hidden" in his society. Specifically with respect to literature, the Jews by virtue of their status as "an internationally insecure group [are] personally acquainted with some of the fundamental themes of insecurity that run through modern literature." This recalls the continuity of some postwar writing with the tradition of contemplation of the abyss which we mentioned earlier in Adams' study, *Nil*. The Jew, adds Rosenfeld in one of his lapidary phrases, "is a specialist in alienation (the one international system they actually control)." The reason is that in our day "nearly all sensibility—thought, creation, perception—is in exile, alienated from society in which it barely managed to stay alive."[26] This idea, which today has widespread currency and is confirmed by our post–World War II literature, has an affinity with the famous saying by Marx that "capitalist production is hostile to certain aspects of intellectual production, such as art and poetry."[27] What Rosenfeld, Schwartz, and others were saying before the relevance of the view gained wide acceptance in the postwar world was that the Jew was peculiarly situated, by virtue of his centuries-old history as the outsider in Western society, to serve as a symbol of the fragmentation of the self under our social conditions. Since the Jew suffered over and above the hardships he shared with others in his society, the exploited workers or victims of the dehumanization of affluence, from a separateness enforced through the socially inherited sentiments of the surrounding non-Jewish world, he was peculiarly fitted to articulate a condition which was now perceived to be general. "Out of their recent sufferings"—Rosenfeld was thinking of Nazism—"one may expect Jewish writers to make certain moral discoveries."[28]

Rosenfeld gave concreteness to the notion of alienation in his sole published novel, *Passage from Home*. This story explores the ultimate homelessness of the fourteen-year-old Bernard Miller, "sensitive as a burn," in the author's unforgettable phrase.[29] This autobiographical novel dramatizes Rosenfeld's own realization of alienation—his "passage from home"—in his teens. The story is propelled by the working out of the Oedipal theme—the boy hates his father and longs to adopt Minna, sister of his non-Jewish aunt Martha, as a surrogate for his own dead mother. He contrives to bring Minna together with Willy, widower of Martha. He leaves home and lives with Minna and Willy. The relations of Minna and Willy are so sordid that Bernard is disillusioned, and he returns home to his father. It soon becomes apparent that reconciliation is futile, and Bernard realizes that he has indeed left home, even if he remains physically present there. His alienation is complete. He has no fulfilling relation with anyone: his efforts to achieve such a relation with Minna, with Willy, and with his father have all failed. What is more, each of these characters is also alienated: Willy is rootless and lacks any attachments in the world; this is also true of Minna; and his father seems incapable of a mutual connection with his son.

Does this failure leave Bernard with no resource whatever? Here Rosenfeld's movement from politics into an adherence to the orgone theory of Wilhelm Reich comes into play. Reich's heretical Freudianism, briefly, maintains that the basic energy of the universe is sexual; sexual maladjustment or deprivation malforms character, and Rosenfeld's fiction explores the effect of an unfulfilled "genitality." Rosenfeld concurred in Reich's universalized concept of "genitality" as the basic form of energy, calling for a natural mode of life, that is, a right relation to nature. This was one aspect of the necessary fulfillment of sexual life which would prevent the distortion of character.

Rosenfeld did not look on religion as in itself a right relation with the cosmos, but substituted for it a sense of community with others. Thus when Bernard leaves Minna and Willy for his father's home, he has a sort of mystical experience of nature, which brings out the healing effects of such a relationship. He stops at a botanical garden and contemplates the flowers. In common with this plant life human life has the "same blindness, the same growing and reaching for the sun and the same meaningless non-being, counting for nothing." Only by expelling the "vision of the jungle" and treasuring "a moment of true life and the true human beauty, greener than the trees...love was a meaning which I would always have to acquire.... For without love, without the signal that one flashed to the other's existence, we died alone." This is, then, the overcoming of alienation. He had known such moments, he writes, "perhaps at home, perhaps in childhood."[30] One such experience is a visit to a Hasidic rabbi on which the boy is taken by his grandfather. Not particularly remarkable in his daily life, the grandfather rises to a spiritual height in communing with his rabbi; he was, writes Rosenfeld, "transformed into a new person. A look of completeness on his face, an expression of gratitude as if for the ecstatic understanding to which Feldman had led him."[31] It was not the theological assumptions of the experience which gave it value for Rosenfeld, but the momentary completeness of being that it gained.

If it was this ecstasy of completeness for which Rosenfeld yearned, his mind and method were still primarily analytical. As in Schwartz' *Genesis*, he was close enough to his Jewish ethnic origin to devote his largest work to the *Bildungsroman* of a second-generation Jew. And like Schwartz' work, his novel breaks with the conventional acculturation novel by interpreting the process of adjustment to generalizing beyond the alienation of the Jew to the general prevalence in modern society of this condition. However it should be noted that the break is more decisive in the Rosenfeld novel because alienation is more deeply and analytically embedded in the story. Curiously neither effort is entirely successful as a work of art. A crucial defect of *Genesis* is its excessive personal viewpoint, which reduces artistic distance. The rather serious deficiency of the Rosenfeld novel is its excessively analytical approach developed at the expense of narrative and fictional interest. Rosenfeld's sense of Jewishness is more active than Schwartz', which is almost wholly passive. The classical Yiddish writers, I. L. Peretz and Sholem Aleichem, interested Rosenfeld, and he wrote about them. He found Hasidism close to his own aspirations as he intimates in *Passage*. Symptomatic of a more lasting literary interest in *Passage* may be the fact that it was reprinted in 1961, for Rosenfeld's intellectuality is of deeper interest than is found in the pervasively personal nature of *Genesis*, and his intellectuality is more interesting and profound than that of Schwartz. Schwartz carried his "deliberate flatness" of style so far as to border on the banal. In Rosenfeld, when the narrative flags, interest is sustained by the evidences of an analytical mind.

While both Schwartz and Rosenfeld were not political in the narrow sense, their doctrine of "alienation" must be recognized as being political in the broadest sense, because it is rooted in the state of society. Thus, Schwartz wrote about the Civil War in his poem "Lincoln" that it was "capitalismus" that finally won the war.[32] A world of politics is also implied in Rosenfeld's title for an essay, "The Age of Enormity," which was appropriately used as the title for his posthumous volume of essays. Indeed, he saw modern society as dehumanized and recognized his being as alienated. This is a "political" judgment on society, and Rosenfeld chose to explore its effects on his inward nature, thereby practicing a cultural criticism. On specific social issues, however, he made conventional errors. When confronted with the challenge of the *Commentary* symposium on "The Jewish Writer and the English Literary Tradition," he was led into a contradiction. On the one hand, he said that in judging the anti-Semitism of great writers like Chaucer, Shakespeare, and Marlowe "historical conditions must be kept in mind," and their anti-Semitism can be understood because "literature is bound to reflect its time." On the other hand, he regarded anti-Semitism as a "symptom of a serious, underlying, psycho-sexual disease of epidemic proportions in our society," a symptom of a disease "just as coughing up blood." He was aware that his argument was "reductive," since he would thereby "reduce a complex cultural problem to a clinical one." Yet he persisted in regarding it as a "disease."[33] He believed, however, that overt anti-Semitism of neighbors or government was far more important than the literary sort.

It is apparent that his view of anti-Semitism as a "psycho-sexual disease" derived from his Reichian convictions. Under this same influence in 1949 he published an article in *Commentary*, "Adam and Eve on Delancey Street," which carried his views to an extreme in a discussion of *Kashruth*. He regards the rituals and taboos connected with food in the Jewish religion as "sexually repressive," and this results in "serious damage" (in the Reichian view, this leads to impaired "genitality"), because the religious and secular life for the religious Jew are continuous, and hence the taboo concerning such a pervasive activity is seriously repressive. This does not apply to Hasidim, he holds, because they have an outlet in "natural enthusiasm." He draws a parallel between the taboo against *treifes* and the sexual taboo against *goyim*. Jewish fascination with *treifes*, he then reasons, is with "the whole world of forbidden sexuality, the sexuality of the *goyim*, and there all the delights are imagined to lie with the *shiksas* and *shkutzim* who are unrestrained and not made kosher."[34] The sexuality of food taboos is symbolized in the prohibition against contact between *milchige*, dairy foods, the feminine side of the taboo, and *fleishige*, meat, or the masculine side. However original or wildly speculative one may regard this Freudian analysis, the American Jewish Committee, the sponsors of the magazine who paid the rather large bill for it, were not pleased. What must have been one of the few, if not the only, effort at interference with editorial policy by the committee, was a letter in the November, 1949 issue signed by its president, Jacob Blaustein, noting that the article had offended "the sensibilities of large numbers of our co-religionists" and had "violated every canon of good taste" and was thus an "abuse" of editorial freedom. Blaustein noted editorial assurance that this sort of thing would not happen again.[35]

But little of Rosenfeld's creative work was so patently derived from psychoanalysis. More apparent is the influence of Kafka on his short stories. In addition there are frequent flashes of humor quite lacking in *Passage*. Both these features are especially strong in two among his best stories, "The Hand That Fed Me" (1952) and "King Solomon" (1956). The first is a series of letters dated during Christmas Eve of 1942 from Joseph Feigenbaum to a non-Jewish girl with whom he had become acquainted in 1939 while they were both applying for WPA jobs. He immediately fell in love with her, but she refused to see him thereafter. Three years later she sends him a Christmas card; this initiates his one-sided correspondence, which she also ignores. Feigenbaum is obviously a *shlemiel*, and his aloneness and the futile persistence of his effort to establish a connection are symptomatic of his alienation: the reader is aroused to quiet, half-suppressed amusement at his obviously futile persistence. The story is Kafkaesque in the unresponsiveness of the addressee, which resembles the failure of Kafka's Joseph K. to establish the connection and explanation he desires. "King Solomon," on the other hand, leading to a similar failure, arouses laughter by its sudden anachronisitc transitions from the biblical Solomon to a weary, alienated, lonely contemporary of our own. For instance: "A pinochle game was in progress when the Queen of Sheba, unannounced and without knocking, came into the room.... The King was in his undershirt, smoking a cigar." The nub of the story is that Solomon is unable, despite all the wiles of the Queen of Sheba, to feel attracted to her—he is finally alienated, unable to establish a connection. She departs, and "King Solomon had leased her oil lands for ninety-nine years."[36] Did this story reflect the lonely, isolated mood of the author in his last years?

The same theme runs through much of Rosenfeld's literary criticism. One of his best-known critical essays is his evaluation in 1952 of Cahan's *The Rise of David Levinsky*. Rosenfeld comes to the conclusion, surprising at first blush, that Levinsky is also typically American in that he ends up a millionaire and lonely and unfulfilled—alienated—like the American millionaire, who "finds nothing but emptiness at the top of the heap."[37] On second thought, however, this is quite explicit in the novel itself, since Cahan has Levinsky himself perceive the futility of passion for success which was the current American goal. "Success! Success! Success! It was the almighty goddess of the hour," wrote Cahan at the end of the novel.[38] But Rosenfeld was saying more. Levinsky, he says, was torn between the desire for wealth and for learning, neither of which he can relinquish: "All things in Levinsky's life are divided," wrote Rosenfeld, "alienated from themselves." Hence, he can never be satisfied, "his hunger remains constant," and he is "driven in an endless yearning after yearning," which Rosenfeld calls a "profoundly Jewish trait." Rosenfeld sees a parallel between this and the constant yearning in the unsatisfied life of the millionaire, to whom indeed "Money isn't everything." Rosenfeld concludes that the "inner loneliness" of both is alike, and that there is "considerable structural congruity that must underlie the character and culture of the two peoples." This putative similarity in my view needs further exploration before one can evaluate it. But insofar as Levinsky emulated the goddess of Success, his story, as Rosenfeld notes, is "an American novel par excellence in the very center of the Jewish genre."[39]

As exemplified in the *Levinsky* review, Rosenfeld integrated his Jewish and American aspects to a far greater degree than Schwartz. He was deeply affected by a realization of the Holocaust, and in an essay, "The Meaning of the Terror," in 1949 he related this to such terrors as the atomic bomb and the breakdown of morality implied in any future use of it. In a review of *Ashes and Fire* by Jacob Pat in 1948 he asks, how could the West have allowed the Holocaust to happen? The breakdown of morality was further shown in the Soviet camps, as his review of the book about them indicated.

In the essay on terror he joined these strategies of terror with the atom bomb and its dire future possibilities.

Rosenfeld did not, like so many of the New York Jewish intellectuals, succumb to the blandishments of acceptance into the Establishment. As with any impressive mind and talent, one wonders how he might have developed had he lived through the 1960s and beyond instead of dying at the age of thirty-eight. He did not leave very much durable writing behind, but I don't think he will be forgotten. Whatever happens to his work, his position as a precursor, together with that of Schwartz, is secure in literary history.

# 5

# From Life to Limbo: Saul Bellow

"I cannot agree with recent writers who have told us that we are nothing," said Saul Bellow in the 1950s. "We are indeed not what the Golden Age boasted us to be. But we are Something."[1] He was thus announcing a sharp turn from major literary tendencies of the past decades (except for the proletarian 1930s). Notwithstanding the worldly wise sophistication of the terrible period following mass slaughter in war, disillusionment with social movements of hope, and Holocaust of a third of the world's Jews, Bellow clung to the basic Jewish affirmation of the value of life. He was in no sense religious, except for vague intimations that he somehow believed in a deity or transcendant being. At the same time he had deeper insight into, and knowledge of, Jewish cultural values than any other major Jewish writer of the time. Nor was his insight into American life any the less profound. He possessed a rare combination of artistic sensitivity, gift for language, and genuine intellectuality that led many, including the present writer, to regard him as the leading American novelist of his time.

But a change came over Bellow in his sixties. As the 1960s drew to a close and the 1970s saw deepening cultural dislocation in the humanistic outlook among students and intellectuals, the suffocating domination of all the arts by the passion for profits, the wholesale evacuation of the inner cities by the white middle class, and by the spread of a Black "underclass" in an increasingly intensive technological society which did not employ them, and by the frighteningly rapid rise in the rate of crime, a change came over Bellow's work. The first signs were apparent in *Mr. Sammler's Planet* (1970). With *The Dean's December* (1982), the sweet flavor of life in his writing was largely gone. Bellow seemed overcome by the profundity of the world's ills. The strong affirmation of life that pervaded his earlier work—basically an expression of the traditional Jewish affirmation—was attenuated and replaced by a near despair for the future of humanity. But this nearness to giving up on humanity did not occur until he had over the previous forty years created a body of seven life-affirming novels.

Although he had declared early in his writing career his discontinuity with recent writers of Nothingness—writers of alienation—there remained a marked continuity. He was a contemporary and close friend of both precursors of postwar writing, Schwartz and Rosenfeld, both of whom ceased creativity in the 1950s, Schwartz through mental illness and Rosenfeld by death. Bellow was a friend of his fellow Chicagoan, Rosenfeld, for twenty-five years and acknowledged his influence. Bellow wrote in his memoir of Rosenfeld that "In some of his strange beliefs I often followed him because I loved him and did not want to lose my connection with him."[2] After Bellow came to live in New York in the 1950s, he became friendly with Schwartz, and in 1952 taught at Princeton for a year as Schwartz' associate. Indeed, a central thread of Bellow's novel *Humboldt's Gift* (1975) is in many respects a historically accurate account of their friendship. Schwartz' chance of immortality is helped by his presence in this work as well as his own writing. Schwartz' preoccupation with his non-Jewish first name (Delmore) is echoed in his name in the novel, "Von Humboldt Fleischer." The "Gift" of the title, among other things, suggests the passage in Schwartz' poem, "Jacob," where Schwartz reflects on his own "gift" in the ambiguities of Jacob's "gift" after usurping Esau's patrimony; the "gift" was "mind," "eminence," "guilt," but why must a gift entail "guilt" and "hurt" to the "gifted"?[3]

If Bellow embraced life and renounced alienation, this by no means signified an absence of the alienated attitude in his fiction. Its renunciation was in every case the culmination of a struggle with strong estranging influences. Affirmation occurs as the conclusion of all too convincing evidence of human fallibility. In *Humboldt's Gift* Bellow examines the nature of "boredom," which, he holds, has bedeviled mankind, and applies his concept about "modern times," in which "the question had been approached under the name of *anomie* or Alienation, as an effect of capitalist conditions of labor, as a result of levelling in Mass Society, as a consequence of the dwindling of religious faith or the gradual using up of charismatic prophetic elements, ... or the increase of Rationalization in a technological society, or the growth of bureaucracy."[4] Considering the ubiquity of this mood in modern man, it is no wonder that the characters in Bellow's novels, so alive to their period, should be deeply influenced by it. They differ from the characters in so many contemporary novels in that they do not succumb to alienation but struggle against it, and are finally determined to overcome it.

Bellow's refusal to acquiesce in alienation, and his affirmation of life, both flow no more from his Jewishness than does his unquestioning acceptance of his Jewish identity. "I've never had a moment's trouble about my identity. I've always known what my identity is," he told a Tel Aviv audience in 1970.[5] His writing fully confirms this assertion. All his novels, except *Henderson the Rain King* (1959) and *The Dean's December* (1982) are steeped in a secular Jewish milieu without any suggestion of self-consciousness. As an artist of integrity he was drawing on his own life experience, which had an essential Jewish component within the larger American environment. Although Bellow was born in 1915 in Lachine, near Montreal, his parents brought him to Chicago when he was nine. There he went to school and college, and returned to live in the mid–1960s after some years in New York and a few years in Paris. From first to last his experience as a Jew is an essential part of his being, and he incorporates this into his fiction. Characteristically, then, his writing is infused with both suffering and its transcendance in the form in which this experience typically occurs in our century, in alienation and the struggle toward disalienation. As the late Abraham Chapman expressed this,

Many of the words that keep recurring in Bellow's works—trouble, grief, disappointment, strife—sound like a search for an adequate English equivalent of the Yiddish word *tzuuress*. As a Jewish-American writer Bellow brings to the postwar scene a vision of life which incorporates his Jewish heritage, the long, historical experience with suffering, scorn, rejection, and the tempering of the soul to confront, live with *and transcend* the suffering and trouble in the very atmosphere of human existence. [Emphasis added][6]

From his saturation in Jewish-American urban experience Bellow also derived the remarkable fusion of demotic with cultivated language which has been so widely remarked upon. The success of the fusion is proved by the absence of strain or incongruity in this new urban style. One element of it is its Yiddish component. Irving Howe has described it:

Bellow's style draws heavily from the Yiddish, not so much in borrowed diction as in underlying intonations and rhythm. Bellow's relation to Yiddish is much more easy and authoritative than that of most other American Jewish writers. The jabbing interplay of ironies, the intimate vulgarities, the strange blend of sentimental and sardonic which characterizes Yiddish speech are lassoed into Bellow's English so that what we get is not a sick exploitation of folk memory but a vibrant linguistic and cultural transmutation.[7]

In addition, Bellow interjected with unforced appropriateness phrases in Hebrew or Yiddish, especially in *Herzog*, which has been regarded by many as his "most Jewish book."[8] Indeed, acceptance of Yiddish phrases, some of which have been adapted into English, is a striking linguistic phenomenon of the past few decades, and American-Jewish writers lend a special flavor to their writing by occasional use of Yiddish.

However, Bellow has resented the characterization of himself as an

"American Jewish writer," regarding it as a "put-down." "One doesn't," he said in an interview, "any longer speak of American Italian Writers or, for that matter, American Wasp Writers." He regards the designation as "without a shred of literary accuracy," since this category includes great variety in style, subject matter, and quality. The "label," he finds, "vulgar, unnecessarily parochializing and utterly without value." For instance, Bellow had been "faintly amused at the curious linkage of Bellow, Malamud, and Roth," which, he added, "always reminded me of Hart, Shaffner, and Marx."[9] And it is, of course, true that these three writers do not form a school, but rather signify the striking emergence of Jewish writers among the leading novelists of their time. Yet Bellow protests too much, for the designation is inevitable, from both the literary and sociological viewpoints. The designation is one means of taking notice—legitimately—of this entry of Jewish writers into general recognition, and hence conforms to the social inevitability of giving a name to a new and striking socioliterary phenomenon. Furthermore, as Bellow himself admitted in a 1968 speech accepting the B'nai B'rith's Jewish Heritage Award "for excellence in Jewish literature," the "contemporary Jewish writer [is] somehow different from others." For the "modern literary tradition," Bellow observed, "is, for the most part, one of negation." But "the negative revolution of 19th century writers," he added, was on the whole not actually shared by Jews. Bellow believes that the Jewish "reliance on God's will [has been] continued into secular Jewish activities in the twentieth century."[10] If this difference exists, as Bellow says he believes, then there is reason to set off the Jewish writers, even from his own point of view, as a special category.

Bellow's observation certainly applies to himself. But other considerations vitiate it. Was not the Jew Kafka one of the main sources of the tradition of "negation" in its twentieth-century guise? And the recognition of the Jew as the prototype of the modern alienated person because of his history of enforced isolation and separation from the general community, which has survived residually to a greater or lesser extent since Emancipation, and the persistence of discrimination and anti-Semitism, are contributory aspects of modern "negativism." Yet it is true that writers who, like Bellow, strive to overcome this negativism, do so by virtue of the deep-seated Jewish conviction of the value of human life derived from the Jewish tradition. In any case Bellow's rejection of the designation of "Jewish-American writer," rather than simply "American writer," aroused considerable discussion. Meyer Levin's contribution was predictably critical of Bellow. In 1971 Levin charged that Bellow's heroes are "thoroughly alienated Jews," and that his novels thus tended to "promote assimilation." Levin complains, accurately enough, that Augie March spends time in Europe at the end of World War II but "has not one encounter with, or reaction to, the Holocaust," and it thus "is avoided as though it had no impact on a sensitive living Jew." Bellow's Jewishness does not impress Levin even in *Mr. Sammler's Planet*

(1970), and Levin concludes that Bellow "fails" as an interpreter of "the Jewish spirit and the sense of Jewishness."[11] No doubt there is justice in Levin's observations that there is no evidence of the Holocaust in the novels until *Sammler*: Bellow admitted this after receiving the Nobel Prize in 1976. In an interview Bellow then said that "at first the Holocaust had passed him by. Now, in a delayed reaction, he felt 'shamed and disgraced' that he had not felt that time in our history with greater intensity."[12]

Notwithstanding Bellow's tardy sensitivity toward the Holocaust, he is nonetheless a Jewish writer. It is probably accurate to say, as he told an Israeli audience, that he was "the only American Jewish writer who knows Yiddish," except for Meyer Levin, whom he excepts as belonging to an older generation. He told them that "the Yiddish writers made a great impression on me as a kid," though he admits that James Fenimore Cooper "excited me more than Sholem Aleichem."[13] That knowledge of, and feeling for, Yiddish resulted in his translation of Isaac Bashevis Singer's "Gimpel the Fool," whose appearance in *Partisan Review* in 1953 spurred Singer's vogue. Ten years later Bellow edited *Great Jewish Short Stories*, a collection of stories written in English in translations from the Hebrew, German, Yiddish, and Russian (Isaac Babel) with a perceptive introduction about Jewish storytelling. His Jewishness is not diminished by the fact that, as he said in 1971, "I have never been a Zionist."[14] He has visited Israel several times, and when the 1967 war broke out, he felt an indefinable necessity to go to Israel. The Long Island daily *Newsday* sent him there as a war correspondent and in 1976 he again visited Israel and promptly published in *To Jerusalem and Back* (1976) his thoughts about the writers and intellectuals he met. This deals modestly with his search for an understanding of Israel's excruciating situation in conversations with, and reading of, scholars and politicians, but he records no meeting with Arabs. The language of the book is instinct with profound concern for the future of Israel and the Jewish people.

Bellow set the direction of his work in his first novel, *Dangling Man* (1944). It is written in the form of a journal, dated from December 15, 1942, with Joseph waiting a call for induction into the army to April 8, 1943, when he leaves to join the army. The story is not a page old before Bellow announces his independence of the prevailing Hemingway manner, an announcemnt that marked a swerve of direction in American literature away from the Hemingway style. For Bellow asserts: "Most serious matters are closed to the hard-boiled. They are unpracticed in introspection, and therefore badly equipped to deal with opponents whom they cannot shoot like big game or outdo in daring."[15] Early in the story his character, Joseph, recalls, in a bitter episode, his renunciation of radicalism and disgust with the Communist party and with his membership in it. "I changed my mind," he writes, "about redoing the world from top to bottom à la Karl Marx."[16] This turn from radicalism, which was the experience of a whole generation of talented writers and intellectuals, was in fact one of the determinative developments of the postwar period. The confident security of a constricted utopian outlook was replaced by uncertainty and the specter of alienation. The novel drew upon one of the fundamental statements of alienation, Dostoyevsky's *Notes from the Underground*. Both are intensely introspective analyses of the emotions and outlook of men who value their personal freedom above all. Joseph's uprootedness, signified by his disillusionment with his friends, his wife, his relatives, and neighbors, is exacerbated by the fact that he must mark time until he is called into the army. "There is nothing to do," writes Bellow, "but wait, or dangle, and grow more and more dispirited." Bellow even goes on to use a term—"spite"—which often recurs in Dostoyevsky's *Notes*. "It is perfectly clear to me," Bellow goes on, "that I am deteriorating, sowing bitterness and spite which eat like acids at my endowment of generosity and good will."[17]

Unlike the *Notes*, however, Bellow's work is not content to rest in an alienated state. He struggles against it and seeks a way out. At the end of the diary, as he is about to enter the army, he is content to suspend the struggle and tolerate the "regimentation" and "supervision of the spirit" which are imposed in army life.[18] But before that he has speculated, "How should a good man live?" Unless measures were taken, "existence could indeed become—in Hobbes' phrase, . . . 'nasty brutish, and short.' " The way to prevent this was to create " 'a colony of the spirit' [Isaac Rosenfeld's phrase] or a group whose covenants would forbid spite, bloodiness, and cruelty."[19] This solution to the alienation of the individual is far from the hope for a radical reconstruction of society which Bellow had believed, like so many leading artists and intellectuals in the 1930s. So great was Bellow's disillusionment that he only passively supported World War II, because, he writes, "As I see it, the whole war's a misfortune."[20] There is no anti-Nazi militance in his outlook. Nevertheless, in this first novel he had already rejected alienation. In a dialogue with "the spirit of Alternatives," the dejected, ruminating Joseph refused "to subscribe to alienation."[21] But he had not come to rest in any position of affirmation and was in fact still suffering from the malaise he rejected. At the end of the story he suspends the struggle by surrendering his freedom to the army. But the novel has announced the basic problems of Bellow's thought and creation.

Although Joseph and other characters in the novel are obviously Jewish, there is no reference to the fact, nor is there any explicit Jewish allusion. The next novel, *The Victim* (1947), however, seemingly centers on the problem of anti-Semitism. But the deeper theme is the ambiguity and complexity of assigning responsibility for human behavior. Who is the victim in the events following an anti-Semitic incident, the Jew or the anti-Semite? In giving the title, *The Victim*, in the singular, Bellow sets the stage for the ambiguities of the situation. In some respects, *both* are victims. Thus an element of psychological and moral complexity is introduced into the problem of anti-Semitism. For the most part the problem is usually viewed as a simple act of individual and social aggrandizement. Bellow's analysis adds another dimension in exploring responsibility for the problem. In the story Asa Leventhal is an editor at a trade paper. At a party at the home of his employer, Williston, his friend and colleague Harkavy and a young Jewish woman are singing spirituals and old ballads. Another guest, a drunken Allbee, interrupts, saying, "It isn't right for you to sing them. You have to be bred to them." His wife, Mary, tells them not to pay any attention to her husband and to go on singing. They resume, but Allbee interrupts again, and demands that they sing a "psalm" or any Jewish song. "Something you've really got feeling for. Sing us the one about the mother."[22] Everyone is embarrassed, and Asa Leventhal is briefly angered. He later leaves his job and, at Williston's suggestion, asks Allbee to introduce him to his employer, the publisher Rudiger. When Asa interviews Rudiger, he finds him rude and arrogant. Provoked, Asa engages the publisher in an intensely angry exchange, and Rudiger orders him out. A few days later Allbee, about whose introduction Asa had reminded Rudiger, is fired.

Did Leventhal unconsciously create this unpleasant scene with Rudiger to generate prejudice against his sponsor, Allbee? This is at least the conviction of Allbee himself. Already bedeviled by a weakness for drink, he becomes a habitual drunkard after failing to get another job; his relations with his wife Mary deteriorate, and she is killed in an auto accident while under the stress of their antagonism. Asa learns this some months later when a derelict Allbee appears at his door and imposes himself on Asa's hospitality for a bed and food, believing Asa is to blame for his loss of a job and its consequences. Asa searches his conscience. Did he really intend this? He asks his friend and colleague Harkavy whether Allbee had not really lost his job simply because he drank too much. Harkavy begins to hedge and tells Asa not to be upset about it, but Asa is insistent, and Harkavy tells him that Williston did think Asa had intentionally antagonized Rudiger. Harkavy assures Asa he thought Williston was wrong but Asa confronts Williston himself and his former employer replies: "Maybe you aimed to hurt him and maybe you didn't. But the effect is the same. You lost him his job." He goes on to tell Asa that he had a talk with Rudiger, who believed that Allbee had arranged the unpleasant episode with Asa. He had wanted an excuse to fire Allbee anyway, in part because of Allbee's drinking. Yet Williston does believe Leventhal responsible for Allbee's loss of the job, and Asa is now really shaken. Was he? "Had he knowingly, that is unconsciously, wanted to get back at Allbee?"[23]

With a psychological detail and subtlety that can only be conveyed by the original text, Bellow shows Asa tormenting himself with the ambiguities of the situation. What Bellow is probing is the nature of responsibility, and Asa is grappling with the question of his responsibility for Allbee's situation. To be human is to accept responsibility for one's actions. " 'Human' meant accountable in spite of many weaknesses."[24] Through such "weaknesses"—anti-Semitism in Allbee, perhaps an unconscious desire for revenge in Asa—both men are "victims," one of the other. To be properly human requires among other things that one does not victimize another. Indeed the search for the meaning of the genuinely human can be said to be the central theme of Bellow's fiction. It is in this context that Bellow explores the problem of anti-Semitism. In *The Victim* he returns to the theme from the suspension in which he left it at the end of *Dangling Man*.

The first two novels gained a considerable reputation for Bellow. They revealed a craftsman of the highest skill as well as a profound mind. The meticulous, dense use of language suggests the influence of Flaubert. In an interview in 1966 Bellow recalled that he was "timid" and "felt the incredible effrontery of announcing myself to the world (in part I mean the WASP world) as a writer and an artist. . . . I had . . . to demonstrate by abilities, pay my respects to formal requirements." When Bellow was starting out, the notion that Jews were not capable of grasping the English language and literature was still widely prevalent. Bellow told an interviewer: "It was made clear to me when I studied literature in the university that as a Jew and the son of Russian Jews I would probably never have the right feeling for Anglo-Saxon traditions, for English words." In his first two novels he had to "fight free" of those prejudices. Once he had proved himself, he threw off, as he says, the "repressive restraints imposed by the Falubertian standard" he had adopted for *The Victim*.[25]

The result of this liberation was *The Adventures of Augie March* (1953). The novel received general acclaim and the National Book Award; it made Bellow widely known to the general reading public. With this work he initiated the remarkable, liberated use of demotic plus Yiddishistic plus fine English style that is one of the great innovations of the novel that so dramatically fulfills the prophecy made by Howells in 1915. This long work is a picaresque novel that takes the reader through a variety of places and experiences in rich detail. The "repressive" manner of the earlier novels, Bellow said, could not encompass the "variety of things I knew intimately" in Chicago as "the son of immigrants."[26] But he felt he had gone "too far" in throwing off restraints, an awareness that accounts for flaws in the novel, perhaps an overextension of its imaginative reach.

One evidence of Bellow's rejection of restraints is the derivation of the early part of the book from his experience in the Jewish milieu of Chicago, the occasional interjection of Yiddish, and the description of Jewish customs that are realistic rather than nostalgic in character. The early part of the story contains dense content of the lives of several Jewish families, Augie's own March family, especially his beloved and colorful Grandmother Lausch, the Einhorns, and the wealthy Magnus family into which Augie's brother Simon marries. But perhaps most distinctively Jewish in the novel is Augie's attitude toward life. This is the most characteristic quality of Bellow's writing, and marks him off from most of his contemporaries.

But search for an affirmative attitude does not necessarily end in finding. Apart from Bellow's certainty that there is "something" in life, and the consequent affirmation of life, one would be hard put to assert definitively that Bellow has ever found the key to the final value he sought. All his works deal with the search. Because he lives in an age of alienation, Bellow— and his characters—are to some extent subject to it. He differs from most others, however, in his deliberate, conscious effort to overcome the alienation. He looks down on those who wallow in their alienation. For his part, he seeks a way out. Augie undergoes many frustrations in his quest. Along the way he attempts a bewildering variety of occupations, experiences, and associations, but refuses to commit himself, since he is prepared to commit himself only to what he is finally convinced is the true object of his quest, "the axial lines of life."[27] It cannot be said that Augie ever really finds it, but he knows in some sense what he is looking for. Late in his adventures Augie says, "I have a feeling about the axial lines of life, with respect to which you must be straight or else your existence is merely clownery, hiding tragedy. I must have had a feeling since I was a kid about these axial lines which made me want to have my existence in them, and so I have said 'no' like a stubborn fellow to all my persuaders." Sometimes he "felt these thrilling lines [which] went quivering right straight through me. Truth, love, peace, bounty, usefulness, harmony!"[28] A man can be "regenerated" and

come where the axial lines are. He will be brought into focus. He will live with *true* joy. Even his pains will be joy if they are true, even his helplessness will not take away his power, even wandering will not take him away from himself, even the big social jokes and hoaxes need not make him ridiculous, even disappointment after disappointment will not take away his love. . . . I bring my entire life to the test.[29]

The goal is not, then, some idealized mode of life but an anchor of assurance amidst all the buffeting inevitable in real life. All this must take place within one's own nature. "I have always tried to become what I am," says Augie.[30] This is consistent with the quest because his "nature" is to strive to live in accordance with the "axial lines of life." All through his adventures he has said "no" to those who would set him on a course of life diverted from the "axial."

Another approach to the quest for humanity, when a man shall feel himself brother to others, is in *Seize the Day* (1956), which some critics regard as Bellow's finest work. Tommy Wilhelm (né Adler) has failed in everything— in everything he has undertaken and in all his personal relations. He lives in a Broadway hotel in New York, separated from his wife and two children. His father, a wealthy retired surgeon, Dr. Adler, heartlessly and contemptuously refuses to help his son Tommy out of his quagmire, personal and financial. Tommy, in his forties, is unemployed. Having failed in trying to be an actor in Hollywood, he had left a job although he badly needed it, and finally he had entrusted his last $700 to the speculative investment adventures of a quack, Dr. Tamkin. All his life he has indecisively yielded to bad judgment. When this money too is lost, he is at his lowest point. His father has refused financial help, and Tommy has nowhere to turn for succor, human or financial. His sense of isolation is nearly total. It is not only his bad judgment in dealing with people, but also his being influenced by the superficial allures of modern society that has led to his present predicament.

Dr. Tamkin is Tommy's "reality instructor," as Bellow called those who tried to instruct Augie March in the ways of the world, and whom Augie rejected. When Dr. Tamkin says he has lost the last of Tommy's money in commodities speculation, Tommy realizes that the psychiatrist is a fraud. He is a "witch-doctor," a smooth talker, a charlatan, but not altogether worthless. Bellow assigns to him the expression of a central thought of the novel, the significance of "seize the day." His wise observations are full of irony, for they are inconsistent with the fraudulent aspects of his character. One can hardly believe that Dr. Tamkin is sincere in the statement: "I am at my most efficient when I don't need the fee. When I only love. Without a financial reward I remove myself from social influence. Especially money. The spiritual compensation is what I look for. Bringing people into the here-and-now. The real universe. That's the present moment. . . . Only the present is real—the here-and-now. Seize the day."[31] Whatever interpretation Dr. Tamkin may put on this passage, Bellow does not intend it in a narrow hedonistic sense, but in the larger sense of seeking the right relationship with people in this life, in being properly human in the life that nature affords us, for there is no other. Again, Dr. Tamkin tells Tommy: "Nature knows only one thing, and that's the present. . . . like a big, huge, giant wave—colossal, bright and beautiful, full of life and death, climbing into the sky, standing in the seas. You must go along with the actual, the Here-and-Now, the glory—."[32] The message is to embrace life. When confronted with a suffering Tommy, Dr. Tamkin enjoins him, "Don't marry suffering. Some people do." For once Tommy agrees. "Yes, thought Wilhelm, suffering is the only kind of life they are sure they can have, and if they quit suffering they're afraid they'll have nothing. . . . this time the fakir knows what he's talking about."[33]

At the nadir of his distress and despair, Tommy wanders along Broadway. At one point he is carried along by a crowd entering a funeral chapel. As the organ sounds, he finds himself in line to view the deceased. While he approaches, the tears start to flow, at first quietly, then more copiously, and he cries louder and louder until "the source of all tears had suddenly sprung open within him, black, deep, and hot, and they were pouring out and convulsed his body.... He cried with all his heart." The pent-up longing for a common awareness of others, and of them as one with himself, at last finds release. The chapel music "sank deeper than sorrow, through torn sobs and cries toward the consummation of his heart's ultimate need."[34] His catharsis had precipitated in him an experience of human affirmation.

While most of the characters in the novel are Jewish and the whole is enacted in the Jewish milieu of upper Broadway, this Jewishness is a simple given of the story, without development of any kind. When Bellow moved on to his next novel, *Henderson the Rain King* (1959), there are no Jews in it at all. Yet Bellow's basic theme, which is his Jewish theme, that is, affirmation of life, is the predominant aim of this novel. Indeed the need that motors the story, Henderson's cry, "*I want! I want!*"[35] signifies a need that is answered by the injunction to "Seize the Day!"—realization of the fullest life of body and spirit. In this instance the quest for the values of life in their fullness is undertaken by Eugene Henderson, a millionaire scion of a family prominent in public life for generations. He leaves his wife and children to find the answer to his "wants" in Africa, and here Bellow brings to bear his interest in anthropology which he had studied as a college student. Henderson's sojourn with an African tribe is an imaginative, symbolic fantasy on presumed tribal ritual and symbolism. Bellow's intention emerges in Henderson's conversation with the old queen of the tribe. She tells him, "Grun—tu-molani," which means, "you want to live." Henderson answers, "Yes, yes, yes! Me *molani*. She sees that? ... Not only I *molani* for myself, but for everybody. I could not bear how sad things have become in the world."[36] Why had he desperately demanded, "I want"? Because "the world as a whole, the entire world, had set itself against life and was opposed to it—just down on life, that's all—but that I was alive nevertheless and somehow found it impossible to go along with it? That something in me, my *grun-tu-molani*, balked and made it impossible to agree."[37] His African search yields an answer, and he returns to the United States to rejoin his wife and children and to enter medical school. Although there is no explicit suggestion of Jewishness in the novel, it is animated throughout by the characteristically Jewish belief in the need to affirm life. Once again, the alienated condition at the start of Bellow's story is overcome by its end.

From the total absence of any explicit Jewishness in *Henderson*, Bellow moved in *Herzog* to what "has been called," wrote Milton Hindus, "his most Jewish book; it is that not in the sense that he has forgotten in it his stance of aesthetic objectivity towards his material but only in the sense that his Jewish material is used more liberally, unself-consciously, and even uncompromisingly than it has ever been used by him before."[38] Many critics consider *Herzog* his finest novel to date, and with this I agree. Its intellectual quality is such that it is perhaps not hyperbolical to call it a magical feast for the mind. In its solidity and depth of intellectuality, it reminds this reader, at least, of the George Eliot of *Middlemarch*. What makes his intellectuality so impressive is the internal rightness of his introduction and analysis of ideas, so that his assimilation of ideas is complete, a part of his own mind, and nowhere intruded on the narrative. This is most apparent in the unsent letters, his highly successful technical innovation. Robert Alter has suggested that "this use of letters ... [is] a *reductio ad absurdum* of the epistolary convention with which the beginnings of the English novel are associated," and his device is "successful in introducing ideas dramatically into a novel."[39] Not only does he pithily comment on ideas in these letters; he also uses the device to explore his relations with other persons in his life. All this is achieved with a remarkable lightness of touch, a kind of informalization of ideas that does not diminish their seriousness in giving them an ironic turn. By mixing ideas in his mind with events of ordinary life he drains all academicism from an approach to them, as in his question for that twentieth-century existentialist, Heidigger, which is actually a subtle philosophical challenge: "Dear Doktor Professor Heidigger, I should like to know what you mean by 'the fall from the quotidian'? When did this fall occur? Where were we standing when it happened?"[40]

There are earlier intimations of this new technique. Did he know of a project of his friend Delmore Schwartz for a poem, "Dear Pope"? James Atlas writes that this unfinished poem "addressed various intellectual and literary heroes in particular Freud," but that Schwartz abandoned it because, as he wrote in a failed poetic invocation to the pope, they were "not within my scope."[41] This is indicative of an important difference in the intellectuality of the two writers: Schwartz' power to absorb ideas was not as total as Bellow's. Schwartz' allusions have an academic, even external, quality, while those of Bellow are completely his own. The idea of the unmailed letter to distinguished people also appears tentatively in *Dangling Man*, when Joseph tells his friend, Myron Adler, that a nurse with a bedpan did more for people than the Communist party. He adds that he "sat down and wrote Jane Addams a letter of apology. ... I never mailed it. Maybe I should have." He later admits to himself that he was "wrong" to have invented a letter to Jane Addams "in order to make a point [but] should have thought of a better way."[42] If we were to inquire how Bellow came to engage in these brief dialogues, often via unsent letters, with thinkers of the past and doers of the present, one may recall that he had been teaching English literature and taught in the Committee on Social Thought at the University of Chicago for over a year while he was writing *Herzog*. It is natural that this least academic of men should fuse into one organic unity his everyday life with his exercise of the mind.

Like all his predecessors in the Bellow novels, Herzog begins in despair and ends in tranquility and acceptane of life. He is an English professor whose wife has left him for his best friend and is suing for divorce. At the outset of the novel, Herzog found his life in chaos and was "overcome by the need to explain, to have it out, to justify, to put in perspective, to clarify, to make amends."[43] This effort takes him from New York, where he is teaching, to Chicago, back to New York, and finallly, at rest, to a ramshackle old house in rural Massachusetts, which he had bought some years before, with the prospect of being joined there by the sensual and intelligent Ramona. In the course of his search for a tranquil acceptance of life he relives his past, skillfully associating back to persons and incidents: from boyhood in an immigrant family, with its frequent use of Yiddish or Hebrew, to his several marriages, divorces, loves, to his intellectual life and his thus far frustrated promise of producing a sequel to his acclaimed book on romanticism, to his quixotic journey to Chicago, where his best friend Valentine Gersbach has taken over his wife and child, and his final return to New York and present female friend, Ramona. At last he comes to rest in his Ludeyville, Massachusetts, house, where Ramona may soon join him. What is the relation between his personal problems and the state of the world? In court during the divorce proceeding Herzog asks himself, though he believes in God, even if he doesn't admit it: "But what else explains my conduct and life?"[44] Do such personal problems result from the outlook brought to bear on them by himself and those with whom he is involved— wives, friends, enemies, colleagues? He wonders if there is a "decay of the religious foundations of civilization. Are all the traditions used up, the beliefs done for, the consciousness of the masses not yet ready for the next development?"[45] He is sure the answer will not be found in the current intellectual fashions, for which he expresses impatience and even contempt. "We mustn't forget," he writes, "how quickly the visions of genius become the canned goods of the intellectuals." What are some of these "canned goods"? "The commonplaces of the Waste Land outlook, the cheap mental stimulants of Alienation, the cant and rant of pipsqueaks about Inauthenticity and Forlornness." Herzog is searching for an answer "after the wars and mass killings."[46] In his present state of receptivity he learns, from a review of the great variety of his past experiences, how he has sought peace within himself. He had intended his answer to emerge from the sequel to his *Romanticism and Christianity*; he had intended to end that work "with a new angle on the modern condition, showing how life could be lived by *renewing universal connections*; overturning the last of the Romantic errors about the uniqueness of the Self; revising the old Western, Faustian ideology; investigating the social meaning of Nothingness" (italics added).[47] His final resolution, rejection of the void of alienation, is in practice, life in his old house, perhaps with Ramona, acceptance of himself and others and nature ("universal connections"), in short an assertion of life, Herzog's—that is, Bellow's—basic Jewish nature.

Bellow has made it amply clear that he rejects social solutions of human problems, that any restructuring of society, in socialism for instance, would not be the answer he is seeking, which must rather be found in an individual conduct of life. The specific character of such a life is rejection of the longing for what is unattainable, and a cherishing above all of our allotted span. This should not be confused with complacency, for it would be idle to suppose that Herzog, for instance, will not in the future meet with severe personal problems or challenges to him as a social individual. What it does mean is that, through all exigencies to come, he will not despair or interpret human life as confrontation with the Void. And in fact, in his next novel, *Mr. Sammler's Planet* (1970), Bellow subjects this view to its severest possible test.

Herzog has worked his way through the inner travails of post–World War II malaise and finally found rest in simple acceptance of life. He survived the illusions fostered by contemplation of the Void. But Arthur Sammler's struggles with despair are different, more acute, more physically testing, more ultimate—he is a Holocaust survivor. He is a Polish Jew who had seen life in its ultimate brutality and degradation under the Nazis. As a correspondent for a Polish paper he had lived in London and become Anglicized. Just before the outbreak of World War II, when he visited Poland with his wife, they were caught by the Nazi invasion, rounded up with many Jews, who were all stripped naked, forced to dig a trench, and shot so that they fell into the mass grave. But Sammler did not die; he crawled out from among the dead bodies, joined the partisans, and survived the war. Despite this ultimately harrowing experience he had not lost faith in man and the value of life. He does not allow this and other subsequent destructive experiences to dispel his Jewish veneration for life. He finds fulfillment not only in intellectual activity, but also in living relationships with others, especially his nephew, Dr. Elya Gruner, a wealthy, distinguished surgeon who has supported Sammler and his daughter Shula in their immigration to America, who is on the verge of death throughout the story, and who dies at the end. *Sammler* is then a judgment on life from one who has virtually returned from the grave, so that it is in some way a final meditation on the evil and good in life from one who has known it under its most brutal, depraved aspect. For Sammler remains sensitive, loving to his friends and close relations, severe but kindly in judgment on some, harsher on others. Together with devotion to abstract, "eternal" values and their exemplification Sammler has a distaste for populist or radical activity, a view shared by Bellow.

But Sammler, now in his seventies, believes that his experience makes him better equipped than most to judge life and its values. The Germans had tried to kill him; the Poles had shot at him when he fought with the Jewish Partisans; yet as a Partisan he was saved from death by a Pole. "I always hated people who declared it [modern life] to be the end. What did they know about the end? From personal experience, from the grave, if I may say so, I knew something about it.... there is still such a thing as a man— or there was. There are still human qualities. Our weak species fought its fear, our crazy species fought its criminality. We are an animal of genius."[48] With all his experience of man at his worst, Sammler has not lost his faith in human possibilities; he would, we assume, agree with the humanist, Hamlet: "What a work is man!" In the end, this novel shows Bellow wrestling with the problem of religion in our intensely scientific, materialistic, and brutal age. Sammler has been reading steadily in the Bible and in the German mystic Meister Eckhardt. As he comtemplates his dead nephew, Elya, he utters what may be the conclusion of the novel. Elya, he believes, knew how to live, did "what was required of him. At best this man was kinder than at my very best I have ever been or could ever be." Then Bellow adumbrates the Talmudic idea of man's accountability to God through their contract. Through the "confusion and degrading clowning of this life through which we are speeding—he did meet the terms of his contract"— his "contract" with "God," or the universe, or whatever transcendant power exists, the contract, "the terms which, in his most inmost heart, each man knows. For that is the truth of it—that we all know, God, that we know, that we know, we know, we know."[49] This final sentence repeats the phrase that some might interpret as strength of conviction of truth, others as an emphatic effort of Bellow to convince himself.

But the novel also reflects Bellow's attitude toward more immediately mundane affairs of the period. For although Bellow's explorations into the moral and intellectual depth of man's being were usually lodged within the most concrete living events, this concreteness did not extend to significant, specific social trends, except in the most general sense, until *Herzog*. The reaction against his early political radicalism left Bellow with a detached attitude toward such politics. Thus, in *Augie*, when Augie very briefly becomes a union organizer, he takes it simply as a job without commitment and he leaves it after a beating from the bosses' thugs; and his brief flirtation with Mexico with an opportunity of traveling with Trotsky has no special significance in the novel, except as more rejection of "Reality Instructors." Then in *Herzog* the titular character writes a letter to himself: "Since when have you taken such an interest in social questions, in the external world? Until lately, you have led a life of innocent sloth. But suddenly a Faustian spirit of discontent and universal reform descends on you. Scolding. Invective."[50] Here Bellow is resisting "the Faustian spirit" in the modern world, but in *Sammler* he engages it in polemic. The conforming and apathetic 1950s were past, the nation was once more awakening to its profound imminent problems. The necessity of grappling with social and political problems—even in their theoretical aspect—in his teaching at the University of Chicago must have confronted Bellow with the necessity of dealing with these problems. As the 1960s wore on, Bellow became increasingly impatient with the student movement and the chaotic mounting social problems, including the Vietnam War. The feelings aroused in Bellow by current radi-

calism came to a head in *Sammler*, in which the conservatism into which
Bellow had fallen becomes evident. This is brought out in two events in the
book.

First is Bellow's account of the disgraceful behavior of students during a
lecture by Sammler at Columbia. They show him no respect whatsoever;
they insult him with obscenities and do not hesitate to let him know they
are not at all interested in the past he is discussing. Perhaps the incident is
close to fact, as well it might be, for the 1960s generation was hardly in
courtesy or cultural interests a model youth generation. But in the story the
reader is left with a totally negative picture, with no mitigation. Further
evidence of the same attitude is Bellow's comment on Marx: "His ideological
hashish was very potent." When Bellow visited Israel in July, 1970 he was
criticized in his talks before Israelis for his attitude toward youth. His
comments then reveal a far more complex view of the youth of that decade
than the categorical condemnation in *Sammler*. Although Sammler is a fully
realized character in his own right, Bellow does to some extent share his
views. In a speech in Tel Aviv in July, 1970 Bellow told his audience that
the accusation which youth "make against the middle class is quite a justified
accusation—that the middle class did not produce values by which these
young people can live." On the other hand the student attack on the universities is harmful because the universities are "the only and perhaps the
last centers of free exchange and discussion in the U.S." In addition, Bellow
held that Jewish parents after the Holocaust "tended to shut themselves up
in suburbs, reviving Judaism and Orthodoxy and removing themselves in
many ways from the main currents of American life,"[51] a course from which
youth were turning away to rejoin the American current. Unlike the treatment of youth in *Sammler*, there are attempts here at least to understand
youth, not simply to condemn it. But it is important to note that Bellow
seems to see little of positive value in the youth revolt of the 1960s. At
almost the same time, in 1966, Bellow told an interviewer: "True radicalism
requires homework—and thought."[52] Did not the 1960s produce, to some
extent, a radicalism of this kind in many young scholars and teachers who
came out of the decade's New Left? Would Bellow acknowledge this as a
positive value of the youth movement of the 1960s, which he condemns in
toto?

We make bare mention here of what seems to me the dubious introduction
of a Black pickpocket in the novel, also signifying Bellow's conservatism,
reserving it for the fuller discussion about the literary relations of Blacks
and Jews.

In the past few decades Bellow has taken every opportunity to urge his
fellow writers to return to questions of criteria for human values. Upon
receiving the National Book Award for *Herzog* in 1965, he exhorted them:
"it is evident now that polymorphous sexuality and vehement declarations
of alienation are not going to produce great works of art."[53] On the other

hand, as he said he told a group of Polish writers in Warsaw in 1966: "it was just too bad people couldn't overcome their political and ideological restraints because there were lots of human problems to be solved in the world. I said that political ideology was a drag."[54] When he received the National Book Award for *Sammler* in 1971, he again told his fellow writers: "there is an ancient belief in art as a remedy for the corruption of consciousness.... If we are not doing something of this sort, we have no business to be writing books."[55] And once again, in accepting the Nobel Prize for Literature in 1976, he urged that "literature might once again engage those 'central energies'—... an immense desire had arisen for a return from the periphery for what is simple and true."[56] Judging from the specific political views professed by Bellow in recent years, from his seemingly total revulsion against the radical youth movements of the 1960s to his sponsorship of Cold War propagandist groups like the Committee of the Present Danger in the early 1980s (he has since resigned), one may be permitted to reserve full judgment on the direction he recommends. Between general statements and their realization in practice there is no straight line. As they apply to creative writing, it seems quite clear that Bellow tended to interpret his view in terms of the profoundly Jewish assertion of the value of life as against resort to the Void.

By making Sammler, survivor of the Holocaust, his spokesman, he gives this conviction a kind of ultimate statement. The renewed peril to the survival of the Jews in Israel from the repeated wars with the Arabs probably compelled Bellow to a concern with the Holocaust. While the 1967 war and subsequent events and visits to Israel have not made a Zionist of him, they have heightened his Jewish awareness. He was led to dispute Hannah Arendt's well-known theory of the "banality of evil," developed in her study of a "banal" mass murderer, Adolf Eichmann. What Bellow seems to be saying is that Arendt was deceived by the Nazis' "idea of making the century's greatest crime look dull." But his is not "banal," he says.

The banality was only a camouflage. What better way to get the curse out of murder than to make it look ordinary, boring, or trite? With horrible political insight they found a way to disguise the thing. Everybody (except certain bluestockings) [Arendt, e.g.?] knows what murder is... banality is the adapted disguise of a very powerful will to abolish conscience.[57]

In other words, banality did not characterize the real situation, as Arendt would have it, but was only the face the Nazis cleverly put on to make their murderous activity viable. "The best and the purest human beings," Bellow adds, "have understood that life is sacred."[58] It is this understanding, in one form or another, that animated the novels of Bellow until the dubieties of *The Dean's December* (1982).

It is not the sacredness of life that Bellow questions in this latest novel but the hopefulness that had been implicit in his embrace of life up to then. For *December* is focused on the seemingly depraved decline of human relations in both communist and capitalist societies, though the capitalist has, at least in some metropolitan countries, the saving grace of some sort of freedom. The prevailing mood of the novel is one of somber, meditative, and problematic apprehension for the future of humanity. There is hardly any lightness in this novel, most unusual for Bellow. It lacks much of the verve of previous books. It seems the work of a man old in spirit and dispirited.

The world perspective is viewed through the mind of Albert Corde, a dean of a Chicago university, of "Irish-Huguenot" ancestry. Aside from the titular hero of *Henderson the Rain King*, Corde is the only non-Jewish protagonist in Bellow's novels, nor is there any explicitly Jewish character in it. But Corde is patently a fictional stand-in for Bellow himself.

The story is set in both major societies. Corde and his wife Minna, a distinguished professor of astronomy who had defected from Rumania years earlier, are in Bucharest awaiting the imminent death of her mother. (Bellow does indeed have a Rumanian wife who is a mathematics professor, and they did go to Rumania in the 1970s to be with her dying mother.) Corde's ruminations on the deterioration of life in his own country are told in flashbacks to his life in Chicago as he waits out the last days of his mother-in-law.

To Corde, both societies are "decadent." The sojourn in Rumania gives Bellow the occasion for an all-too-credible picture of a morally repungant, repressive society. This is obvious from his observation of callous bureaucracy, rigid conformism, perpetual intimidation, integrity corrupted by fear of reprisal, as well as a resolute few who are immune from corrupting influences and suffer the consequences. The capitalist side of the world picture is filtered through controversies provoked by several articles Corde had published about the squalid and criminal corruption pervading Chicago and by Corde's involvement in the case of the alleged murder of a white college student by a Black pimp and his Black prostitute. Corde is directly interested in the case because the allegedly murdered student had a pregnant wife and because his nephew, Mason Zaehner, is a close friend of the arrested Black, Ebry. The novel's account renders Ebry's innocence of the murder dubious. All these circumstances form a microcosm through which the state of society is evaluated.

In *December*, again as in *Sammler*, Bellow's critique of his own country is channeled in part through Black criminality and student radicalism through his nephew Mason. This time, however, Bellow introduces positive Black influences in three exemplary Black characters. As in *Sammler*, Bellow makes clear his bitter condemnation of student radicalism through the intensely unfavorable character of his nephew, who is depicted as lacking any redeeming features. He is "a cruel kid,"[59] aspires to be an "honorary black,"⁶⁰ and his radicalism is extremist. Bellow's antagonism to student militancy leads him to put the worst possible face on it. Whatever he may feel about social activism, the parlous state of the world he depicts in this novel leads him willy-nilly into involvement. Bellow's unfriendliness to social activism had already been expressed when Herzog writes to himself: "Since when have you taken such an interest in social questions? ... a Faustian spirit of discontent and universal reform descends on you."⁶¹

The total outcome of *December* is little short of despair. But is there no possibility of social amelioration? Does Bellow believe in some undefined non-material forces of whose existence we have no conception? Or is this "spiritual" factor only a name for stubborn and extremely complicated social problems which are nevertheless deteriorating the moral fiber of both communist and capitalist societies? Toward the end Bellow admits his inconclusiveness about the sad state of civilization which has occupied him. Of course no one can expect finality. But one can ill afford to ignore or undervalue the necessity for the application of whatever "material" remedies are at hand.

In this novel Bellow is overcome by the world's ills. The strong affirmation of life which pervaded his earlier novels, an expression of his essential Jewishness, is now weakened and replaced by a near despair for the future. His novelistic technique has not lost its closeness to earthy reality, but the sparkle and exuberance are muted. Has Bellow given up on people too easily?

But Bellow is irrepressible. His humor, irony, and exurberance return in full force in his next book, *Him with His Foot in His Mouth* (1984), a collection of short stories written over the previous decade. The first and titular story is one of the funniest of his career. Then follow others based on deceased friends, two of whom can be identified by those familiar with the avant-garde cultural life of past decades. One is the famous art critic Harold Rosenberg, coiner of the phrase "action painting" and the other his close friend from adolescence until death at thirty-eight, Isaac Rosenfeld, the critic and writer. These portraits are far from hagiographic—they are dense with the concrete reality of each person. In addition, many others appear in these stories who are said to suggest other friends and relatives of the author. But these stories are not explicitly sordid nor do they verge on the despair felt in *December*. Neither do they recover the earlier mood of affirmation, for they are pervaded with a sense of mortality. Where will Bellow go from here?

# 6

# From *Shlemiel* to *Mentsh*: Bernard Malamud

Like his distinguished contemporary Saul Bellow, Bernard Malamud has asserted, "I belong to American writing. I am unaware of a school of American-Jewish writing."[1] Indeed, American-Jewish writers have proliferated in a great variety of styles and modes. Yet it is striking that these two leading American-Jewish writers, who are also among the leading American writers of their time, should start from similar premises not shared by most of their non–Jewish-American contemporaries. For both resist the nihilistic trend of the immediate past, not to mention the more than century-old attempt to confront the Nil, Nothingness. We have already seen this in Bellow. And quite independently of Bellow, Malamud has in his own terms emphatically renounced dehumanizing tendencies. When he received the National Book Award for *The Magic Barrel* (1958), Malamud stated his credo in his acceptance speech: "I am quite tired of the colossally deceitful devaluation of man in this day." After detailing the familiar reasons given for this—war, totalitarian dehumanizing processes, values of our "thing-ridden society," threat of human extinction—leading to the self-description "fragmented, abbreviated, other-directed, organizationally anonymous man, a victim." Malamud's conclusion is: "The devaluation exists because he accepts it without protest."[2] The essence of Malamud's work is to raise the devalued man to a being of dignity, to transform, as Ihab Hassan has noted, "a man into a mentsh."[3]

If it is true, as we tried to show in dealing with Bellow, that his central theme is the affirmation of life in the face of a world that seems bent on denying it, then we may perceive in him an underlying agreement with the quest of Malamud's characters for human dignity. Is not the basis for this agreement the two authors' indefeasible sense of their Jewishness, of which a central tenet is the value of life? But their respective styles, manners, approaches are extremely different. Robert Alter has no doubt well observed that "concentration on Jewish social environments" in recent American writing has not "led to anything like a distinctively Jewish mode of imaginative writing."[4] Bellow's style is in the realistic tradition, while an aura of fantasy suffuses the style of Malamud. Yet both styles are distinctively products of American-Jewish writers, and each has its special Jewish quality, though they are different from each other.

Although Malamud is a year older than Bellow, he began publishing in literary magazines about a decade later and came to general public attention five years later than Bellow: Bellow received the National Book Award for *Augie March* in 1954 while Malmud's *The Magic Barrel* won the award in 1959. Malamud was born in Brooklyn in 1914 of Russian-Jewish immigrant parents. His father eked out a living for the family as the proprietor of a small grocery store, no doubt supplying some of the experience that went into the concept of Morris Bober, grocery store owner of *The Assistant*. At Erasmus Hall High School he was an editor of, and wrote stories for, the school magazine. He graduated from the City College of New York in 1936; in 1945 he married Ann de Chiara, daughter of Italian parents, and taught, first at Erasmus High School and then from 1949 to 1961 at Oregon State College (the "Cascadia College" of *A New Life*); then he joined the faculty of Bennington College in Vermont. His first paid-for story was published in *Harper's Bazaar* in 1949, and his first novel, *The Natural*, appeared in 1952. It is of some interest that a sensitive, compassionate writer, who lived through the Great Depression, the war against Nazism, and the Holocaust, scarcely allows these events to figure in his early fiction. Granville Hicks has observed that in his younger years Malamud, "Unlike many of his contemporaries, . . . never became interested in radical causes. He had his own problems, and he distrusted the Communists, especially after the Moscow trials."[5]

His writing was modernist under the influence of writers like Dostoyevsky, Chekhov, Gogol, James Joyce, and, among Americans, Maxwell Anderson. T. S Eliot must have been an early influence, for Malamud's first novel, *The Natural*, which contained no Jews, is a baseball story grounded in the myth of the quest of the Holy Grail. In 1963, Malamud told Ihab Hassan that he was not involved in social problems "outside of writing." Malamud said that "the writer's involvement in writing *is* involvement with social problems; he doesn't need political involvement." What then, asked Hassan, of his involvement with social problems? "A writer must say something worthwhile," replied Malamud, "but it must be art; his problem is to handle social issues so imaginatively and uniquely that they become art. Otherwise I'm not interested."[6] Social issues do indeed figure in some of his later stories, like anti-Semitism and the Holocaust in some of the short stories; the central importance of the social in his tale of pogromist Tsarist Russia in *The Fixer*, and Black-white relations in the United States in a few short stories and *The Tenants*. But they are concentrated in the moral conflict they generate in individuals, and they are unfailingly "art." They are evidence of his struggle to repress immediate social and political interests. It is not reading too much to identify the author's own feelings in this passage from *A New Life* (1961): Seymour Levin (Malamud) at the Oregon College

felt comparatively at peace with himself, more than for years. To stay at peace he let days go by without opening a newspaper or turning on a broadcast. He knew what the news was and preferred to forget it. The cold war blew on the world like an approaching glacier. The Korean War flamed hot, although less hopelessly for America. The country had become, in fear and self-accusation, a nation of spies and communists. Senator McCarthy held in his hairy fist everyman's name. And there were rumors of further frightening intercourse between scientists and atomic things. America was in the best sense of a bad term, un-American. Levin was content to be hidden amid forests and mountains in an unknown town in the Far West.[7]

But this degree of sociopolitical specificity is rare in his fiction (except for *The Fixer*). During the 1970s, however, as president of American PEN, he frequently signed his name to appeals for freedom to jailed or persecuted writers and intellectuals in many parts of the world.

But precisely how does he fulfill the Jewish part of his American-Jewish heritage? If his writing is a completely different kind from Bellow's, what is there in his manner and matter that justifies the designation Jewish? Obviously, Jews populate most of his works, and allusions to Jewishness abound. No one reading his work would take the author for anything but a Jew. He was asked in an interview the reason for the interest Jews in his fiction despite the fact that his rearing was not especially Jewish. Malamud replied, first, that it was "the pity I have felt for the suffering of too many Jews during the time of the Nazis"; second, "One of the things about writing is that you write about things you know.... I know Jewish people, and therefore I write about them"; third, "To me the Jew is a symbol of existential man as he becomes aware of his destiny"—a basic statement; and, fourth, his marriage to a non-Jewish Italian wife compelled him to examine his "relationship to the Jewish people," and he was driven "to read, ponder, understand, and direct my sympathies in this direction." While dilution of his Jewishness is generally expected as a result of intermarriage, it was the reverse in his case. These four reasons for the interest in Jews in his fiction comprehend the several levels of Jewish significance of his writing. The ambience of much of his fiction, whether real or fantastic, is Jewish. Yiddish-inflected English is occasionally used where appropriate. But most important is his use of the Jew as "symbol of existential man."[8]

Observation of this symbolism in his work has led a succession of critics to characterize his use of Jewishness as "metaphor," or as Robert Alter says, an "ethical symbol."[9] As Theodore Solotaroff phrased the idea, Jewishness functions in Malamud's fiction as "a type of metaphor... both for the tragic dimension of anyone's life and for a code of personal morality."[10]

While the essential Jewishness in Bellow's fiction is his espousal of a direct Jewish prime value, embrace of life, Malamud's Jewishness is mediated by metaphor. That is, by projecting the Jew as the universal existential man—he who asserts human dignity by rejecting domination by the false values of his society and by transcending the consequences—the author exemplifies this idea through Jewish characters. These characters are given in most of the fiction the nature of the *shlemiel*, the Jewish folk figure who is frustrated, blundering, and generally lacking in social status. He is also often a *shlimazel* as well, he to whom injurious things happen as if by his choice. He may be both victim and victimized. The *shlemiel* is a traditional figure of Jewish folklore, and he has become especially familiar to us through his extensive presence in classical Yiddish literature. He has been variously used, sometimes for satire, as, for instance, in Mendele Mocher Sforim's *The Travels of Benjamin III*, which satirizes the shortcomings of the Jews of the *shtetl* while also exhibiting their aspirations. I. L. Peretz's Bontshe Shweig is a quintessential *shlemiel*. Sholem Aleichem's Krasilevka has the *shlemiel* among its citizens, like his Menachem Mendel, another of his famous characters. More recently, Isaac Bashevis Singer's Gimpel the Fool, the town fool much put upon by everyone, but who bears no one ill-will, is perhaps the best-known example to English-speaking people. Victimization of the Jews over centuries of persecution has given rise to the use of irony and satire as a measure of emotional protection against the effects of this persecution. Hence the typicality of the *shlemiel* as a Jewish literary device. In a period, as Malamud said, of "the universally deceitful devaluation of man," he has brought Jewish experience to bear "in order to survive morally."[11]

The universality of Malamud's pervasive theme, suffering and its transcendance, is employed in his first novel, *The Natural* (1952), without use of its Jewish metaphor. There are no Jewish characters in this baseball story with its mythical underpinnings of the hero's quest to overcome suffering. In a crucial conversation, the central character, Roy Hobbs, reveals to the woman who helps him evoke his vision of his Grail, a decent life, in whose attainment he has always in the past been frustrated (the *shlemiel* theme); he wonders why he has this vision. She tells him, "Perhaps it was because you were a good person," and, going on, "Experience makes good people better." "We have two lives, Roy, the life we learn with and the life we live after that. Suffering is what brings us toward happiness."[12] Perhaps this could stand for the essential idea of Malamud's fiction. This is, as Sidney Richman calls it, "redemption through suffering,"[13] which is a universal experience of which Jews have had abundant experience. In the short stories and in his second novel, *The Assistant* (1957), Malamud extends his exemplification of this condition by linking it with the experience of Jews and thereby using Jewishness thus experienced as a metaphor for the universal condition. We can look further into this by an examination of *The Assistant*.

The "happiness" of which Roy Hobbs' woman friend spoke as maturation through suffering can be interpreted in several terms. It may be regarded as the redemption through suffering, or, as Morris Bober, the Jewish grocer of *The Assistant* appreciated, a realization of "the magic quality of life" in which suffering is transcended.[14] This is what his Italian "assistant," Frank Alpine, learned from Morris at the end. Frank is morally adrift, but basically a decent person. After participating in a robbery of Morris' impoverished grocery, during which Morris is beaten by Frank's vicious partner, Frank is consumed with remorse. Unrecognized by Morris, he is accepted as grocer's assistant for practically no wage except board and room. He falls in love with Morris' young daughter Helen, who is both attracted and repelled by him because he is a "goy." She finally falls in love with him, but they conceal their feelings for each other from her parents. In the park one day, when Helen is prepared to yield to his importunities, he tries to rape her. Calling him "Dog—an uncircumcised dog," she withdraws from him in loathing.[15] Again absorbed in his remorse, he confesses his part in the robbery to Morris and then is caught pilfering the cash register. Morris fires him. Morris soon dies, and Frank contrives to be allowed to work devotedly for Helen and her mother in the grocery; Helen gradually softens her attitude toward Frank, and the prospect of a reconciliation is left open at the end.

The pattern of offense and remorse in his relation with Helen is even more central in Frank's relations with Morris. He comes gradually to admire and to emulate Morris' humaneness. By his contrition Frank reinforces his own sense of decency. One sign of his painful progress to wisdom is the gradual breakdown of his folk anti-Semitism. When Helen rejects him after his attempted rape, he tries to mitigate her estrangement by thinking, "what was the payoff... of marrying a dame like her and having to do with Jews for the rest of his life?"[16] But he is drawn increasingly to the Jewish ethic as practiced by Morris. He observes that what Jews "live for... [is] to suffer."[17] He draws Morris out about his conception of Judaism. Morris is indifferent to *Kashruth* but does regard Torah as the law. "This means to me," he tells Frank, "to do what is right, to be honest, to be good. Why should we hate somebody else? For everybody should be the best not only for you and me. We ain't animals. That is why I need the law. This is what a Jew believes." When Frank replies that other religions also have similar ideas, he asks why "the Jews suffer so damn much, Morris? It seems to me they like to suffer, don't they?" Morris responds that "they suffer because they are Jews," and not because they like to suffer. And finally, "if a Jew don't suffer for the Law, he will suffer for nothing." When Frank asks what Morris suffers for, Morris replies "I suffer for you." When Frank asks what he means, Morris replies, "I mean you suffer for me."[18] Human beings are willy-nilly locked into mutual consideration. The final paragraph of the novel reads: "One day in April Frank Alpine went to the hospital and had himself circumcised. For a couple of days he dragged himself around with a pain between his legs. The pain enraged and inspired him. After Passover he became a Jew."[19]

Of course Malamud was aware of what he was doing with his conception of the good, as is evidenced by Frank's remark to Morris that his ideas are present in other religions, or we might add, ethical philosophies. In Judaism, as in any set of ideas enduring over centuries and institutionalized, many traditions are formed, not all consistent with one another. (The same could be said for Christianity or of any other religious outlook.) The particular tradition to which Morris belonged was characterized by the rabbi at Morris' funeral. "There are many ways to be a Jew," said the rabbi: even one who

lived and worked among the gentiles and sold them pig meat, trayfe,... and not once in twenty years came inside a synagogue.... Morris Bober was to me a true Jew because he believed in the Jewish experience, which he remembered, and with the Jewish heart. Maybe not our formal tradition—for this I don't want to excuse him—but he was true to the spirit of our life.... He suffered, he endured, but with hope.[20]

The essence of this concept is that aspect of Judaism which is universal. This is the meaning of Malamud's use of Jewishness as a metaphor. Through its exemplification in Jewish experience, a universal ethical outlook is set forth as the essence of Jewishness.

Much of Malamud's fiction depicts a struggle of his main characters to realize the kind of life he thus describes as Jewish. The extent to which it can be fully realized is doubtful. The suffering aspirant is hemmed in by doubts and frustrations and relapses. To symbolize these obstacles to realization, Malamud often employs the image of the prison. For instance, in *The Assistant*, the image of a prison and an alternative form, the coffin, recurs. Frank thought Morris, in his bondage to the store, lived in "an overgrown coffin.... The answer was not hard to say—you had to be a Jew. They were born prisoners."[21] And when Frank took to studying the history of the Jews, he "read about the ghettos, where the half-starved, bearded prisoners spent their lives trying to figure out why they were the Chosen People." When expelled from the Bober family, Frank "lived in his prison."[22]

This imagery appears in the next novel, *A New Life* (1961). Although there is only one allusion to the Jewishness of the central figure, Seymour Levin, it is a highly significant element of the plot, which again pursues the theme of redemption through suffering. Levin has broken away from a stagnant life in New York through his appointment to teach English in Cascadia College in Oregon. He falls in love with Pauline Gilley, wife of the college dean who appointed him. Toward the end of the story Pauline, who now loves him and plans to go away with him and her children and divorce her husband, reveals that it was she who was decisive in getting him appointed. "Your picture," she tells Levin, "reminded me of a Jewish boy I knew in college who was very kind to me during a trying time in my life."[23] This, in turn, is then linked to Levin's bringing love to her. Levin is the characteristic suffering Malamud character, but one who transcends his suffering at the last. After their decision to go away together with the children and to marry, Levin is not sure of the ultimate wisdom of the decision. "His doubts," writes Malamud, "were the bricks of a windowless prison.... The prison was really himself, flawed edifice of failures, each locking up tight the one before. He had failed at his best plans, who could say he wouldn't with her?... He would look like a free man but whoever peered into his eyes would see the lines of a brick wall."[24] But he will not go back on the responsibility to Pauline and her children he has now acquired, and in this lies his transcendance of suffering. The "tragic quality of life" remains. "The prison," writes Robert Alter, "like the *shlemiel*, who is usually its chief occupant, is Malamud's way of suggesting that to be fully human is to accept the most painful limitations; those who escape these limitations achieve only an illusory, self-negating kind of freedom for they become less than responsible human beings."[25]

The same themes as those of the novels are adumbrated in Malamud's short stories, of which he is a master. Surely one of the finest of these stories is "The Magic Barrel," which is also the title of his first collection of short stories. As in so many of the stories, the atmosphere of the Yiddish folk tale pervades it, but they exceed the folk tale in subtlety and, above all, in the ambiguity that marks them as modernist. In "The Magic Barrel," Leo, the rabbinical student, decides he should marry in order to become more eligible as a practicing rabbi. He engages the *shadchen* Salzman to find him a suitable wife, but the search is at first fruitless. Then in looking through the photographs left by Salzman, Leo comes on one with which he falls in love—it is the daughter of Salzman. She is, alas, a prostitute, and Salzman is persuaded to arrange a meeting only by Leo's vehement insistence. The meeting is set for a street corner where the girl Stella leans against a lamp-post, smoking. "She waited uneasily and shyly. From afar he saw that her eyes—clearly her father's—were filled with desperate innocence. He pictured, in her, his own redemption. Violins and lit candles revolved in the sky. Leo ran forward with flowers outthrust."[26] Redemption, then, is no simple achievement. Together with Stella's "desperate innocence" is her violation of her womanhood in prostitution. Salzman has witnessed the meeting. "Around the corner, Salzman, leaning against a wall, chanted prayers for the dead."[27] Redemption through love is not divorced from tragedy.

Most of the stories depict the suffering of a *shlemiel* character, who endures continual frustration but is redeemed by his transcendence of that suffering, often through love. Despite the depth of suffering, the narration never loses its humanity and sympathy for suffering felt and inflicted. So in the story, "The First Seven Years," the middle-aged Polish refugee Sobel labors long hours as a shoemaker for very little out of love for his employer's young daughter, hoping desperately that she will reciprocate his feelings when she is old enough to marry. Consider these thoughts passing through the shoemaker's mind when he learns what Sobel is hoping:

The shoemaker's ... teeth were on edge with pity for the man and his eyes grew moist. How strange and sad that a refugee, a grown man, bald and old with his miseries, who had by the skin of his teeth escaped Hitler's incinerators, should fall in love ... with a girl less than half his age. Day after day, for five years, he had sat at his bench, cutting and hammering away, waiting for the girl to become a woman, unable to bare his heart with speech, knowing no protest but desperation.[28]

This moving compassion is followed by "a strange and gripping sorrow" at the thought that his daughter's life with Sobel would be far from "the better life" he had dreamed for her.[29] Malamud never succumbs to sentimentality because he never fails to confront the inexorable negative component of any life situation in which its tragedy consists.

This story is one of the best of those in a Jewish milieu, which Malamud knew well. Indeed, all his writings had to touch on some aspect of his own experience. Thus, his characters are either Jewish or Italian because he knows these peoples. His Italian characters—Frank Alpine, for instance, and a number in the short stories—derive from his experience gathered from his life with his Italian wife, Ann de Chiara. Stories set in Italy, particularly in Rome, are accounted for by his residence in Rome and year-long travels in Italy on a *Partisan Review* fellowship. For some of his Roman stories he created the character of Arthur Fidelman (his mother's maiden name was Fidelman), a *shlemiel* whose travails are recounted in a half-dozen stories. Of these, "The Last Mohican," published in *The Magic Barrel* and reprinted later in *Pictures of Fidelman* (1969), is one of the best, and could be called "Variation on the Theme of the *Shlemiel*." Fidelman, in Rome to write a book on Giotto, is harassed by Shimon (later called "Virgilio") Susskind, a Holocaust survivor, for money and for a suit. Fidelman gives him a coat and money, but refuses to turn over his best suit, and Susskind gives up and disappears. But Fidelman's briefcase containing the unique copy of his first chapter has also disappeared with it. He sets out to find Susskind to retrieve his work. After an agonized search, the refugee is found, the briefcase is restored to its owner, but the chapter is missing. "I did you a favor," says Susskind, "... the words were there but the spirit is missing." The enraged Fidelman pursues the fleeing Susskind until he has "a triumphant insight." "Susskind, come back," says the "half-sobbing" Fidelman, "the suit is yours.... All is forgiven."[30] The "insight" is Fidelman's final grasp of reality and acceptance of it. His Virgilio has led him through Purgatory to a realization of his real self and an acceptance of it—redemption through love of his fellow man (the gifts to Susskind) and transcendence of the limitations of reality. Tragedy lies in the conquest of reality by acquiescence to its limitations. However, in the five remaining Fidelman stories Malamud's fantasy runs rampant, and it is difficult to find one consistent thread. As one might expect, there are a number of trenchant lines and thoughts. For instance, in "A Pimp's Revenge," a desperate Fidelman, in love with an eighteen-year-old Florentine whore, tries to paint her as Madonna with a Child. But he cannot succeed; paints it out and tries, "Sister and Brother"; fails again, and tries, "Prostitute and Procurer." The author comments, "How can you paint a *Kaddish?*"[31] However what does remain constant throughout is the desperate frustration of the *shlemiel* character through fantastic erotic and other adventures in a strange combination of fantasized stark realism suffused with tender human feeling.

Other themes enter some of the stories. Two deal with Jewish self-hate. The first, "Lady of the Lake," set in Italy, is a straightforward narrative that follows the young New York Jew, Henry Levin, on his quest for love. He finds it in an ancient castle on the Island del Dongo in Isabella, whom he supposes the daughter of the del Dongo. He has called himself Henry R. Freeman to conceal his Jewishness, which he believes will render him less eligible as a suitor. When Isabella asks him if he is Jewish, he denies it because of his suspicion that she is anti-Semitic. The affair advances to the point where he asks her to marry him, and she asks him once more if he is Jewish, which he again denies. She then reveals to him her tattooed Auschwitz number and tells him that she lost her whole family there, and is only the caretaker's daughter. Isabella is prepared to marry an American in order to be able to enter the United States—but not unless he is Jewish, in deference to her martyred family. She refuses him. He returns, determined to retract his lie, but Isabella had disappeared, and he is denied fulfillment. The other story, "The Jewbird," in the collection *Idiots First* (1963), is one of the most fantastic. The locus is the East Side apartment of Harry Cohen where there appears a "Jewbird" whose name is "Schwartz" (blackbird?), who talks, to no one's surprise, in a Yiddishized English. The talkative Schwartz is placed in a cage and helps Cohen's son Maurie with his lessons. But when Maurie gets a cat, Schwartz refuses to go on with his tutoring, and Harry is furious with Schwartz for refusing to help his son. Harry has hated the Jewbird anyway (symbol of self-hatred?). He throws Schwartz out of the window and Maurie, finding him dead, cries, "Who did it to you, Mr. Schwartz?" His mother says the murderers were "Anti-Semeets."[32] The Jewbird can be interpreted as the victim of Jewish self-hatred at the hands of Harry Cohen, for on first flying into the apartment he is attacked by Cohen, cries, "Gevalt, a pogrom!" and is finally driven out to his death by Cohen—Jew rejecting Jew—at the end.

Just as *The Assistant* can be regarded as an elaborated announcement of the complex of themes which Malamud was to pursue, so *The Fixer* (1966), for which Malamud received the Pulitzer Prize, epitomizes his themes most inclusively by an explicit addition of the sociopolitical dimension. There had been attempts at a social dimension earlier (in stories like "Black Is My Favorite Color" and, in a limited way, "Angel Levine"), but "The German Refugee" in *Idiots First* is the most explicit. In a technique unusual for Malamud, the story is a first-person narrative by a New York college student, Martin Goldberg, who has undertaken to help a distinguished refugee scholar, Oskar Gassner, prepare to deliver a lecture in English about the influence of Walt Whitman on the Germans. Gassner has left his non-Jewish wife and mother-in-law behind in Germany on the suspicion that his mother-in-law is anti-Semitic, and he is steeped in such profound guilt and despair over this that he seems unable to master English enough to give the lecture. He is overcome by despair to virtual mental paralysis over the enormity of his situation when Martin discusses some ideas of Walt Whitman. The German suddenly realizes that "it wasn't love of death they got from Whitman—that ran through German poetry, but it was most of all his feeling for Brudermensch, his humanity," and sadly, adds, "But this does not grow long in German earth."[33] This awareness releases Gassner, he learns English, and successfully delivers the lecture. Several days later, he is a suicide, and Martin discovers a letter from his mother-in-law informing Gassner that his wife had converted to Judaism and was taken away by the Brown Shirts and shot.

Malamud was aware that with *The Fixer* he had launched into a "new direction," which, he told an interviewer in 1967, was a "change perhaps that began with 'The German Refugee.'... I wanted to broaden my subject matter."[34] Perhaps it was the wave of social awareness of the 1960s that accounts for this change, and when it occurred, Malamud occupied himself with the specific problem of Jewish persecution, perhaps in belated assimilation of the Holocaust, as in the self-confessed instance also of Bellow. In so doing Malamud did not abandon his determination "to handle social issues so imaginatively and uniquely that they became art."[35] Critical opinion of *The Fixer* varied widely. Philip Rahv judged it "the weakest of his longer narratives,"[36] while Robert Alter thought it "clearly Malamud's most powerful novel" and "his first wholly successful one."[37] Alter seems nearer the truth because Malamud has succeeded in making art of a sociopolitical episode. As Alter points out, the pervasive Malamudian symbol of imprisonment as the metaphoric situation of the Jew is here fused with the actuality of physical imprisonment, thus lending social depth to the original idea. Malamud's running theme is one of suffering in a situation, confined by character and external events, which is finally transcended and given a densely social meaning.

The author chose as his vehicle one of the most notorious cases of the fake charge of ritual murder. In 1911 in Kiev, the simple Jew Mendel Beiliss was charged with murdering a Christian boy in order to use his blood in the making of *matzos* under the preposterous, ignorant delusion of anti-

Semites that this has been a standard Jewish ritual in preparation for Pass-over. Despite an intense, Russia-wide anti-Semitic campaign and Black Hundreds persecution, with the participation of even the Tsar himself, a jury acquitted Beiliss. The most brazen lies, bribed witnesses, as well as hysterical popular agitation did not succeed in convincing a carefully selected jury that Mendel Beiliss was the agent of a conspiracy of the Jewish people as a whole to carry through an annual "ritual" of murder. Quite by chance *The Fixer* appeared within a few weeks of the thoroughly researched, acutely analyzed, and well-written study of the case by the Jewish scholar and critic Maurice Samuel, entitled *Blood Accusation: The Strange History of the Beiliss Case*. His exposure of a totally vicious, contemptibly corrupt, in-human, unjust effort by Tsarism to arouse the masses of Russians against the Jewish people is devastating. For the fictional re-creation of the episode Malamud retains the bare facts of the crime and imprisonment of Beiliss and the Tsarist attempt to make a case that will hold. But the individual victim, named Yakov Bok (*Bok* is the Hebrew term for fool) by the author, is wholly invented by Malamud and bears no resemblance to the original Beiliss. The Beiliss character seems rather to have been given to Yakov's father-in-law Shmuel. Bok is a typical Malamud study: "My story," Ma-lamud wrote, "is about imprisonment and the effort of liberation through the growth of a man's spirit. He is able to defeat his captivity by becoming a greater man than he was before he was imprisoned."[38] Bok changes from *shlemiel* to *mentsh*.

Yakov Bok is an unremarkable Jew, a "fixer," a term which I remember as regularly used on the East Side for a repair man. But Malamud char-acteristically qualifies his notion of "the fixer": "I fix what's broken—except in the heart."[39] After his wife deserts him in the *shtetl*, he himself leaves and succeeds in living illegally in the Jewish district of Kiev. One day he comes on a Russian in the street, dead drunk with his face in the snow. The man's daughter asks Yakov to help her get him home, and asks him to return next day, presumably for his reward. Yakov had noted the drunk's Black Hundreds pin, indicating a rabid anti-Semite, but he sees no harm in getting a few rubles to live on from this man. Instead he is offered a job as superintendent of a brick factory in Kiev. Yakov accepts, having meanwhile passed himself off as a non-Jew with an appropriate last name. A few months later he rescues an old Hasidic Jew from the taunts of some boys and invites him to rest in his rooms before resuming his journey. Returning, he finds his rooms have been searched. A few days later it becomes apparent that his foreman had observed his hospitality to the old Jew, and Yakov is arrested for the ritual murder of a Christian boy who had been killed a few days earlier. He cannot understand why he is in jail, revealing how little he comprehended his situation as a Jew. It "was not enough," he thinks, "to explain his fate" simply because he was a Jew, "willing or unwilling." All he feels is resentment. "I'm a fixer but all my life I've broken more than I fix."[40] Under interrogation he confesses he is a Jew but maintains that he is innocent.

Then follow two years of beatings, privations, solitary confinement, a life in chains, and continual pressure to confess that he was part of a Jewish conspiracy to murder the Christian boy. Despite his early confusion as to just what his position is, he stubbornly asserts his innocence. The authorities hold out the lure of release if he will involve the Jewish community in the "plot," but he remains firm. Under this cruel instruction Yakov changes: he realizes the reality of what is happening to himself and the Jewish community at the hands of anti-Semitic persecution, official and unofficial. The Malamudian theme of suffering and its conquest is thus blended into a social situation, instead of remaining within the individual orbit. Individual redemption is gained through a socially responsible heroism. In a dream Yakov sees his still living father-in-law Shmuel in a coffin, and then awakens saying, "Live, Shmuel, live. Let me die for you."[41] He realizes that even if he dies, Jews may still be killed in pogroms, "but if I must suffer, let it be for something. Let it be for Shmuel."[42] Shmuel here stands for the Jewish people as a whole. Yakov will not "help them kill me."[43] His resistance to the anti-Semites lies in not helping them, in refusing collaboration, and in surviving as long as possible. He has indeed grown through suffering from a Jew indifferent to his identity as such to a Jew with a primary sense of responsibility to his people. Although he does not fear to commit suicide to end his suffering, he will not because "there is no way of keeping the consequences of his death to himself. To the goyim what one Jew does is what they all are," just as the death of Christ is "the crime of all Jews."[44] Yakov did not think of himself as a thorough Jew, but even though he was "half a Jew, . . . yet enough of one to protest them all. . . . He believes in their right to be Jews and live in the world like men." He has "made a covenant with himself" to endure until their lies confirm his innocence.[45] Once he overcomes the desire to commit suicide to escape suffering so as not to make things worse for the Jews, he expresses his awareness of the meaning of his life especially of what has been done to the Jew in history. "We're all in history, that's sure," he thinks, "but some are more than others, Jews more than some."[46] If he were not a Jew, he would not be where he is— for he is there for no other reason than that he is a Jew. No matter where he was, whether among his own people in the *shtetl* or out of it, "a Jew wasn't free. Because the government destroyed his freedom by reducing his worth. . . . A hand had reached forth and plucked him by his Jewish beard . . . to be imprisoned, starved, degraded, chained like an animal to a wall although he was innocent . . . because no Jew was innocent in a corrupt state, the most visible sign of its corruption its fear and hatred of those it persecuted. . . . Those who persecute the innocent were themselves never free."[47]

Thus, an enormous growth has taken place in Yakov from his initial puzzlement over why he should find himself in prison for nothing, to his final understanding under pressure of events and direct experience of the machinations of anti-Semites. He emerges to pit an unbreakable will as Jew against the most drastic measures to induce him to betray his people. It is therefore curiously imperceptive that Philip Rahv should assert that Yakov has been "deprived" by the pain he has undergone "of the chance to exert his will and make moral choices." Yakov is, Rahv says, a "victim pure and simple," and as such "cannot attain the stature of a hero of a work of art." Despite Rahv's recognition that in the "closing pages" Yakov "is transformed by a frenzied revolutionary imagination, he remains inert as a character."[48] But Yakov has emphatically been making "moral choices" from the moment he was arrested until the end by refusing to swerve from his assertions of innocence and, when he achieves understanding, by rejecting suicide and rejecting the anti-Semites' temptation to betray the Jewish people.

Yakov himself is fully aware that he has undergone change. In a dream, he says "something in myself has changed. I'm not the same man I was. I fear less and hate more."[49] Above all, he has emerged from a personal cocoon and perceived himself willy-nilly as part of history, has relocated himself in the social dimension. "To his painful surprise," he had "stepped into history more deeply than some."[50] His arrest, because of his peculiar circumstances, was "history's doing." No matter what he did or where, he carried on his back "a condition of servitude, diminished opportunity, vulnerability."[51] Gone was the earlier indifference to social matters and movements. Early in the novel Yakov rejects his father-in-law Shmuel's advice to go to *shul*. Yakov replies that he should rather go to a meeting of the "Socialist Bund." But he doesn't like politics, especially since it's futile "if you're not an activist," and Yakov is surely not that.[52] Later, when his Black Hundreds employer asks about his politics, whether he is a Socialist, Yakov truthfully replies that he is "not a political person. . . . it is not my nature."[53] But the torture he has undergone has changed him. The novel ends with Yakov on the way to trial, determined to resist the anti-Semites, thinking, "As for history, . . . there are ways to reverse it. . . . One thing I've learned. . . . there's no such thing as an unpolitical man, especially a Jew. . . . You can't sit still and see yourself destroyed. . . . Death to the anti-Semites! Long live revolution! Long live liberty!"[54] With *The Fixer*, the literary use of the Jew as metaphor is conjoined with the Jew as a specific category whom history has chosen as victim with the opportunity of surmounting his victimization.

The account of the trial itself is now needless to realize the full fruits of the experience Yakov has undergone, and the novel ends on his way to the trial. His momentous personal choices have not only been moral; their morality actually issued from the sociopolitical situation. Robert Alter has not fully understood what Yakov has learned when Alter limits this "to the necessity for moral involvement." Yakov has also quite literally learned the necessity of *political* involvement. This was a new note in Malamud's fiction, but Alter's observations about Yakov's newly perceived need to "retain his self-respect" by accepting "the entanglement in the worst of history" does not make up for the absence of the specifically political phase of Yakov's new knowledge. It is evasive to say, as Alter does, that Yakov's rejection of the "unpolitical man" "nicely states the relationship between the partic- ular and the universal in this novel."[55] Yakov unequivocally states that human life is inevitably *political*, especially in the case of Jews.

Malamud did indeed go on in his next novel to address aspects of Black- Jewish relations in *The Tenants* (1971), which we shall discuss in a later chapter. But this phase of his literary inspiration did not enter *Dubin's Lives* (1979). Despite many fine passages of natural description, especially a grip- ping account of exposure to a snowstorm, the story is a self-indulgent picture of middle-life crisis and obsession with aging. It is a late Malamud version of the *shlemiel* who ends in defeat and frustration. Although Dubin, the central character, is indubitably Jewish, Jewishness hardly figures in the novel. Anti-Semitism appears in one incident during the snowstorm when Dubin kills an attacking dog in self-defense, causing the farmer who owns the dog to go after him with a shotgun shouting, "I'll get you, you Jew son- of-a-bitch, one way or t'other."[56]

While the *shlemiel* figure in *Dubin's Lives* ends in frustration, many of these figures in the earlier work do not fail. Yakov Bok is the most striking example of this transformation from *shlemiel* to *mentsh*, and parallels a similar pattern in the best of Saul Bellow's work: the alienated man, most often a Jew, transcending his alienation by affirming life. There are, it would therefore seem, several species of *shlemiel*, those who remain immersed in their frustrations and those who emerge from them with a liberated con- sciousness which has escaped from self-enclosure. Jewish writers, especially Bellow and Malamud, were among the leaders of this liberation, which they achieved by affirming Jewish attitudes.

# 7

# Confessions of Philip Roth

The third of the triumvirate of leading American-Jewish writers since the late 1950s is Philip Roth. He is almost a generation younger than both Bellow and Malamud, and his outlook is so different from theirs as to fortify emphatically the observation that they do not form a "school" of Jewish writing. What they do have in common is their frequent use of Jewish characters, central and peripheral, throughout their writings. Further, they all share the sociopolitical disillusionment that pervaded post–World War II literature, and all are touched in some way by literary modernism. But each writer has a distinctive manner and approach to the predicaments of our commercialized, high technologized, sex-obsessed, *angst*-ridden society.

Popular recognition came to Roth in the 1950s, the "Jewish decade" in American literature, as it did to the older Bellow and Malamud, in each case signaled by a best-selling book given the National Book Award. Roth was in his middle twenties while the others were in their late thirties. Actually Roth had caught popular attention in 1959, before his first book appeared in that year, with the short story, "Defender of the Faith," in *The New Yorker* of March 14. Most of the English-Jewish press and many Jewish publicists bitterly criticized the story as anti-Semitic. It concerned the small group of Jewish trainees at an army camp during World War II. They are led by Grossbart, a schemer who gains privileges for the group by exploiting the reawakened Jewish awareness of their sergeant, Nathan Marx, a combat veteran assigned to a training company. When Grossbart contrives to have his name removed from a list of trainees assigned to the Pacific Theater, Marx discovers it and manages to have Grossbart's name restored to the list. Grossbart curses Marx. When the trainees leave, "Grossbart swallowed hard, accepting his" fate. And Marx—"resisting with all my will an impulse to turn and seek pardon for my vindictivenes, I accepted my own."[1]

When the story first appeared, I was among those who declared this story anti-Semitic. I granted that the Jews in the story were not improbable characters—"there are such people," I wrote. The point was, rather, that the story concentrated a number of unfavorable aspects of Jewish life and character. The rabbi at the training base incites the Jewish soldiers to protest absence of kosher food despite the well-known fact that religious Jews had special dispensation in this matter during wartime. Each trainee corresponds to a Jewish stereotype: one of the Jewish trainees is "obsequious"; another is "spiritually soft," a "Yeshiva-boy"; Grossbart is the shrewd, self-aggrandizing, scheming Jew. As for Marx, he is victimized *because of* his Jewish awareness. My conclusion was that "the concentration of these traits within a tightly knit framework tends to confirm in the reader—Jewish and non-Jewish—an unfavorable, untrue, and harmful picture of the Jews."[2] While I no longer hold this view with the same conviction as when I first advanced it, I still believe it to be one possible interpretation of the story. Some may have regarded the frustration of Grossbart's attempt to evade Pacific service as deserved punishment, but this was not of course Roth's intention. On the contrary, for Roth this was, on Marx's part, an act of "vindictiveness." Did Marx then "accept his fate" as a Jew, or as a morally flawed person, at the end? In any case the ambiguities of the story and of the ending seem to signify an unfavorable attitude toward Jews. We may believe Roth when he says he didn't intend this: he didn't, he writes, "see Marx's problem as nothing more than Jewish," but rather one of "confronting the limitations of charity and forgiveness in one's nature," the moral problem involved in the relationship of Marx and Grossbart.[3] It can be argued, I think, that the story carried it beyond this, despite what Roth believed his intention. Some estimable critics differ. Irving Howe, for instance, despite his unfavorale "reconsideration" of Roth's quality as a writer, believes this story exempt from the strictures he passes on most of Roth's other work and calls it "a distinguished performance." He further holds that Marx' sense of guilt at the end is "perhaps, of the same Jewishness that had first made him susceptible to Grossbart's designs." The story, concludes Howe, yields successfully a "texture of reality."[4]

However, when this story was published in Roth's first book, *Goodbye Columbus* (1959), the torrent of criticism and abuse poured on his head by the Jewish community seemed to be quite unjustified. Unlike "Defender of the Faith," the other stories seemed to me valid satirical depiction of much of the postwar Jewish middle class with much of its empty, conformist, suburban values and to challenge religious obscurantism. Indeed, reality in the form of the revolt of such a large proportion of Jewish youth in the 1960s was to confirm the validity of much of the criticism of the Jewish middle class in Roth's stories. Much of the Jewish community interpreted Roth's unsparing satire as anti-Semitic and self-hating. Yet Roth was awarded not only the National Book Award for this book in 1960, but also the Jewish Book Council's award for the best work of Jewish fiction in that year. This Jewish award, too, was criticized. Samuel Margoshes, a leading Yiddish journalist, charged Roth with anti-Semitism, and described his book as "a document redolent of Jewish self-hatred." Margoshes asserted that to make "the picture all black without a single ray of light is not to indulge in good literature or social criticism, but to insinuate that Jews are a hopelessly bad lot."[5] Margoshes here missed the point that the central figure of "Defender," Marx, is surely not a "bad lot," but that it was the consequences of the *Jewishness* of Marx that opens the story itself to anti-Semitic interpretation.

In any event, *Goodbye Columbus* announced the advent of a new, significant talent, Jewish in origin and employing Jewish material, on the literary scene. That talent already exhibited a strong, unsparing satiric bent. The titular story, "Goodbye, Columbus," a novella, recounts a frustrated love affair between Brenda Potamkin, daughter of a nouveau riche Jewish man, and Neil Klugman, a poor young Newark librarian, in which the empty, mindless, false values of this new middle class created by World War II, of which the Jewish sector had its special features, are satirized. The satire is serious, acute, and often funny, an early manifestation of Roth's comic vein, which was to be so marked as his work progressed. Besides "Defender of the Faith" there was "The Conversion of the Jews," depicting the revolt of a thirteen-year-old boy in Hebrew school against religious intolerance and obscurantism. Already, also, Roth's often excessive preoccupation with sex appears in this story. He later told an Israeli audience that he may have been led to writing "Conversion," by the fact that Jews "can be so intolerant of dissent" and was "about a boy who becomes so awestruck by the possibility of God that he believes that God had even done the unforgiveable—what the Christians allowed to happen here—which is, to allow one woman to have a child without first having the pleasure of intercourse."[6]

Another story, "Epstein," is a relentless exposure of a deteriorated marriage of petty bourgeois Jews, the free sexuality of their radical children, and the death of Epstein in adulterous intercourse. While Roth and some critics see this picture of Epstein as slightly comic, it seemed to me too pathetic to evoke even a smile. This story was especially excoriated by some hypersensitive Jews, as if no Jews commit adultery. "Eli the Fanatic," like the titular story, is a further exposure of the contemptible conformism in a middle-class suburban Jewish community and their desperate effort to prevent a Hasidic community from buying a house in their town lest "the goyim" confuse their own manner of life with that of the exotic Hasidim. Like so many talented writers of the postwar generation, Jewish and non-Jewish, Roth rejects the spurious and superficial values spawned in the tidal wave toward suburban middle-class life, and like most of his generation he is in a quandary. Where to turn? Like most writers, he rejects social radicalism. What is left in Roth's case is an affirmation of personal integrity lacking any general outlook or philosophy.

Unlike both Bellow and Malamud, Roth does not accept characteristic Jewish values as fundamental to his outlook. As we saw, for Bellow the tenacious Jewish affirmation of life is basic; for Malamud, Jewishness stands as a "metaphor" or symbol for the transcendance of suffering. Roth has no such large associations with his Jewishness, which he regards as simply a fact of his life. He was confronted with the question of his Jewishness not only by the attack made on him but also by a symposium in Israel, in which he participated, sponsored by the American Jewish Congress on "The Jewish Intellectual and Jewish Identity," in the summer of 1963. Israeli and American writers and intellectuals exchanged views. An Israeli writer bluntly stated that he considered the American participants "Jewish intellectuals in terms of intellectuals who happened to be Jewish. I do not consider you to be Jewish intellectuals as all."[7] Roth just as bluntly replied that he did not object to this distinction. "I am not a Jewish writer," he added. "I am a writer who is a Jew." What, then, does Jewishness have to do with his writing? He candidly acknowledged that he had not inherited Jewish law and learning, even that his knowledge of the Bible is "nil." "So," he concluded, "there is no body of law, no body of learning and no language, and finally, no Lord." But that did not mean an end of Jewish awareness for him, for "there were reminders constantly that one was a Jew and that there were *goyim* out there." What was finally left, he believes, "was a psychology, not a culture and not a history in its totality." And since what he *had* learned he reports as a fact of his life, is only that "Jews are better," that "what he had to do as he grew up was to create a moral character"—that is, "one had to invent the Jew." Since he then inherited a "psychology without a content, or with only the remains of a content," he had to "invent" off this impoverished state of affairs.[8]

All this is honest and true, but incomplete. For Roth's preoccupation is with personal psychology and seems to scant the sociology of ethnicity which is also involved in the content of his writing. His depiction of Jewish characters and of a Jewish milieu, even if it is deprived and diminished by its call upon only a residue of a rich Jewish culture, is nevertheless an ethnic phenomenon. Relics of language and ritual and social custom survive. The "invented" Jew of Roth is a species of assimilated Jew who may himself retain traits or turns of mind inherited from a family closer to a fuller ethnicity. Sometimes Jewishness is minimal and consists only in an awareness of being regarded by others as a Jew. But the "psychology" to which Roth refers as the only Jewishness left in him is only the subjective aspect of a social, ethnic situation. This is the meaning of what Roth granted later in the symposium. "It may appear that some of my stories appear to deal with Jewish life, and in certain ways they do," but many of the concerns in his longer narratives, he adds, were not specifically Jewish. Of course it is true that many concerns are not unique to any ethnic group but partake of universality in some respect. While he did not set out to write "Jewish" stories, "the American Jewish scene was more important to me when I was close to it," that is, when he started to write, "so my first stories were written out of facts and people I knew, places I went, things I had feelings for."[9] And as he moved, both geographically and into varying milieux, his stories changed accordingly. But we now know, several decades later, that he kept returning to Jewish characters and situations because these were so deeply ingrained a part of him. He exhibited the "psychology" of one who is *ethnically* Jewish, no matter what the degree of intensity.

Roth's concentration on the psychology of the individual—Jewish or non-Jewish—entails artistic risks which Roth has not, I believe, entirely escaped, and which in the end prevents him from being as great an artist as a Bellow or Malamud. The risk is in fact dual: it may deprive a work of social richness and depth, and the writer may fail to cut the umbilical cord with the artist's personal consciousness. I think Roth's work is diminished in both respects. It is necessary here to caution that his entire corpus roughly divides into two aspects, probing of individual consciousness and satire, and that these are frequently intermixed in the same work. But in both aspects Roth is not entirely in control of his abundant talent and allows it to run away with him, so that he either attenuates the satire or cannot prevent his own personality from intruding on the writing. The result is that his writing is never far from the *personal*, both in relation to the characters depicted and to himself, so that it is robbed of that broad human significance which constitutes the element of greatness in art. Perhaps this is the reason for the widely held belief, which I share, that Roth has not thus far fully realized the promise of his talent. These observations may acquire substantiation as we look further at his writings.

While the stories in Roth's first novel were impressive, certain danger signs appeared. It was as if the author could not suppress his own tendency toward a sour attitude toward people. "Why do you always sound a little nasty to me?" Brenda asks Neil in "Goodbye Columbus."[10] The reader is also inclined to ask this of Roth. A similar attitude seems to inform his second novel, the 630-page *Letting Go* (1962). Roth would, I think, agree with the dictum of the cynical Asher of this novel: "We're on earth to take it."[11] All around one finds circumstances that can ultimately be met with fortitude if one determines to be utterly oneself, to adhere to the dictates of conscience. This means "letting go," conducting one's personal life in accordance with one's own nature. The character who enunciates this central doctrine of the book is Gabe Wallach, who is thoroughly disillusioned with life—as is Roth—and the only thing left for him is to act with integrity within the orbit of his personal relations. His absorption is with his personal self. The whole complex of relations with the outside world is minimal.

Involvements with politics or social movements, in those few passages when they enter the story, are alluded to with scorn. "But in the end I knew," says Wallach to himself, "it was not from my students, or my colleagues or my publications, but from my private life, my secret life, that I would extract whatever joy—or whatever misery—was going to be mine."[12] This comes close to a wholly egotistical conclusion.

The trouble is that it seems to reflect Roth's own approach, which seeps into his writing as well. Even though it may be true that Roth's writings are not as autobiographical as they seem to many, they do read like confessionals, not of the fictional characters as such, but of Roth himself through the medium of his characters. The artist in him has not sufficiently distanced himself from the person. The result is that Roth's concentration on personal salvation is closer to the pathetic than the tragic. As one follows the story of *Letting Go*, for instance, one feels that Roth is intruding on the reader with details of grossly mismanaged lives rather than illumination of human relations. But the misfortunes in the lives of the characters are developed with such power that the reader becomes empathically involved and shrinks in horror at the unfolding of one personal catastrophe after another. It is as if one were a first-hand witness of disaster on the street without being illuminated as to the implications, as if one were seeing a case of bad luck. And this is the difference between the pathetic and the tragic—the former is an individual accident while the latter is a situation in which the nature of life and the relation of the individual to the order of nature and society are probed and perhaps revealed.

Jewishness in various degrees and types appears throughout the novel. Two of the main male characters are Jewish, but their wives or mistresses are not. Roth captures traits of a variety of Jews of different social strata from middle class to working class, Central Park West to Brooklyn: a cynical artist, an unscrupulous lawyer, a small businessman, and others. Both Catholic and Jewish parental intolerance of a mixed marriage is an important plot element. The Jewish husband of this marriage observes that the failures of the marriage are not to be blamed on the parents, but on their own maladroit way of dealing with their lives. Thus Jewishness is not the theme of the novel but rather the personal mismanagement of lives that is responsible for their unhappiness.

Roth leaves the Jewish community altogether in his next novel, *When She Was Good* (1967), which contains no Jewish characters, and explores ordinary midwestern life with unrelieved grimness. The reader closes this psychological portrait of a stifling moralistic but essentially egotistic central female character only depressed. As in the previous novel, the personal involvement of the reader does not transcend the naturalism of the novel. Whether or not Roth realized that he was least successful when he left the Jewish community altogether and did not use his talent for comedy, the fact remains that never again in his fiction (as distinct from his satires) did he stray from engagement with Jewish characters.

*Portnoy's Complaint* (1969) returned to the Jewish theme with a vengeance. The confessional trend of Roth's stories is here exploited to the full. All of his strengths and weaknesses are exemplified in abundance in this notorious novel—his comic talent, the natural fluency of his first-person narrative—the confessional—his satiric touch, his sexual obsession, his ambiguous attitude toward Jewishness. As Dwight Macdonald wrote, "after a decade of false starts he found his true voice with *Portnoy*."[13] This novel is an attempted Freudian account of Portnoy's sexual impotence with Jewish women owing to the "castrating" effect of smothering attention by his Jewish mother, his sense of guilt over sexuality, and his successful but unsatisfying sexual pursuit of *shiksas*, non-Jewish women. Added to the shock the novel administered to the Jewish community was the almost unprecedented freedom from sexual restraints in description which probably extended to a new level of explicitness in the treatment of sex in widely read literature, for *Portnoy* promptly became a best-seller. As Roth noted in one of his many defenses of his writing against Jewish critics, *Portnoy* sold 420,000 copies, "seven times as many as had purchased my three previous books combined," and "half of them within the first ten weeks" of publication.[14]

The story unfolds in an unbroken stream of monologue by a patient to a psychoanalyst, and is impressive in its unflagging conversational tone. The deeply troubled Alexander Portnoy, now in his mid-thirties (as was Roth), conveys the, to him, repressive atmosphere of a working-class Jewish family of first-generation parents. What he most rebels against is the smothering love and attempt to dominate by his mother. To make the "castration" idea clear, Roth even has Portnoy's mother force the boy to eat when he doesn't want to, seated "in a chair beside me with a long bread knife in her hand." This stereotypical mother and her "Philistine" husband badgering Alex with commands and prohibitions, he tells his psychoanalyst, "are the outstanding producers of guilt in our time!... I'm living in the middle of a Jewish joke! ...Please, who crippled us like this? Who made us so morbid and hysterical and weak?" Complaining about his obsessive masturbation even then, in his thirties, Alex asks, "Is this the Jewish suffering I used to hear so much about? Is this what has come down to me from the pogroms, the persecution? from the mockery and abuse bestowed by the *goyim* over these two thousand lonely years?"[15]

Psychologizing could go no further. This sort of hyperbolic comment goes beyond caricature to lack of comprehension of social objectivity. When the sick, sex-obsessed Portnoy casually mentions his work as Assistant Commissioner of Human Opportunity in the reform Lindsay administration of New York City, it is hard to take this seriously, so totally absorbed does

Portnoy seem in his sexual preoccupations, and so little does any other consideration seem to matter in comparison. One cannot help feeling that Roth tends to trivialize social activism whenever it is encountered in his stories. Thus Roth interprets Gabe Wallach's father's political activity in *Letting Go* as merely personal therapy, and similar allusions in the later novels get the same casual treatment. In Israel, the kibbutznik who ridicules his sick offer of marriage just after he meets her, tells him something that often applies to Roth's prose: "Everything you say is somehow always twisted some way or another, to come out 'funny.' "[16]

Since he believes his neurotic eroticism stems from the inhibitions generated in him by his parents, which can be evaded only in his sexual relations with *shiksas*, could his condition be cured by marriage to a conflict-free Sabra Israeli? Can the impotence he experienced with an Israeli woman be overcome? He picks up a hitchhiking kibbutznik, tall, strong, healthy, socialist. His abrupt, desperate proposal of marriage, really his search for a "mother-substitute," as he says, and his effort to bring her to bed are contemptuously rejected.[17] Portnoy craves salvation from the effects of a constricted Jewish upbringing. Perhaps Spielvogel, the psychoanalyst, can help him extricate himself?

The shock of sexual explicitness and anger at the novel's one-dimensional picture of a Jewish mother's destruction of the erotic morale of her son caused the book to become an important topic of general concern, mostly unfavorable. The Jewish establishment was especially indignant. As a character of a later novel says, "it is already the main topic of discussion at every Jewish wedding, bar mitzvah, social club, women's club, sisterhood meeting, and Hadassah luncheon in America."[18] The reaction to "Defender of the Faith" was a ripple compared to the tidal wave of protest that swept over Roth with *Portnoy*. Practically every Jewish publication had its article on the subject. Roth had some defenders, but most were critical. In literary circles many regarded the novel as a liberating influence. The personal notoriety into which Roth fell was more than he could endure, and he retreated to the Yaddo colony for a few months. Many had understood the novel as a personal confession, and the author was often accosted by strangers with sexual taunts. His absence from his New York apartment gave rise to unfounded rumors that he had suffered a breakdown and was hospitalized. The public had, to quote Roth, set upon "a voyeuristick kick," especially as, he added, "going wild in public is the last thing a Jew is expected to do—by himself, by his family, by his fellow Jews, and by the larger community of Christians whose tolerance for him is often tenuous to begin with, and whose code of respectability he flaunts or violates at his own psychological risk, and perhaps at the risk of fellow Jews' physical and social well being."[19] Roth attributed the strenuous rejection of the novel by many middle-class Jews to the fact that Portnoy's own hysterical sense of guilt at the end of the novel confirmed their own view that "a preoccupation with the flesh is as compromising to the safety and well-being of a Jew in America as was Arnold Rothstein's fixing—of all the stupid things for a Jewish boy to go and fix—a whole World Series."[20]

It was Roth's depiction of the Jew lusting after *shiksas* that especially engaged the wrath of Marie Syrkin, an editor of the Zionist *Jewish Frontier* and a professor of English. Roth's treatment on this point, she wrote, yields the "obscene and baleful stereotype which emerges from the banter. The dark Jew seeking to defile the fair Nordic is standard stuff.... There is little to choose between his [Goebbels'] and Roth's interpretation of what animates Roth."[21] She later rephrased this charge in a letter to *Commentary* in March, 1973 climaxing a series of attacks on Roth in that journal, which probably prompted Roth's response, "Imagining Jews," in the *New York Review of Books* for October 3, 1974. Syrkin there characterized the book's descriptions of sexual encounters with a *shiksa* as a "classic description of what the Nazis call *rassenschande* (racial defilement)... straight out of the Goebbels-Streicher script.... The anti-Semitic indictment straight through Hitler is that the Jew is a defiler and destroyer of the Gentile world."[22] Roth replies that Syrkin has ignored the fact that sexual involvements between Jewish men and non-Jewish women may be tinged with conflict and strain just as centuries of anti-Semitism and persecution have affected Jewish–non-Jewish relations of any kind: he instances the strain between Allbee and Leventhal in Bellow's *The Victim* or between Morris Bober and Frank Alpine in Malamud's *The Assistant*. What Syrkin has done here, adds Roth, is to impose her own conception of Jewish behavior on Portnoy—and Roth. It seems to me that Roth is correct in assigning what amounts to overzealous nationalism to Syrkin's extreme parallel with *Rassenschande* of the sexuality in *Portnoy*.

Where Syrkin is on firmer ground, however, is in her condemnation of the caricature of the Jewish mother stereotype in *Portnoy*. It is true, I think, that the irrepressible comic strain, often turning to the nasty, in Roth's talent, could not resist the conjunction of the Jewish mother stereotype with the Freudian notion of the castration complex attributed to the hyper-solicitous mother. Syrkin further emphasizes that the *Jewish* character of his family is responsible for his neurotic state. "Roth is relentless," she writes, "in driving home the thesis that the factors responsible for Portnoy and his ways are peculiarly Jewish," and she quotes Portnoy, "Dr. Spielvogel, this is my life, my only life, and I'm living it in the middle of a Jewish joke. I am the son of a Jewish joke."[23] She grants that the book is occasionally funny, has "stunning verisimilitude in trivia," and some "externals of Jewish middle class life... are neatly caught." But in the end, she holds, the work is "superficial" and "within it lurks a savage anti-Jewish stereotype."[24]

While Syrkin's onslaught is probably excessive, there is no doubt that Roth means the special Jewish features in Portnoy's upbringing—his family pressures and taboos—to be held responsible for the sexual problems rooted in the guilt experienced by Portnoy, who is, after all, revealing his innermost perplexities to his psychoanalyst. It was therefore not surprising that an actual psychiatrist should undertake the challenge. The noted Freudian psychologist Bruno Bettelheim undertook it in an article, "Portnoy Psychoanalyzed." The subject chose a *Jewish* analyst because "deep down he does not want to transcend his background, but chose an analyst who . . . would not alienate him from what he pretends to hate." Portnoy further assumes that "the cliches of a spoiled Jewish boyhood" regarding his mother and father are "valid."[25] But in fact he is incapable of loving anyone, and by "thinking himself liberated" by the use of obscenity, "he expresses his loathing of himself."[26] His sickness, says this presumed psychiatric report, lies in his refusal to recognize his parents' love for him because that would obligate him to love them in return, which he cannot do. "All human relations," he believes, " . . . are exploitative power plays." He is locked into ambiguous involvement with Jewishness: he realizes that he feels "Jewish inferiority" but resents anti-Semitism, and hence "cannot find sexual satisfaction except through seducing his gentile partners into practices which to him are degrading."[27] Bettelheim ends by expressing uncertainty as to whether in *Portnoy* the writer was merely telling a story of himself, genuinely engaged in self-analysis. In other words, is he or is he not "just another case then of the self-hating Jew living in exile?"[28]

What is Portnoy's relation to Roth himself? In one of his several essays in self-defense against the onslaught of bitter criticism of his book by the Jewish community and others, Roth implicitly denied the autobiographical identity of himself with his notorious creation. Was the novel a personal "confession"? Roth called it "this supposed confession."[29] One of the reasons why his novel was so shocking, Roth wrote, was that, while "the postholocaust decades" have seen the Jew "identified in American fiction with righteousness and restraint, with the just and measured response rather than with those libidinous and aggressive activities that border on the socially acceptable and may even constitute criminal transgression,"[30] Portnoy has thrown off all restraints and delved into hitherto taboo regions like masterbation. In terms of our own analysis in this present work, while Bellow and Malamud had in their fiction exemplified exploration into the Jewish relation to an ethical life and transcendance of suffering, Roth has seen in Jewishness the source of maladjustment and psychological aberration. And since in Roth's case the direction of this maladjustment was so obsessively sexual, it is hard to separate what Roth calls the "voyeuristic" from the literary attraction of the novel. Among the literary critics, the response to the book was mixed, and many gave it high praise. No doubt the novel has a certain historical importance as a nodal point in the release of popular literature from sexual inhibitions. It also revealed the direction of Roth's talent for the comic and for fluidity of first-person narrative which he was to exploit in coming novels, in addition to the satiric gift evident in his early stories. The promise of his early writings, however, remained unfulfilled. He had produced impressive fiction, but not yet a masterpiece.

In his next book *Our Gang* (1971), Roth indulges his satiric bent to the utmost. He could not contain himself in the face of the staggering hypocrisy, double-talk, and deviousness of the then President Richard Nixon, especially when, within one week, Nixon declared his undying opposition to abortion in view of his belief in the "sanctity of human life" and then released Lieutenant Calley from the stockade after he had been declared guilty in connection with the My Lai massacre. One would have thought that no better satire could be found than Nixon's own words and deeds, self-satire in its purest form. But Roth's satirical compulsion won out. Critical opinion may have been more negative than positive about *Our Gang*. It ranged from Dwight Macdonald's characterization, "far-fetched, unfair, tasteless, disturbing, logical, coarse, and very funny . . . in short, a masterpiece,"[31] to Murray Kempton's "a lame journey indeed" and "a dreary interlude" in Roth's work.[32] Although it is full of funny turns, the central point of the satire, Nixon's straight-faced hypocrisy, is belabored beyond the point of sustaining interest, and becomes boringly repetitious. In a later satire on a much larger scale, *The Great American Novel* (1973), the problem is different. Can a satire on many aspects of American life, down to the vicious inanities of the McCarthyite crusade, be based on an intense interest in and knowledge of baseball? Is it un-American to suggest that baseball does not possess the universally accepted and familiar basis as a satirical reference point for general comprehension and appeal? More serious, however, is that the satire is overly long, attenuated, and hence becomes tiresome, as could also be said of the much shorter *Our Gang*.

Unfortunately, unlike *Our Gang*, there are a few Jewish characters in it. Why did Roth find it necessary to include a tired stereotype of an immigrant, accented-speaking, "oily, overweight, excitable little Jew" who becomes the owner of the "Greenback" baseball team, and his mathematical prodigy of a son, Isaac, who could manage the team and its plays by intricate mathematical formulas? The Jewish owner, called Ellis (so named because the immigration official could not spell his name), takes on a young baseball genius and, to make the stereotype quite clear, himself adjusts the recruit's uniform. "Ain't the seat kind a' baggy?" says the boy. "The seat I can take in," says Ellis. "And the waist—." "De vaist I can fix, please." He calls his wife Sarah to look at the new player. "Toin around', show her from de back." But the boy is concerned about the seat. "Dun *vurry* vit de seat. De important thing is de shoulder. If it fits in de shoulder, it fits."[33] Was it necessary to introduce Jewish stereotypes—and did they have to be owners of the "Greenback" team, too—to carry the satire forward?

Roth's obsession with sex and his satirical proclivities are fused in *The Breast* (1972), which, despite its brevity, proves attenuated. The professor of literature, David Kepesh, undergoes a profound organic disturbance and wakes up in the hospital to find himself transformed into a breast. Kepesh speculates that his teaching for some years with great conviction of Gogol's "The Nose" and Kafka's "Metamorphosis" induced the change. His doctor dismisses this idea, but Roth's association of his story with these classic tales, when examined, reveals Roth's basic weakness—self-absorption on the part of his character so as to deprive his stories of universality. Gogol's story concens a search by a Russian petty official Kovalev for the nose which his barber had presumably inadvertently cut off. Kovalev briefly meets his nose walking about the city, but loses sight of it, seeks it through an attempted advertisement and at last by police help, until one day the nose reappears on his face. What's the point? Gogol makes it clear at the end. The absurdity of the story is a lampoon of his critics who deplore the subject matter of his grimly realistic and satiric exposure of Russian officialdom. For the real content of the story itself is the smugness and self-importance and stupidity of Kovalev—in other words, a story under the guise of a preposterous situation of the very kind for which Gogol is criticized. Gogol's satire is thus compounded in this story.

In the Kafka story—widely regarded as his masterpiece—the clerk Gregor Samsa suffers under a dual oppression, from his authoritarian father and from the mechanical and bureaucratized nature of his office work, and is metamorphosed into an insect, the symbol of dehumanization. Thus Kafka fused two central intellectual currents of our time, Freudianism and the notion of alienation in both philosophy and literature. Both stories are big with social and individual implication. Furthermore, the natural absurdity of the transformations in both is essential to bring out these large meanings. But there is nothing of this sort in *The Breast*. The story satirizes sexual obsession, but has no social resonance to extend it beyond this limited context. The subject was hardly worth more than the kind of succinct, expressive sentences which Jean Stafford in one of her stories used to describe an obsessive craving for food: "what it was like to be ruled by food and half driven out of one's mind until one dreamed of it and had at last no other ambition but to eat incessantly with an appetite that grew and grew until one saw oneself, in nightmares, as nothing but an enormous mouth and tongue, trembling lasciviously!"[34] Obviously, Roth has written better novels than *The Breast*, but none reveals his weakness so blatantly as the comparison with Gogal and Kafka he himself invites.

From the beginning of his career Roth was buffeted by adverse criticism, not only from those who deplored his attitude toward Jews and Jewishness, but also on literary grounds. In articles and interviews he responded defensively to these criticisms. Indeed, so many of these appeared that he gathered them into a book of over 250 pages, *Reading Myself and Others* (1975). Most of the book is an attempt to refute these criticisms, many of which were either excessive or wrong-headed. But Roth is not willing to grant that his treatment of Jewishness generally allows the dynamic energy of his satiric bent to take over and land him into caricature, when he writes of Jews— or anyone else, for that matter. He was voluminous in his attempts to refute criticism, but was he responsive to it? In this book he wrote, "The direction my work has taken since *Portnoy's Complaint* can in part be accounted for by my increased responsiveness to and respect for, what is unsocialized in me."[35]

By this I take him to mean he would henceforth "let go" in his fiction and give free rein to the sexuality of his nature, as indeed his subsequent work did. But he no longer blamed his parents or Jewishness for his problems as he did in *Portnoy*. In *My Life As a Man* (1974) he returned to the confessional narrator. Sexual involvement is still at the center of the novel. The narrator, Tarnapol, does not blame his parents for his problems, and he loves his mother and father. This character now has achieved enough objectivity about his personal state to aspire, he says, to be "humanish, manly, a man . . . nor did I pursue a career in which being married and then trying to get unmarried would become my predominant activity and obsession . . . in the way that exploring the South Pole had occupied Admiral Byrd—or writing *Madame Bovary* had occupied Flaubert."[36] His success is dubious. Both women with whom he is involved, his wife and her successor, are non-Jewish. The narrator has now for some years been seeing Dr. Spielvogel, the psychiatrist of *Portnoy*. But the burden of responsibility for the writer's obsessive preoccupation with his marital problems is turned inward on himself, and his Jewishness is no longer to blame. Most of the characters are Jewish except for his wife and lover, but Tarnapol is still obsessed with his personal problems. Beginning with *My Life As a Man* nearly all the novels are erotocentric but without the nastiness or resentment at parents, especially the Jewish mother, which had shocked so many.

Perhaps the feeling that he had not suffiently explained why David Kepesh in the earlier novel, *The Breast*, was transformed into a breast, Roth returned in *The Professor of Desire* (1977) to the life of Kepesh up to the eve of his transformation. The mellowing tone continues more distinctly, even though the sex is no less tortured and sexual problems with women remain central. A psychiatrist, a Dr. Klinger this time, is Kepesh's outlet for emotional relief. After a sexually perverse affair with two Swedish girls in London, then with an exotic non-Jewish woman whom he marries in Stanford and divorces to preserve his sanity, he finally comes upon a lovely, gentle non-Jewish girl and has a fulfilling affair which is interrupted by Kepesh's development of impotence, a condition which leads into the transformation into *The Breast*. If Roth intended to make the bizarre story more meaningful by its antecedents in *The Professor of Desire* there is no reason to suppose him successful. There is a vivid account of David's parents' resort hotel in the Catskills, in which David's youthful fascination with social director Herbie

Bratatsky's antics, especially his uncanny skill with scatalogical noises, provides an outlet for Roth's satirical treatment of middle-class Jews at a Catskill resort. However, David's relations with his parents are loving.

The earlier ridicule of Jewishness reappears, but this time it is repudiated. Now a professor of literature, David becomes friendly with a crude, antisocial poet, Ralph Baumgarten. To David's question why the poet had never written about his family, Baumgarten replies, "Spare me the subject of the Jewish family and its travails. Can you actually get worked up over another son and another daughter and another mother and another father driving each other nuts? All that loving, all that hating; all those meals. And don't forget the *menschlichkeit*. And the baffled quest for dignity. Oh, and the goodness."[37] This sounds like early Roth. But the narrator, David, says of the poet's attitude, "There are times when, listening to him speaking with such shamelessness of the wide range of satisfactions, I feel I am in the presence of a parodied projection of myself. . . . I am a Baumgarten locked in the Big House, caged in the kennels, a Baumgarten Klingered."[38] The erotic drive and sense of guilt felt by Roth's characters remain, but he has turned the blame on himself. In the book which began this trend, *My Life As a Man*, Roth had involuted his personal analysis by preceding Peter Tarnapol's own struggles for a satisfactory sexual relation without guilt under the unsuccessful treatment of a Dr. Spielvogel with Tarnapol's two stories about the sexual vagaries of the writer Nathan Zuckerman.

Roth now launched on a trilogy which is a deliberate attempt to come to terms with the bitter fruits of *Portnoy's* success. On the one hand, the protagonist must defend himself against the guilt for the profound hurt which the cruel portraits of Portnoy's father and mother had inflicted on them. Whether there is some element of autobiography here or not, I do not know. And on the other hand, Roth needed to deal with the unwelcome notoriety released by the sexually obsessed, unbuttoned *Portnoy*. These two themes were then developed in the ensuing trilogy.

The first is *The Ghost Writer* (1979), written in a quieter and more controlled vein than any of his previous novels. It takes the first-person writer back to his early twenties, before his enormous success with *Carnovsky* (*Portnoy*). Although the Pulitzer Prize judges for fiction unanimously selected *The Ghost Writer* for the prize, they were overridden by the Pulitzer board. There is no psychiatrist-auditor in this first-person narrative of Nathan Zuckerman's visit with an established writer in his fifties, E. I. Lonoff, a transparent representation of Bernard Malamud, whom Zuckerman deeply admires. Lonoff sees much promise in Nathan, whose writing, he says, has a "voice: something that begins at around the back of the knees and reaches well above the head."[39] The tribute to "Lonoff" is deep and sincere, and the literary conversation of the two writers is vital. The narrative, encompassing a brief week-end visit with Lonoff and his WASP wife during which Nathan falls in love with a European refugee student, Amy

Bellette, who is helping Lonoff order his papers. This student is in love with Lonoff, who has been her lover, but Lonoff now sends her away in order to save his marriage. Roth introduces the Holocaust through Nathan's fantasy that Amy Bellette was Anne Frank, who accordng to the fantasy, really survived, but has refrained from revealing her identity to avoid disturbing the aura and mystique grown up around the famous diary.

Nathan, in love with Amy, during his fantasy that she is Anne Frank, imagines he will marry her. One may suppose that this is an attempt to refute the charge by his father in the novel and many of the public that he really hates Jews. The deep hurt Nathan has inflicted on his parents is also introduced by his father's shocked response at a short story he had asked his father to read. His father believes his story is crassly and injuriously critical of the Jews. At the end of the novel Lonoff says to Nathan, "I'll be curious to see how it all comes out some day. It could be an interesting story. You're not so nice and polite in your fiction. You're a different person."[40] In other words, either the fiction is not autobiographical or it represents repressed inner being. This work was made into a beautifully realized television drama.

How it all comes out is related in the next two novels. Roth continues to insist that his critics confuse the literary character and the author. In his next novel, *Zuckerman Unbound* (1981), the author is still trying to come to terms with the confusion between his fictional and personal life. His critics may not be altogether mistaken. For this reader, at least, the separation of author from fictional character is not convincing. This has seemed to me Roth's failing from the start of his creative career. The signs of autobiography in *Zuckerman Unbound* are especially strong. This is not to say that in any literal sense his novels are one continuous autobiography, but that the writing persuades us that aspects of Roth's personal inner and external lives are the kernel of much of his writing, organized, and elaborated with his exuberant imagination and fluent descriptive powers and comic gift. The signs of autobiography are so strong in *Zuckerman Unbound* that one may venture to see it as Roth suffering the consequences of his writing which alienated so many readers and perhaps his family as well.

The book opens in 1969, with the sensational success of Zuckerman's outrageous novel, *Carnovsky*, precisely like the unpleasant notoriety that followed *Portnoy*. Nathan is divorced from Laura, a committed anti-war activist lawyer deeply involved in legal aid to draft resisters, because he is bored by her. In light of the short shrift that Roth gave to social activism from *Letting Go* onward, this is not surprising. Like all Roth's surrogates in the novels, Nathan is in deep conflict over the breakup of his marriage. But his thoughts are perhaps those of his characters in the 1970s, rather than in the 1960s.

The woman's too good for you, he told himself. . . . It isn't even Laura's virtue which bores you to tears—it's the reputable, responsible, drearily virtuous face that's your own. It should bore you. It's a goddam disgrace. Coldhearted betrayer of the most intimate confessions, cutthroat caricaturist of your own living parents, graphic reporter of encounters with women to whom you have been deeply bound by trust, by sex, by love.... Hers is the cause of righteousness, yours the art of depiction.[41]

This would seem is recognition that he has been ruthless in exploiting his personal life for novelistic purposes, and that he is therefore not justified in making so much of his guilt feelings. The counterpart of this disreputable aspect of Nathan's character is his fellow "Newarker," Alvin Pepler, who is a sexually deprived, down-and-out, once brief celebrity. He had been the star performer of a quiz show and was summarily displaced by a socially more eligible performer who had to be coached on the answers. By the end Nathan realizes that his influence on Pepler is one of the results of his fiction. Under the inspiration of *Carnovsky*'s success, Pepler tells Nathan, "I'm trying to write myself," to expose how he had been cheated of his success.[42] When Nathan again meets Pepler, whose association he accepts: "Enough taking cover from his own corruption. Receive what has been given! Accept what you inspire! Welcome the genies released by that book!"[43] Pepler breaks the news that he is attempting a review of Nathan's *Carnovsky*; he is especially interested in the "hang-up."[44] Nathan's discouraging response to Pepler's effort arouses Pepler to the fury of confession. "Those hang-ups you wrote about happen to be mine, and... you knew it.... you stole it. ...From what my Aunt Lottie told your cousin Essie that she told your mother that she told you.... About my past."[45] The nagging question remains, is Roth entirely innocent of guilt for such or is Roth writing so critically of Zuckerman (and Roth) with tongue in cheek?

An even more persuasive revelation occurs at the death of Nathan's father. Nathan had been a loving son to his parents. But he had not begun to realize how the caricature of the parents in his writing had devastated them; they had both kept this knowledge from him while they lived. As Nathan sits at his father's bedside in the last moments, he hears something that sounds like "Bastard!" and can hardly credit his ears. But after his father dies, his brother Henry sets upon him with fury:

You *are* a bastard. A heartless conscienceless bastard. What does loyalty mean to you? What does responsibility mean to you? What does self-denial mean, *restraint*—anything at all? To you everything is disposable! Everything is *ex*posable! Jewish morality, Jewish endurance, Jewish wisdom, Jewish families—everything is grist for your fun-machine. Even your shiksas go down the drain when they don't tickle your fancy any more. Love, marriage, children, what the hell do you care? To you it's all fun and games. *But that isn't the way it is to the rest of us.* And the worst is how we protect you from knowing what you really are!... You killed him, Nathan, with that book. *Of course* he said "Bastard." He'd seen it. He'd seen what you had done to him and Mother in that book!... What you write about people has *real consequences*.[46]

A profoundly shaken Nathan is on the verge of breakdown in the third and last novel of the trilogy, *An Anatomy Lesson* (1983), which takes place four years after his father's death and one year after his mother's. The terrible expletive that was the father's dying word to Nathan, and his brother Henry's condemnation for the injury his parents suffered from *Carnovsky* has ridden Nathan with guilt. Henry told him that his mother had suffered terribly from public identification with Carnovsky's mother, and that his father had died from a coronary brought on by that book. Nathan is now wracked with an excruciating pain in the neck and shoulder, which all his doctors have diagnosed as psychosomatic. Zuckerman believes his psychiatrist is confusing the author with the book character *Carnovsky*. But why, Nathan thinks, does no one understand that "life and art are distinct... that writing is an act of imagination seems to infuriate everyone."[47]

Added to the obsessive guilt feelings over his parents was another traumatic injury. This was a devastating reevaluation of Zuckerman's writing by a former admirer, the critic Milton Appel. From this harsh judgment only one short story emerged unscathed. The real counterpart of this event was the actual "Reconsideration" of Roth's work by his former admirer, Irving Howe, published in a *Commentary* article. The parallel is transparent. Nathan says to a girl who ministers to him in his pain and immobility, and who refuses to type his splenetic reply to Appel, "I'm a petty, raging, vengeful, unforgiving Jew, and I have been insulted one time too many by another petty, raging, vengeful, unforgiving Jew."[48]

Nathan's consuming obsessions and unrelieved pain are even more important than sex in this novel. There are four women who help Nathan to cope with his conditions, but they are not essential to the central theme. At the age of forty Nathan decides to abandon literature and begin the study of medicine. Curiously, in the process Roth seems to be confessing his absorbed preoccupation with his own life in his writing so as to obscure the distinction between himself and his fictional character. Indeed, this seems to be the meaning of the story, namely, that Roth as a writer has reached a dead end. The entire story is grappling with the consequences of past writings very similar to Roth's own. Nathan says to his old college roommate, now a doctor advising him about a medical career, "I'm sick of raiding my memory and feeling in the past. There's nothing more to see from my angle; if it ever was the thing I did best, it isn't anymore."[49] The novel signifies that Nathan—and Roth—have exhausted their vein of story telling. The story leads us to conjecture that Nathan will persist in pursuing medicine. But one may also conjecture that Roth himself will continue as a writer—at least one clear difference between the author and his fictional character.

And he does. In 1985 Roth published his trilogy in one volume under the title *Zuckerman Unbound* and added an epilogue to the trilogy, "The Prague Orgy." The experiental basis for this story is Roth's editorship of a series of fiction works in English translation by contemporary Eastern European authors. He has therefore visited these countries in past years for material, and one would suppose has gained intimate knowledge especially of their cultural life. In "The Prague Orgy" the narrator (Roth) is in Czechoslovakia to find and take out fiction work by a dead Jewish author whose work, written in Yiddish, cannot be published there, for translation and publication in the United States. In the course of this search for the manuscript he becomes acquainted with a decadent, dissolute cultural community which flourishes among the repressed artistically frustrated life of cultural figures—the "orgy." In all candor, it is difficult to understand why this forms an "epilogue" to the trilogy, except, perhaps, as a cautionary tale against effects of cultural and social oppression.

Roth is still a young man. His power to entertain is undiminished, and one perceives a growth in maturity in the trilogy. One looks to his future with decided interest.

# 8

# The Jew Manqué: Norman Mailer

Just as each of the major Jewish writers—Bellow, Malamud, and Roth—has a different specific relation to his Jewishness, so also with Norman Mailer. It should be clear at once that, as he wrote, "I would never say I was not a Jew," but he adds, "I looked to take no strength from the fact." What precisely the relationship of his writing and viewpoint to his Jewishness was we shall explore. He was born in Long Branch, New Jersey, but his family moved to Brooklyn when he was four, and it was there that he received what little Jewish education he had. His parents, he has written, were "modestly Orthodox, then Conservative"; he went to *heder* and was put through the *Bar Mitzvah* ritual. Whatever Hebrew he learned "was set out to atrophy." When he went to college, he "left what part of me belonged to Brooklyn and the Jews in the streets of Crown Heights," and he "had less connection to the past than anyone I knew." In the mid–1950s, like so many young Jewish writers and intellectuals, he discovered Martin Buber's version of Hasidism and "dipped" into Buber's translation of Hasidic tales while "riding the electric rail of long nights on marijuana." This "Jewish devotional prose," he notes, was the first of this kind he ever read which "were not deadening to me."[1] However, it was the existential, rather than the Jewish, aspect of these writings which appealed to him. His relation to Jewishness remained minimal.

But it would be next to impossible for a Jew in the United States, especially if he is a writer, to sever himself totally from his identity. Since a writer, especially in his early work, usually draws heavily upon his own experience, Jewish characters turn up at least in his early work, and so it was with Mailer. While still at Harvard (1939–1943), Mailer wrote voluminously under the influence of Ernest Hemingway. What he now regards as "the best" of this writing was a novelette, "A Calculus at Heaven," a tale of the

Pacific War first published in 1944 in *Cross-Section: A Collection of New American Writing*, edited by Edwin Seaver, a volume that also introduced several other important American writers to the literary public. Mailer imitated not only Hemingway's style, but his macho attitude as well, and this was obviously manifested in his one Jewish character, "blond Jewboy Wexler," a star football tackle in his New Jersey high school.[2] But Wexler regarded himself as a Jew in name only. While in action against the Japanese, he flexes his macho consciousness. "He didn't have a big Jewish nose," he thinks, "that was one help.... Minnesota hadn't given him the scholarship cause he was Jewish, but for crise-sakes what was in a name? He had blond hair, didn't he?... Jewish, hell, in Freehold they said he played like a big Swede."[3] Caught in a tight spot, the men in his unit are given the choice of surrendering or staying to fight their way out. Wexler elects to stay, but during a lull he exposes himself to the enemy while showing his comrades how he threw a forward pass and is killed. A more mature Mailer, sobered by his experience as a rifleman in the Pacific where he served eighteen months, returned to write a war novel, *The Naked and the Dead* (1948), which will surely rank as one of the best American novels on World War II. Several Jews figure importantly and with considerable realistic accuracy, as we described at some length in our discussion of the war novel.

Never again in his fiction, unless one adds his existentialist comment on Martin Buber's tales of Hasidism, would Mailer treat Jewishness with the specificity of *The Naked and the Dead*, which was written while the experience of a war against Nazism was still fresh. Furthermore, anti-Semitism was so pervasive in the United States Army during this war against Nazism—a paradox that highlights the complexity of social affairs—that the writer, Jewish or non-Jewish, could hardly avoid it. Even so, his connection with Jewishness after the war, except for that in the first novel, was minimal. Yet he felt that he was "some sort of dispossessed American" and "had at least a rudimentary sense of clan across the century." He had a positive sense of being a Jew in one respect: "I was a Jew out of loyalty to the underdog."[4] And, in fact, he has been a radical of one sort or another, or at least a non-conformist, throughout his career, however much one may at times have questioned the benefit to the "underdog" of his approach, or who indeed the "underdog" might be. For some years he considered himself a socialist of sorts, and was from 1957 to 1963 a member of the editorial board of *Dissent*, a monthly professing democratic socialism through a broad spectrum of interpretations. For a few years after the war he was under the intellectual influence of Jean Malaquais, a Trotskyist. Mailer was active in the Progressive party's campaign for the Henry Wallace candidacy for president but left "rather abruptly at the time of the Waldorf Peace Conference in 1949."[5]

This break betokened a turn to anti-Stalinism, probably under the influence of Malaquais. In any case Mailer was not drawn into the conformity and the cold war attitude that seized so many writers and intellectuals of the period, as evidenced in *Partisan Review*'s symposium of 1952, "Our Country and Our Culture." His contribution to this symposium registered "shock" at its "assumptions."[6] Mailer there agreed with Edmund Wilson that the revival of American literature of the half-century past was a "literature of alienation and protest, disgust and rebellion. The writer had a sense of the enemy, and it could nourish him. Today, the enemy is vague."[7] Many intellectuals, wrote Mailer, are now "within" the society, and have eschewed criticism of the most urgent problems facing it. Mailer's second novel, *Barbary Shore* (1951) is a transitional novel between the social concern of the political Left-wing writer up to then and the changing outlook toward a primary concentration on the spiritual state of the individual, issuing in existentialism and hipsterism. Perhaps it would be accurate to describe Mailer's basic interest at this point as the spiritual state of the political individual. For in this anti-Stalinist novel he explores "the psychic mysteries of Stalinists, secret policemen, narcissists, children, Lesbians, hysterics, revolutionaries," as he wrote in retrospect.[8] In one regard at least *Barbary Shore* was a sharp turning point—there are no Jewish characters in it.

In much of his important fiction thereafter the Jew was not again to be totally absent even though often only minimally present *qua* Jew. For several years he floundered. He published short stories, one of the best of which, written under Reichian influence, is "The Man Who Studied Yoga" (1952). It deals with an evening of three couples who gather to witness a pornographic movie. Two of the husbands' names are obviously Jewish—Marvin Rossman and Alan Sperber—and the third, the central character, Sam Slovoda, is one-quarter Jewish. No comment is made on the Jewishness of the first two, but of Slovoda, Mailer writes, that though "a quarter-Jew, yet he is a Jew, or so he feels himself, knowing nothing of Gospel, tabernacle, or Mass, the Jew through accident, through state of mind."[9] Nothing more is made of this, and one wonders whether this sense of being a Jew, no matter how tenuous, does not apply to Mailer himself. In any case, this story was in the line of Mailer's entry into a new Reichian mode of writing, when he wished, as he says, to enter "the mysteries of murder, suicide, incest, orgy, orgasm, and Time."[10] One wonders if "mystification," rather than "mysteries," would not be a more accurate characterization. To this element was added a return to the fore of the macho Hemingway hero. When he was revising *The Deer Park*, he writes, he realized that "I shared with Papa [Hemingway] the notion, arrived at slowly in my case, that it was more important to be a man than a very good writer."[11] In *The Deer Park* (1955) Mailer introduced the macho character, Sergius O'Shaughnessy, who was to reappear in his future fiction, and the Jew drops into a secondary or peripheral place. In this Hollywood novel an absence of Jewish characters would have been an obvious anomaly, and Mailer does include the secondary characters of Collie Munshin, a producer, and his father-in-law and studio head, Herman Teppis. Both are depicted in the deserved self-satire of such types. Except for speech mannerism, and some pious allusions by Teppis, there is no Jewishness in the novel.

It is O'Shaughnessy, however, who represents Mailer's thinking at this point, and in succeeding fiction. This fact alone indicates the distance which Mailer had placed between himself and Jewishness. O'Shaughnessy is an orphan who became a combat flyer in World War II and has a breakdown after he realizes the horror he has inflicted in fire-bombing a Pacific village. It can be said that this experience has made an existentialist of him; that is, he strives to achieve the free choice to live by the severe requirements of his authentic self. Thus, living at Desert D'Or, near Hollywood, after the war, he refuses to allow Hollywood (Munshin and Teppis) to exploit and falsify his wartime air force experience, an existential choice of the free man, and decides to devote himself to serious writing. The false ("inauthentic," in existential terms) values he rejects are represented by his break with his Hollywood actress-lover Lulu. He is contrasted with the writer-director Charles Eitel, who finally caves in before the House Un-American Affairs Committee after a year of refusing to testify and thereby has "lost the final desire of the artist" to face and depict "the real world."[12] In reality this signifies the artist's utter freedom to pit himself against the interferences from the social world to his self-realization.

During this period, also, the influence of Wilhelm Reich (1897–1957), for whom sexuality was the basic and pervasive nature of human beings, and a sexually satisfying life was the guarantee of individual happiness so that social amelioration should be directed toward this end in all human beings. For Mailer, the quest for the "apocalyptic orgasm"[13] became the central objective of his fictions, as he expressed it in his most important short story following *The Deer Park*, "The Time of Her Time." So strong was this influence that Mailer was to write, in "The White Negro," that the "good orgasm opens his possibilities and bad orgasm imprisons him."[14] O'Shaughnessy in "The Time of Her Time" lives the Beat life in an East Village loft, and meets a rather unpleasant, tough Jewish girl, a student at New York University, with "an ugly New York accent with a cultured overlay." He had found an "excess of strength, complacency and deprecation which I found in many Jewish women—a sort of 'Ech' of disgust at the romantic and mysterious All." He is full of comments about her Jewish identity: she "adored" T. S. Eliot, but O'Shaughnessy was "tempted to tell her how little Eliot would adore the mannerless yeasts of the Brooklyn from which she came, and would prefer her to appreciate his poetry only in step to the transmigration of her voice from all urgent Yiddish nasalities to the few high English analities of relinquished desire."[15] She was being psychoanalyzed by a Jewish analyst ("they were now working on Jewish self-hatred") whom she admired equally with Eliot. "How I envied the jazzed-up brain of the Jews," O'Shaughnessy thinks, as he takes her to his loft for a sexual bout.[16] The two are antagonistic, but their sexual duelling leaves the girl without an orgasm, which she confesses she has never experienced. O'Shaughnessy's macho prowess is challenged, and they have two more encounters. The second is again a failure, but the third coupling, long, labored, extremely strenuous, indeed heroic, brings her near, when O'Shaughnessy's "You dirty little Jew" whispered in her ear carries her to orgasm.[17] But judging from the mutual contempt with which they leave one another, one can hardly credit his response to her parting shot that her analyst thinks O'Shaughnessy's life is a "lie" because he's trying to run away from his homosexuality. She arouses his admiration by this remark: "She was a hero fit for me."[18] One wonders at the desirability of the life-style implied in the story. The technique of the story is tight and controlled and worthy of Mailer's impressive talent. But the content does not have comparable value.

Clearly Mailer's attitude toward Jewishness is detached and neutral. He maintains a tenuous connection of de-emphasizing Jewishness in his characters (the Jewish girl in "The Time of Her Time" is perhaps an exception), by making central characters only part-Jewish—like Slovoda in "The Man Who Studied Yoga" or an unfavorable character as in *Why Are We in Vietnam?* (1967). There, a Jewish psychiatrist, a "Texas Jew," is a cynic. In *An American Dream* (1965) the central figure, Stephen Rojack, is half Jewish. The only mention of Jewishness in the novel is at an early point where Rojack first meets his wife, Deborah. She detested "Jewish Protestants and Gentile Jews" who, she added, "know nothing of grace."[19] At the end his father-in-law, Kelly, tells Rojack, "Deborah once explained to me how you would like to blow up poor old Freud by demonstrating that the root of neurosis is cowardice rather than brave old Oedipus.... I always say it takes one Jew to do in another."[20] The connection with Jewishness in these fictions is thus slim indeed. The novel is Mailer's attempt to exemplify the hipster, whose nature he had been delineating for about a decade. After the publisher, Rinehart, had rejected his *The Deer Park* because Mailer refused to make recommended changes, Mailer was learning that "my fine America ...did real things and ugly things to the characters of more people than just the characters of my book."[21] Added to this personal shock of awareness was the extreme situation of all humanity following World War II. As Mailer expressed it in his famous essay, "The White Negro" (1957), in which he set forth his conception of the "hipster": We may "never be able to determine the psychic havoc of the concentration camps and the atom bomb upon the unconscious mind of almost everyone alive in those years."[22] While he felt the full impact of the depth of human depravity signified by the concentration camps, one may assume that the specific—and special—Jewish aspect, the Holocaust, did not loom large in his awareness. "Special" because the Jews were targets of total annihilation as a people, unlike victims of other nationalities (except gypsies). In addition, universal death hung like a sword of Damocles over the human race. For all of us, Mailer added, had to face, "the suppressed knowledge that . . . we might still be doomed to die as a cipher in some vast statistical operation."[23] Mailer's answer is "to accept the terms of death" by divorcing oneself from society, "to set out on that uncharted journey into the rebellious imperatives of the self," no matter where such a life may lead, even when it might lead to crime, if only one lives in "the enormous present." The hipster, Mailer readily grants, is then "to encourage the psychopath in oneself."[24]

The resultant mode of life, "hip," is "an American existentialism."[25] This type of existentialist, the "hipster," believes he may die at any instant from the atomic bomb or be confronted with death in a concentration camp, or live under forced captivity and suppressed creativity. Further, Mailer argues, the American Negro has known what it is to live a life in an American society "between totalitarianism and democracy," and he has therefore served as the source of the hipster life-style. Now the entire American people, like the Negro, live in imminent daily danger. The hip subculture was "a wedding of the white and the black (and) it was the Negro who brought the cultural dowry. . . . Any Negro who wishes to live must live with danger from his first day."[26] Hence, the hipster is a "White Negro."[27] One would hardly expect most Blacks to agree with Mailer's sweeping characterizations of the Black sources of hipsterism. The hipster seeks absolute freedom, especially in sex. Mailer would apparently put no limits on the hipster's freedom of action, concerned only with free, uninhibited, unrestricted realization of his own self. He is undeterred by the prospect of crime, rape, incest, murder. Above all, "the Hipster moves through his life on a constant search with glimpses of Mecca . . . (Mecca being the apocalyptic orgasm)."[28] Mailer was undoubtedly correct in locating the source of hipsterism in the extreme state of world affairs in the 1950s, with the trauma of the death camps relatively fresh, the threat of atomic annihilation, the Cold War, and the quite real generally oppressive atmosphere. Mailer was also in fact drawn toward hipsterism by the basic influence of the Hemingway macho temperament which he emulated.

While the term "hipster" passed out of usage with the intervening resistance to the Vietnam War, the rise of the New Left in the 1960s, and the recession from radicalism in the 1970s, Mailer tried to glorify the hipster in the character of Rojack in *An American Dream* and subsequent writings. This story was probably intended to be weighted with symbolic existential significance, but it is closer to a parody of a lurid, amoral melodrama than to serious philosophical fiction. One can only believe that Mailer's artistic sense was skewed by an attempt to exemplify the overblown rhetorical mode of thought which has at times overtaken him. He is very far in this novel not only from *The Naked and the Dead*, but even from *The Deer Park*. In an interview in 1958, Mailer was asked directly if he himself advocated hipsterism, and his reply was equivocal. However, Mailer's stabbing of his wife would indicate that his hipsterism was more than theoretical. Aware of a largely unfavorable reception to *An American Dream*, Mailer replied that "the difficulty for many people . . . is that I started as one kind of writer, and I've been evolving into another."[29] He refused to say directly that he advocated hipsterism, but he was drawn to it as a fertile source of "expression." Since "experience," he said, has an "umbilical relationship" to expression, and the hipster's experience has "extreme awareness,"[30] this mode offers the novelist materials which Mailer has used. The interview was then directed to Mailer's conception of God. His notion bears no relation to Judaism, but is rather a form of Manichaeism, the doctrine that God and the Devil are independent powers in conflict. That any transcendant power is even potentially greater than God is heresy not only for Judaism but for Christianity as well. Indeed, Mailer asserts that "the burning pinpoint of the vision of Hip" is that "God is in danger of dying."[31] Because of this limited nature of God, an antagonist, the Devil, a principle of Evil whose "signature is the concentration camps" and to pervert realization of God's purposes. Evil is "a record of the Devil's victories over God."[32] Mailer's theological viewpoint is not developed, but he told an interviewer directly that "I do believe in it."[33]

It would be a mistake, I think, to regard Mailer's interest in Hasidism in Martin Buber's version as an expression of interest in Judaism. This interest is only minimally Jewish. What drew Mailer to Hasidism was rather, as he wrote, because "the tradition of the Hasidism was naturally and passionately existential." When he undertook to do a series of brief articles in *Commentary* beginning in December, 1962, quoting from Buber's *Tales of Hasidism* and adding his own commentary, he wrote with his customary candor on matters relating to Jews. *The Tales*, he wrote, "did not make me feel like a Jew" today,[34] but rather how he might have felt as a Jew a few hundred years earlier. What did touch him about the *Tales* was the relevance they might have to existentialism, not their Judaic origin, although there probably was some inclination to attend to them because they were Jewish *and* could be interpreted existentially. Nevertheless, he used the occasion of this commentary for his most extended public discussion of the situation of the Jew in a hostile world. Significantly, however, he considers the Jew not alone, but as a "minority" along with the Blacks. When Mailer republished the five "Responses and Reactions" in book collections of his work, he did some editing and added highly speculative comments, which are not those of the Jew as such, but of a presumably detached observer of both the Jews and the Blacks. Hasidism appealed to him as existential, but it suggested to him the problem of "minorities," Blacks as well as Jews, which he explores in his preface to the series. This gives him an opportunity to subject the problem to existential phenomenological analysis, and it turns out in places to be so speculative as to verge on the absurd. Consider the excess in his statement, "No white man, for example, can hate the Negro race with the same passionate hatred and detailed detestation that *each Negro* feels for himself and his people; no anti-Semite can begin to comprehend the malicious analysis of his soul which *every Jew* indulges every day"[35] (emphasis added). Or, for example, the Jews might have difficulty recognizing themselves in Mailer's assertion that "the Jews have staggered along for centuries wondering to their primitive horror whether they have betrayed God once in the desert or again twice with Christ."[36]

There is truth in his assertion that the Jew or the Black, because of his insecure place in a predominantly Anglo-Saxon society, tends to be more intensely self-aware and even self-critical than the more secure white non-Jew although Mailer generally states this, like other theses, in an extreme, overgeneralized manner when he allows his speculation to run away with him, which is often. This is what occurs in assimilation, and in this respect he has an interesting view. The feeling of insecurity among minorities, he says, leads the majority to them "to manufacture a mediocre personality which is a dull replica of the manners of the white man in power. Nothing can be more conformist, more Square, more profoundly depressing than the Jew-in-the-suburb, or the Negro as member of the Black Bourgeoisie. It is the price they pay for the fact that not all self-hatred is invalid."[37] Assimilated Jews or Blacks are "colorless."[38] Democracy, he holds, should not strive for this effect, but rather for equality without such assimilation, with an enriched mode of life that incorporates the special qualities of each minority. This view suggests the idea of cultural pluralism, but Mailer gives the notion what he believes to be a hipsterish existential turn by urging that minorities must achieve more than their "rights," but should "search to liberate the art which is trapped in the thousand acts of perception which embody their self-hatred, for self-hatred ignored must corrode the roots of one's past and leave one marooned in an alien culture, . . . in the complexity, the intensity, and the psychistic brilliance of a minority's inner life."[39] It then becomes evident why Mailer's prefatory remark to his comments on Hasidic tales is appropriate: the Hasidim, who, he wrote, "embodied the most passionate and individual expression of Jewish life in many centuries,"[40] represent to him a type of Jewishness which should be a part of the American amalgam which he is seeking. It is the *existentialism* that can be generalized out of Hasidism which he would incorporate. Mailer's admiration is for Hasidism, its existentialism stripped of Jewishness.

Mailer is full of high-flown, often portentous, rhetoric about the Jews—as about many other matters in his existential mood. It is hard to grasp any specific meaning in many of his generalizations. For instance, the Jews, he wrote, "have an irreducible greatness . . . in the devil of their dialectic, which places madness next to practicality, illumination side by side with duty, and arrogance in bed with humility."[41] However, in the third of his "Responses and Reactions" he makes several interesting realistic observations. Mailer quotes the Hasidic passage, "Before the coming of the Messiah," a condition in some ways suggesting the pre-Holocaust condition of the Jews. "Yet," comments Mailer, "to our knowledge no Messiah was brought forth from the concentration camps."[42] (A novel by Arthur A. Cohen, *In the Days of Simon Stern* [1973], is built around the emergence of a Messiah from the Holocaust.) "Or," adds Mailer, "were a hundred delivered to die with the victims, secret Angels of Death?"[43] Thus, like Bellow and Malamud, Mailer voiced his awareness of the Holocaust in the 1960s. Mailer suggests that Judaism may have suffered a fatal blow from this failure. He suggests that it may be more urgent for the Messiah to appear "where souls are becoming dead rather than lives being lost."[44] Mailer speculates that the Holocaust may signify a victory of the Devil over God, and that "a portion of God's creative power was extinguished in the camps of extermination." On the other hand, if Jews hold to the idea of an "all-powerful" God, they must be led to the "bitter recognition" that God "considered one of His inscrutable purposes to be worth more than half His chosen people."[45] This may have "paralyzed the organized religious spirit of the American Jews,"[46] if one is to judge, says Mailer, from the primarily recreational activities of the new synagogues. The rest of this "Reaction and Response" is given over to elucidating the character of God's antagonist, the Devil, who is the animus behind debilitating "repetition," and "insomnia," which may be "the anger of the Lord."[47]

Is there a gap between Mailer's attenuated speculation and his consistently and genuinely held beliefs? Or is he momentarily seized by his speculations? I don't know. How much has he rejected of "his private mixture of Marxism, conservatism-nihilism, and parts of existentialism" in the early 1960s, as he wrote in *Armies of the Night* (1968)?[48] He has also lived in a mixture of existentialism and social activism as dissent intensified in the 1960s. Except for his roseate view of the Kennedy administration, he has steadily been an enemy of the Establishment, and participated in active resistance to it. His decidedly superior journalism was a dissenting influence in those years, with his *Armies of the Night*, an account of the March on the Pentagon of March, 1968, and especially of his own arrest to symbolize resistance, and his books about the Democratic and Republican conventions in that year. Other than referring to himself as "the nice Jewish boy from Brooklyn"[49] and referring to his having learned "something of Jewish genius and of revolutionaries and large indiscriminate love for the oppressed from his first wife,"[50] the one and only Jew among his six wives, there is only one other reference to Jewishness in *Armies of the Night*. Mailer gets into a fist fight with an American Nazi counterdemonstrator who Jew-baited him while they were both waiting in a van to be taken to jail, a fight averted only by the intervention of a United States marshal. The Nazi initiated the encounter with anti-Semitic epithets quite gratuitously, but Mailer gave verbally as well as he received and was ready for the fight. With his penchant for teetering on the edge of the meaningless in his speculations, he refers to himself in this account as a "Left Conservative," so it is not surprising that he would write that "there was no one in America who had a position even remotely like his own."[51]

Mailer is a writer of abundant but often undisciplined talent, which he has not always used to best artistic advantage, especially in the 1970s. That talent is diverse, as he proved by his first three novels, by his superb journalism which transcended the limits of that genre to achieve literature in *Armies of the Night*, which he subtitled "History as a Novel; the Novel as History," and the imaginative flair of his true-life story of a murderer, *The Executioner's Song* (1980). While his Jewishness momentarily reappears in some of his work after *The Naked and the Dead*, he has perhaps allowed it to influence him only as a component of the insecurity in his personality which has all too often led him into speculative flights difficult to decipher. He is willy-nilly a Jew as a person, knowing that he cannot shed his Jewishness, nor would he want to. Instead he resides in a limbo of indifference to it.

# 9

# The Religious Trend

Once the euphoria of victory over Nazism and Japan and peace had passed, to be quickly followed by the Cold War, it became apparent to many that something had gone seriously wrong in Western society. An increasing number turned for reassurance to religion. In a 1957 article, "The Religious Revival in Contemporary Literature," Charles I. Glicksberg saw the reasons in "the unsettled condition of the world, the unsettling threat of another world war, the bankruptcy of the Marxist eschatological vision, the revolutionary changes that have taken place in the scientific outlook, the splitting of the atom and the manufacture and use of the atomic bomb."[1] By the 1950s it was acknowledged in all thoughtful circles that "an alarming malady of nihilism" was epidemic, with its anxiety, anguish, spiritual fatigue, existentialist dolor, and despair. The literary response was to elaborate on human alienation. The figure of the Jew as alien in Western society over the centuries and most emphatically under Hitlerism just past was taken as a symbol or prototypical model. Glicksberg observed that "writers of the twentieth century have again raised the question of the religious consciousness, which seems virtually to have disappeared. There are...signs of a religious revival in literature but not in a doctrinal sense."[2]

The response among writers and intellectuals was varied. Some returned to their ancestral Christian and Jewish religions. Many resorted to Oriental religions. Others were inspired by existentialism in the versions of Sartre or Camus. Norman Mailer adopted an existentialism of his own, sometimes under the inspiration of Martin Buber's version of Hasidim, sometimes in the form of the "hipsters," extreme outlook of anomie plus drugs and a Manichaean view of God and the Devil. We cannot expect intellectual or theological discipline in literary figures like Mailer or Ginsberg in their formulation of personal religion. Ginsberg was once asked by some Episcopalian clergymen what his religion was, and he answered, after a little thought, that he was probably a "Buddhist Jew" or a "Buddhist Jewish Jew."[3] But his religious practice in the long run turned out to be Oriental.

Like Mailer and Ginsberg, other Jewish writers turned eastward in their newly adopted religious beliefs. One of the most noted of these was J. D. Salinger, who eschewed use of drugs or any form of violent behavior. He had an Irish mother and a Jewish father. His series of stories about the Glass family seems to have been an amalgam of Christian and Eastern religions, Christian and Zen. The Glass children, Zooey, Buddy, and Franny, looked to their deceased oldest brother Seymour as their guru. In *Franny and Zooey* (1961), his last published book before his virtually total withdrawal from open society and publishing to an isolated home in New Hampshire, Salinger gives an account of Franny's religious crisis, which might well be a rendering of his own. Like Franny, this extreme measure was taken to escape, as Franny expressed it when she abruptly left college, escape from "egomania.... I mean all the *ego* ... I'm just sick of ego, ego, ego. My own and everybody else's."[4] Whatever lies behind Salinger's seclusion to this day, which he has never discussed anywhere, is likely to be religious, Eastern, Christian, or both in some combination.

But by no means all Jewish writers were turning toward Eastern or Christian or eclectic religious views. A significant trend toward Judaism itself occurred among a number of younger serious writers in response to a world in crisis and a problematic outlook for humanity brought on by the Damocles sword of atomic annihilation and the increasing perversion of all values under domination by money and every manner of dehumanizing influence. To the motivating influence of general crisis, Jews had the added stimulus of the hardly conceivable Holocaust of the 6 million, and one of its by-products, establishment of the State of Israel. The consequence was not only adoption of practicing Judaism, but of active support of Israel and reassertion of Jewish identity.

Among the writers affected we find, not surprisingly, variety in quality both religious and literary, from Herman Wouk to Chaim Potok to Cynthia Ozick to Arthur A. Cohen and points between. The modish, largely socially oriented return to the synagogue of the 1950s had its most popular representative in the work of Herman Wouk, spokesman of the suburban, affluent recruits for Judaism. His *Marjorie Morningstar* (1955) was a fictional effort to demonstrate the validity of a middle-class, conformist, quietistic, Orthodox mode of existence as the solution to life's problems. Wouk followed his popular fiction successes with a non-fiction best-seller, *This Is My God*, in which he propagandized for Judaism. He reassured his middle-class audience that Orthodox conformity was not hard, entailed no sacrifice, was easily surmounted when inconvenient.

A number of other post–World War II writers fell into the religion trend— Myron Kaufmann, Hugh Nissenson, Jay Neugeboren, Mark Helprin. I shall, however, here limit my discussion to three of the best-known and perhaps most important, at this point, Chaim Potok, Arthur A. Cohen, and Cynthia Ozick. The 1950s were the period of gestation for these three Jewish writers who treated Judaism with special authority rooted in knowledge of Jewish religious traditions and practices. All three were born in New York City, Arthur A. Cohen and Cynthia Ozick in 1928 and Chaim Potok in 1929. Cohen and Potok studied at the Jewish Theological Seminary in the 1950s; Potok was ordained a rabbi in 1954 and then obtained his Ph.D. in philosophy in 1965. Ozick was largely self-taught in traditional Jewish writing. All three are talented writers; what they have in common is a deep involvement in Judaism which is integral to their writing. In this sense, they can be said to be religious writers, though not all their fiction is directly and explicitly relevant to their religious convictions.

It was Chaim Potok's *The Chosen*, published in 1967, whose immense success and months-long presence on best-seller lists startled the literary world—at least the less secularly doctrinaire—with the knowledge that something new had entered American writing. All other popular American works on Judaism, from Lewisohn to Kaufmann, had been set among acculturated Jews within the large American context. But Potok had written a work whose plot and argument was acutely focused within Orthodox and even ultra-Orthodox Judaistic society and on its specific problem of fundamentalism in that milieu. It is a story of the American form taken by the struggle between ultra-Orthodox Hasidism and the more flexible Misnagdim, not imprisoned within tradition. The plot deals with the attempt to reconcile sophisticated modern minds to the methods of studying the Torah, as opposed to the fundamentalist literal belief in the Bible and its view that examination of texts by scientific methodology was a profound blasphemy, tampering with the word of God.

Potok had already, before the appearance of the novel, made his position clear in this struggle. In a symposium on "The State of Jewish Belief" in *Commentary* (August, 1966), Potok wrote, "My Judaism being in the balance for a long anguished year" until he found that he could reconstruct his views "from *within* Judaism," he finally decided to subject "the sacred texts of Judaism" to modern scientific textual criticism.[5] Thus the basic conflict of *The Chosen* is autobiographical, if not the literal actuality. Two brilliant teen-aged yeshiva students, the one, Danny Saunders, prospective heir to the office of his father, Hasidic Tsaddik Reb Saunders, the other, Reuven Malter, the son of a great Misnagid Talmud scholar. The conflict is posed at the opening with a baseball game between the students of the yeshivas of the opposing camps. Strange as it may seem, this game seems to me the most imaginative, gripping, and best-written passage in the entire fictional work of Potok to date. The intolerance, even hatred, with which each group regards the other exposes the depth of the traditional antagonism. The Hasidim regard their opponents as *apikorsim*, renegades from

Judaism. But the two boys became close friends, and Danny's intellectual curiosity and budding interest in psychology, clandestinely helped by Reuven's father on Danny's initiative, results finally in his renunciation of the inheritance of his father's place as Tsaddik, his abandonment of rabbinical studies in favor of pursuing a career in psychology. For his part, Reuven, who shows promise as a mathematician, continues his rabbinical studies.[6]

If Potok is scientifically modern, he yet seems unaffected by literary modernism. His style is plain and direct, and his meanings are explicit. There is no obscurity, and his language is unadorned. This is not to say that his observation is superficial: no, it is substantial and is a serious treatment of real problems within a specific sphere of society which illuminates human character. The fact that his narrative moves quickly makes his popularity comprehensible. Potok followed *The Chosen* with a succession of novels. *The Promise* (1969), *My Name Is Asher Lev* (1972), *In the Beginning* (1975), and *The Book of Lights* (1981), and more. *The Chosen* is arguably the best so far. The truth is that all have essentially the same theme—the conflict of Torah as the word of God with Torah as an ancient human document subject to textual criticism, with all its doctrinal, ritual, and social implications. Despite the variations introduced into each successive novel, the basic conflict in each is essentially the same, exposing Potok's limited imaginative range.

Arthur A. Cohen is a "religious" novelist by virtue of one important novel thus far in this category. But he is generally a religious influence in the intellectual community, and hence falls within this tendency. He was a fellow in Jewish philosophy at the Jewish Theological Seminary from 1951 to 1953, and has written books on theology and other topics as well as fiction and has been a book publisher as well. In 1959 he set forth his outlook in an article in *Harper's Magazine* (April), "Why I Choose to Be a Jew." He maintains that only with the third generation of American Jews—his own generation—was it possible to choose *not* to be a Jew. Before this, no matter what one's personal predilections, the Jew could not make such a choice because the world would regard him as a Jew no matter what he himself believed or did. Today, Cohen writes, "the irresistible forces of history no longer *compel* the Jew to choose Judaism."[7] He can choose Christianity or atheism or religious indifference. For himself, Cohen has chosen to embrace Judaism. He explains, "I have not done so out of loyalty to the Jewish people or the Jewish state. My choice was religious."[8] He arrived at his decision after considerable and intense study, through reflection and deliberation. He projects four structural pillars of his belief. First, "I choose to believe in the God of Abraham, Isaac, and Joseph," which means for him "to affirm the reality of a God who acts in history and addresses man."[9] Second, "The Law of Moses is the Word of God," which is conveyed through the Torah, signifying "*any* teaching which brings man closer to the true God, who is the God of Israel and the Lord of History." Third, "the Jewish people have been chosen as a special instrument of God," that is, chosen by God himself. This chosenness should not be confused with arrogance or racism, but means that a Jew was put in possession of "important truth which is available to all."[10] Fourth, "Jesus is not the Messiah of which the Bible speaks.... A Messiah is yet to come who will redeem history."[11] To Jews, Jesus was "one in the line of 'suffering servants' whom God sends forth to instruct the nations," not the "Christ" into which St. Paul transformed him.[12]

Cohen does not confine his writings to theology, of which he has written several volumes. His large mind extends also to writing art criticism as well as fiction. His novel, *In the Days of Simon Stern* (1973), is an important work, an impressive imaginative feat in the projection of a theological view of messianism in genuinely artistic terms. The "Messiah" with whom this novel is concerned is one of the thirty-six wise men who appear in each generation and keep the world on an even keel, are "the vanguard of the Messiah,[13] ... the *sotto voce* of divinity,"[14] the "little Messiahs"[15] who prepare the way for the true Messiah.

Stern's story opens in Poland, where a humble couple marry on instructions from a prophet, who foretells that their son—Simon Stern—will be one of the thirty-six, a little Messiah. The first-person narrator is blind Nathan Gaza (suggestive of that seventeenth-century Nathan of Gaza who was Sabbatai Zevi's most important theologian and propagator). In due time the Stern family immigrates to the United States and settles on the East Side of New York. Simon is a financial genius who becomes fabulously wealthy, his fortune over a $100 million from real estate, which he achieves without ever leaving the East Side. He is not aware of his destiny as little Messiah until World War II, when a letter left for him by his dead father informing him of his Messiahship appears, and he realizes that he has been amassing a fortune unknowingly for a divine purpose, to establish in the United States a community of survivors of the Holocaust, all the while he was simply living on the East Side. Blind Nathan comments, "Prophets... don't, for a moment, know that they're saving the universe." The Messiah, Nathan says, is no tranquil, serene, integrated man, but, like Simon himself, "shakes with the anguish of the world."[16] What they aim for on behalf of the world is "the surcease of pain, the remission of violence, the removal of hunger, the release from venom, rancor, fury."[17] Once Simon is made aware of his mission by his father's letter, he sets in motion, with his vast wealth, the rescue of survivors and assembles them in an enclave on New York's East Side.

But the little Messiah is fallible, and he makes a fatal mistake. He has chosen as a leading manager of the survivor community a half-Jewish survivor, who had as a matter of fact been a cruel kapo in a death camp, one Janos Baltar, who is the devil in the garden, a force of evil. After Baltar is exposed, he sets fire to the community and destroys it. But this is not unexpected. The little Messiahs are capable of achieving "a correct moment ... but time slips over the moment, and the Messiah, waiting ready in the shadows, does not appear." In accordance with Jewish religious traditions, the thirty-six righteous men hold mankind off from ultimate catastrophe until the Messiah comes, and as such they are "little Messiahs." During such unfulfilled moments, such as the failure of the project of Simon Stern, "God flees" and "we have tragedy," but that moment also "holds back tragedy until God regains his courage and returns."[18] With the collapse of his project Simon Stern leaves the East Side and moves uptown, his mission ended in failure as was inevitable.

The novel won the Edward Louis Wallant prize in 1974 for the best Jewish novel of the year, and one can understand why. Without submerging the esthetic structure and failing in the advancement of his theological ideas, by employing fantasy as an aid in presenting the supernatural aspects of Judaistic belief, and by imbuing the novel with a "modern" feeling, Cohen achieved a successful religious fictional work which was welcomed by an established Jewish institution.

One of the most brilliant of recent Jewish writers, Cynthia Ozick, falls within the religious trend in a unique way, since she is reticent on her explicit religious belief. She was the recipient of the Jewish Book Council Award in 1972 for her *The Pagan Rabbi and Other Stories* (1971), but to date her books have sold only modestly. She is also a prolific writer of essays and reviews; indeed her essays often exhibit an unusual mode of intellectual imagination, and sometimes the imagination predominates. One suspects from her occasional references to herself as an "autodidact" that she achieved Jewish learning by personal efforts rather than formal instruction. She is one of the better informed among contemporary Jewish writers on Jewish history and learning. What she has said about Yiddish literature also applies to her own viewpoint: "*Mamaloshen* doesn't produce *Wastelands*. No alienation, no nihilism, no dadaism."[19] Like Bellow, she has swerved from the post–World War II adoption of the alienation theme. Instead, she is a passionate exponent of a literature in English that aims to be Jewish in its essence. What "Jewish" means in this context is a constant element in her thought and writing.

This course was by no means clear in her first book, *Trust* (1966), a 568-page novel in the Jamesian manner in which she explored various forms of betrayal of one person by another. Her virtuoso command of English is perhaps too apparent in this overwritten story. It conveys a sense that the author revels in her virtuosity. In an early programmatic essay, "America: Toward Yavneh" (1970), she wrote candidly, "Until very recently, my whole life was given over to the religion of Art. . . . I had no other aspiration, no other commitment, no other creed." She had begun the book, she says, "for the Gentiles," but by the time she was ending it, it was "finished" for the Jews.[20]

By the time she finished *Trust*, she was weary of its "mandarin" style and aspirations to "High Art."[21] Her subsequent fiction indicates the drastic change in strategy—to the short and the novella, after turning "in relief" to the short stories of Frank O'Connor for inspiration.[22] By 1970 she had worked out her conception of the Jewish perspective (at that time) in literature, and took the occasion of her participation in the Eighth Annual American-Israel Dialogue in Jerusalem to present it in her elaborate paper, "America: Toward Yavneh." The Diaspora, she holds, can be like a "Jerusalem Displaced," like the cultural renewal at Yavneh after the destruction of the Temple. Similarly, she holds, "America shall, for a while, become Yavneh" until Israel "consolidates itself against savagery."[23] She asserts that the language of this Yavneh would be a Judaized English, what she calls the "New Yiddish."[24] She admits to being "cramped" by English sometimes because, being a "Christian language," it is inadequate for words to encompass "the oceanic amplitudes of the Jewish Idea," as, for instance, the inadequacy of any English term for "Torah."[25] Further, she held that such an English must be "liturgical," animated by "moral imagination" and is a "communal voice, the echo of the Lord of History."[26] She goes so far as to maintain that such a language cannot be "secular," for if it is, it is no longer Jewish. However, she renounced this idea of the "New Yiddish" in a *Commentary* article in February, 1983, as "my old fantasy." She now calls for a "fusion of the Enlightenment... with Jewish primary," a combination of the "intellectual power" bestowed by the Enlightenment with profound immersion in "Jewish sensibility" and study of the holy books.

In her speech of acceptance of the Jewish Book Council Award for *The Pagan Rabbi* in 1972 she held that the Jew must follow history, not nature, that is, adherence to Jewish historical religious practice rather than a pagan naturalism. "The God of the Jews" she writes, "must not be conceived as belonging to nature."[27] She is concerned that Jewish writing must have moral content traditional to Judaism. She interprets the Mosaic commandment against idolatry to mean not only to reject worship of material objects or images, but also not to pursue anything for its own sake apart from its moral or religious status. Thus literature enjoyed for its own sake as an aesthetic object is "idolatry." "Storytelling," Ozick has written, "...is a kind of magic act.... The story-making faculty itself can be a corridor to the corruption and abominations of idol-worship, of the adoration of the magical event."[28] Can one therefore be a storyteller and remain a Jew?

It should be apparent that her conception of the "Jew" is drastically constricted, that it is limited to one who practices conformity with the traditional beliefs and regulations set forth in Torah. In actuality, however, one gathers—though she is not explicit on this point—the "Jew" may exercise judgment on which items of *halakhah* he observes. Indeed, it would not even be necessary for the Jew to *believe* in God. He must only perpetuate the spirit of the tradition.

One of the most serious consequences of her passionate Jewish identification with tradition is the absence in her writing, essayistic or creative, of a world in crisis, except as it bears on the danger of anti-Semitism or what she stigmatizes as anti-Israel or a renewal of the Holocaust. The possibility of world destruction from nuclear action seems not to exist for her. Her apprehensions about the future are limited to the Jewish future. In "Diaspora," she writes, her determination is to read and write as urgently as she can—"before the coming of the American pogrom! How much time is there left? The rest of my life? One generation? Two?"[29] Concern about Jews in the Diaspora is surely a vital matter, but Jews are just as susceptible as their non-Jewish fellow citizens to the effect of general social events, to repression or enslavement, to destruction in war, to responsibility for oppression of one's non-Jewish fellows, and in the end to atomic annihilation—before the "pogrom." But these obligations upon Jews as human beings and citizens are outside her scope, or even concern, if one is to judge from her writing.

It is in her short stories, none longer than a novella, that Ozick's language skills, inventiveness, and imaginative power appear to best advantage. In her essays she seems at times to have allowed these qualities to submerge logic and intellectual discipline. The meaning of her stories in some cases becomes clear fairly quickly, but in others, it is obscure. Sometimes, indeed, meaning may be ambiguous, as for instance in "The Suitcase" (*The Pagan Rabbi*). In the confrontation in the 1960s between Genevieve Levin, Jewish mistress of the painter Gottfried Hencke, and Gottfried's father, who was born in Germany but who had lived in the United States and England since the 1920s, she charges him with having been an anti-Semite during the Hitler days, and he becomes pathetically confused and defensive in denial. It had seemed to me that the story did not justify Genevieve's accusation. Ozick intended Mr. Hencke to have been guilty of Genevieve's charge.[30] Yet, the story is susceptible of a contrary interpretation.

If one were not aware at the time of Ozick's theoretical aspirations to a New Yiddish, one would say simply that many of her stories are deeply informed by the Jewish tradition and by explicit Jewish content, and that the author was a fine practitioner of the English language. Her commitment to a pervasive Jewish spirit in her fiction also emerges from many of her stories.

Among the best of her stories are two in her first volume of short stories, *The Pagan Rabbi and Other Stories* (1971), "The Pagan Rabbi" (1966) and "Envy: or, Yiddish in America" (1969). "The Pagan Rabbi" epitomizes her conception of the opposition between embrace of the natural which we know "intuitively somehow feels different from being a Jew."[31] By fixing the Sabbath as a day of rest, she holds, the Jew has opposed himself to nature, in which one day is indistinguishable from another. So, if one chooses to be a Jew, one must choose "holiness" *against* nature. This "struggle" is given its rendering in the fantasy, "The Pagan Rabbi."

While the story vivifies the struggle between the Orthodox tradition and the allure of a pagan love of nature, another Ozick story, on quite another plane of writing, "Envy: or, Yiddish in America," is a brilliant evocation of the plight of a language which has lost its main constituency through the Holocaust and is conceived as losing viability as an everyday language among acculturating later generations. In a mordantly comic vein Ozick exemplifies this struggle for the life of a language by pitting a fully translated Yiddish writer against another who cannot find a translator. The antagonism of the enormously successful Yankel Ostrover, Yiddish writer translated copiously into English and many other languages, and Hershel Edelshtein, a Yiddish poet who cannot get a translator and is bitterly envious of Ostrover's success, is familiar to those acquainted with the Yiddish-speaking community. It is no secret that this story conveys a thinly veiled view of the relations of most Yiddish writers to Isaac Bashevis Singer.

More important, however, is the use of the story's theme to bring to life the predicament of Yiddish in the modern world. The audience of the writer in Yiddish is not only small now, but shrinking, although it now seems to be gaining new life among the younger generations. When one compares the author's command of such basically different tones as the religious fantasy underlying "The Pagan Rabbi" and the bitter, deeply ironic humor of "Envy," one realizes the versatility of Ozick's talent. "Envy" is a masterpiece and will stand as a definitive literary evocation of the pathos of Yiddish in post–World War II United States.

In a strange way Ozick's basic theme of authenticity can be seen in "Envy" in the impurity of the passion for translation on the part of both Ostrover and Edelshtein. Devotion to the language—Yiddish—is set over against material success and fame, and in the dubious criticism of Ostrover's literary quality under the guise of envy of his success. But the center of the story is the plight of Yiddish in the modern world. In another story, "Virility," inauthenticity is conveyed through the misappropriation by the erstwhile immigrant Edmund Gate (né Elia Gatoff) in New York of volumes of poetry sent to him by his old Tante Rivka in England. Until he began to receive poems from his aunt, his own attempts at poetry had been a failure. But he decides to offer her poetry as his own, and they prove a great success and Gate becomes a world celebrity. When his aunt dies, the flow of poetry stops. He confesses the deception. Some poems remain and are published with Tante Rivka as author, and the point of the story emerges. Whereas the poems published under Gate's name had been regarded as "The Masculine Principle personified, verified, and illuminated," or "Robust, lusty, male," and published six volumes under the title, "Virility," it was otherwise when the poetry of the same author, published under her name is characterized as "thin feminist art."[32]

While the feminism in the poem is brought out perhaps too obviously, Ozick expressed herself in the strongest feminist terms and importantly later in relation to the sexism of Judaism during a visit to Israel in the summer

of 1978. Her address to a seminar on Judaism and Contemporary Thought
at the Bar-Ilan University must have shocked her audience. In light of the
incalculable loss of potential Jewish talent from the Holocaust, she said,
the Jews can no longer afford not to encourage the fullest contribution from
women. She quotes the great contemporary Talmudic scholar Adin Stein-
saltz' statement, among others, that the Talmud "is the collective endeavor
of the entire Jewish people." This, she says unequivocally, is "a plain whop-
ping lie on the face of it." It is now, she says, a "necessity—*having lost so
much and so many*—to share Jewish history to the hilt" with Jewish women.
For the Talmud is the product of only "the male half" of the Jewish people;
"Jewish women have been excluded—by purposeful excision—from this
'collective endeavor of the Jewish people.' " Failure to allow Jewish women
to participate has meant "the mass loss of half of the available Jewish
minds." She calls on Torah scholars to stop offering Jewish women "stopgap
tactics, tinkerings, placebos, and sops, all in the form of further separation
and isolation—So far, we can only refer to the 'Jewish half-genius.' " Only
when complete and untrammeled access is permitted to women, will it be
possible to speak of a "Jewish genius."[33]

Ozick's more extended analysis of the place of women under Judaism,
published in the Jewish feminist magazine *Lilith* in 1979, is even more deeply
critical in what she calls "fifteen brief meditations."[34] Only a skeleton of
her argument can be suggested here. She first dismisses as a "wrong question" whether God should be considered a "He" or a "She" because "the
Creator of the Universe" is neither, is beyond pronouns. Further, it is the
"wrong question" to regard the woman problem as "theological"—it is
rather "sociological."[35] After a strong, cogently argued thesis, she concludes
that Torah does not differ in its view of women from the rest of the world.
This "scandal ... calls Torah itself into question." The Torah must seek a
Yavneh in which conditions exist for a new Commandment, "*Thou shalt
not lessen the humanity of women.*"[36] For her, the necessity for this
change is nothing less than the preservation and strengthening of Torah
itself.

In her second volume of short stories, *Bloodshed and Three Novellas*
(1976), Ozick delineated duplicity in several forms, variations on the theme
of inauthenticity, or betrayal of "trust." One story in *Bloodshed* is "A
Mercenary," an ironic description of a self-hating Polish Jew, an ambassador
at the United Nations—not of Poland, not representing Jews either, but of
a small African country. As a child he had been left with a Christian-Polish
family during the war, but they abandoned him in the forest, where he
survived. Telling about his survival on television, he is "all mockery and
parody, ... the man telling about the boy, Pole putting himself out as African, candor offering cunning."[37] At the UN, he was known as the "P.M.,"
standing not for "Prime Minister" but for "Paid Mouthpiece."[38] His mistress
Lulu, derived from a titled German family, taunts him with evading his

Jewishness. "I know what *you* hate," she says. "You hate being part of the Jews." He replies, "I am not part of the Jews. I am part of mankind." "Practically no one knows you're a Jew," she added.[39] The author comments further: "Always he was cold to the Jews. He never went among them. In the Assembly he turned his back on the ambassador from Israel." His mistress had seen it, and "heard the gallery gasp. All New York Jews in the gallery."[40] The title story "Bloodshed" (1970) brings out once again Ozick's view of Jewish authenticity by challenging a secular Jew with a passionate Chassid, who denies his right to call himself a Jew. Again, with allusive richness, Ozick iterates her approach to the problem of who is a Jew, with the same astringent insistence of immersion in and pursuit of life according to the tradition of the sacred Jewish texts.

The final story, "Usurpation (Other People's Stories)," attacks the problem from another angle, the antagonism of art and Judaism, or, put more precisely, the danger of allowing the allure of art to be sought for its own sake, thus making of it an "idol." To the Jew, stories "ought to judge and interpret the world."[41] So great is the danger of "idolatry" that the whole project of literary art is put in question. In the story "Usurpation," she adapts Malamud's short story, "The Magic Crown" and David Stern's "Agnon, A Story." The crown is the symbol for the attainment by the story-writer of false "idolatrous" values. The magic crown is passed on from one writer to another as prestige passes—"When a writer wishes to usurp the place and power of another writer, he simply puts it [the crown] on."[42] Most fundamentally, however, there will be "a cage for story writers" in Paradise, and they will be taught that "All that is not Law is levity."[43] In the end, storytelling is at the least trivial, at worst "idolatry." Obviously, Ozick herself cannot abandon storytelling, but uses it to warn of its violation of Law. She recalls that even if Ibn Gabirol "felt the same," he still "wrote poems." "Why do demons choose to sink their hooves into black, black ink? As if ink were blood."[44] Now we know why she titled her book *Bloodshed*.

The fertility of her imagination and virtuosity of language continue undiminished. She is capable of ruthless, if deeply compassionate realism as in her short story, "The Shawl" (*The New Yorker*, May 26, 1980), in which a brutal death march of some Jewish women, especially a young woman and a child, driven by the Nazis, is related with relentless, chilling effect. In 1982 she published her *Levitation: Five Fictions*, containing stories published since 1977. She maintains here her amalgam of realistic detail with an almost imperceptible slide into fantasy. Any attempt to reduce her stories to their meaning leaves a sense of inadequacy because it misses the lively sense of reality from moment to moment of her narrative, and of the wit that frequently erupts. However, the meaning of some stories continues to be obscure to some readers (like myself), as in several sketches in this collection.

Ozick seized the opportunity in her next novel, *The Cannibal Galaxy* (1983), to introduce her latest idea of a modern Jewish culture. Her central character, a French Jew, Joseph Brill, is a Holocaust survivor. During the war he is hidden in the basement of a convent in Paris. There the nuns supply a library which includes the works of the French–Jewish-conscious intellectual, Edmond Fleg, who combined within himself the culture of the Hebrew and Enlightenment traditions, which Ozick has presented in her 1983 essay. When years later Brill has become founder and principal of a private elementary school in the midwest United States, he introduces a dual curriculum of Hebrew and Western studies along the lines of the Fleg approach. But she misses the opportunity in this story to give more body to the idea of a viable Jewish culture in terms of the Dual Curriculum.[45]

This relatively new tendency of Jewish writers to pursue—or believe they are pursuing—religious themes, or deal with religious characters continues unabated concurrently with the return to religion among the younger generations. However, it must be emphasized that, as was the case with the previous generations of Jewish writers, they do not form a "school."

# Conclusion

As the twentieth century wore on, one may witness the growing maturation of Jewish writers as writers together with that of American writers as a whole. We need to bear in mind, however, that this applies to techniques and sophistication, so that it would be debatable to assert that growth in the technical level necessarily implies an access of wisdom. In one respect, however, the fiction marks a long step forward: the numerous Jewish stereotypes were much less often met with; Jewish characters were more generally treated by both non-Jewish and Jewish authors in rounded human terms as individuals. Anti-Semitism, while occasionally manifested by a fictional character, is rarely shared by the author. Indeed, anti-Semitism in general tended to become simply unacceptable in the literary community.

All through the century many works by Jewish authors were concerned with the acculturation theme, emphasizing the durability of this type of literary material down to our own day. This is scarcely remarkable, since this mode of social change is an ongoing personal experience for several generations after immigration.

Some of the lines of development of Jewish writing in this period can be discussed within a paradigm of the sequential relations of three publications, the *Menorah Journal, Partisan Review*, and *Commentary* (at least until the 1960s). These journals were the bearers in important respects of the three components of Jewish writing in the course of the century: generally left politics, modernist literary values, and Jewish ethnic interest. Of course there were other tributaries. Jewish literary ethnicity derived great stimulus from the Holocaust of Jews revealed after World War II and from the struggle for the birth and existence of Israel. The post–World War II period witnessed even more deeply disillusioned generations than those experienced after World War II, for they know the uncertainties around the very future of humanity in the shadow of the Bomb. By our own day modernism has almost completely swept the field with an existential component and in some cases an almost nihilistic outlook. Jewish writers shared in all these trends, but one striking difference may be noted. Major Jewish writers like Saul Bellow and Bernard Malamud, as well as others, declared their refusal to acquiesce to this trend and succumb to a mood of alienation and complete loss of faith in man. Instead they clung, not consciously perhaps, to the salience of the value of life in the Jewish tradition.

By the 1950s, emergence of Jewish writers within the entire range of American literature, most particularly as major fiction writers as well as best-selling popular authors justifies our designation of the 1950s as the "Jewish Decade." Once and for all the Jew was recognized as a full citizen of the American republic of letters and situated together with non-Jewish writers as belonging to the mainstream of our nation's literature. From among Jews came major, minor, popular, and even trashy fiction writers as members of a fully franchised group in the country.

No Jewish writers of the stature of the major figures of those who emerged in the 1950s seem to have appeared since (in my opinion). Yet the uninterrupted flow of competent writing of high quality by Jews continues to appear in a steady stream and are generally accepted, no longer looked upon as a phenomenon evoking special comment. A decade or two later the process was repeated with the emergence of many Black writers who received general recognition, as well as numbers of female writers. These "minority" writers have produced a number of significant works in all literary areas. The last few decades have also witnessed a revival of writing oriented toward religion of one kind or another, including Judaism. This trend is in large part precipitated by the ominous threat of a global nuclear Holocaust and a deterioration of the environment which threatens the very survival of life on the planet.

In the third and final volume of this series, *Dramatic Encounters*, we look at the Jewish literary experience with humor, poetry, and in more detail, the theater, as well as the special relationship between Blacks and Jews, as can also be perceived in social life itself.

# Notes

## 1. THREAD OF INFLUENCE: FROM *MENORAH JOURNAL* TO *PARTISAN REVIEW* TO *COMMENTARY*

1. William Dean Howells, "Editor's Easy Chair," *Harper's Monthly Magazine*, Vol. 130 (May, 1915), 958.

2. Robert Alter, "Epitaph for a Jewish Magazine: Notes on the 'Menorah Journal,'" *Commentary*, Vol. 39, No. 5 (May, 1965), 51. I have drawn on the informative monograph by Alan M. Wald, "The Menorah Group Moves Left," *Jewish Social Studies*, Vol. 38, Nos. 3–4, (Summer-Fall, 1976). See also Mark Krupnick, "The Menorah Journal Group and the Origins of Modern Jewish-American Radicalism," *Modern Jewish Studies*, Annual III (1979), 56–67; and Lionel Trilling, "Afterword," in Tess Slesinger, *The Unpossessed* (New York, 1966 [c1934]).

3. "Ten Years of the Menorah Journal: An Editorial Statement," *Menorah Journal*, Vol. 11, No. 1 (February, 1925), 1–2.

4. Letter from Elliot Cohen to Isidor Schneider, November 27, 1929, and Isidor Schneider's reply, November 28, 1929, Isidor Schneider Papers, Butler Library, Columbia University. By permission of Columbia University Library.

5. Lionel Trilling, "Afterword," in Slesinger, pp. 319, 320, 322.

6. *Menorah Journal*, Vol. 14, No. 1 (January, 1928), 108.

7. *Menorah Journal*, Vol. 18, No. 4 (April, 1930), 381, 382.

8. *Menorah Journal*, Vol. 14, No. 6 (June, 1928), 604–5.

9. *Menorah Journal*, Vol. 17, No. 3 (December, 1929), 294.

10. *Menorah Journal*, Vol. 15, No. 5 (November, 1928), 483, 484.

11. *Menorah Journal*, Vol. 19, No. 1 (October, 1930), 88.

12. *Menorah Journal*, Vol. 14, No. 2 (February, 1928), 218, 219.

13. *Menorah Journal*, June, 1931, 470, 471, 471–72, 472.

14. Slesinger, p. 78.

15. Ibid., pp. 33, 37.

16. Trilling, "Afterword," p. 326.

17. Ibid., p. 327.

18. Slesinger, p. 283.

19. "Under Forty," *Contemporary Jewish Record*, Vol. 7 (February, 1944), 3, 4, 15.

20. See, for instance, Gertrude Selznick and Stephen Steinberg, *The Tenacity of Prejudice* (New York, 1966), and Charles T. Glock and Rodney Stark, *Christian Beliefs and Anti-Semitism* (New York, 1969); and Will Herberg, *Protestant-Catholic-Jew* (New York, 1955).

21. Norman Podhoretz, *Making It* (New York, 1967), p. 288.

22. Leslie Fiedler, "The State of American Writing," *Partisan Review*, Vol. 15, No. 8 (August, 1948), 872, 873.

23. Leslie Fiedler, "What Can We Do About Fagin?" *Commentary*, Vol. 7, No. 5 (May, 1949), 418.

24. "The Jewish Writer and the English Literary Tradition," *Commentary*, Parts I (September) and II (October), Vol. 8 (1949), I, 209.

25. Stanley Edgar Hyman, "The Jewish Writer," I, 214, 215.

26. Irving Howe, "The Jewish Writer," II, 365.

27. Saul Bellow, "The Jewish Writer," II, 367.

28. Harold Rosenberg, "The Jewish Writer," I, 218.

29. Harry Levin, "The Jewish Writer," II, 363, 364.

30. William Phillips, "How *Partisan Review* Began," *Commentary* (December, 1979), p. 44. It is relevant that the Hungarian Marxist Georg Lukacs, confronted with a similar dilemma in 1929 when he was obliged to publish a "self-criticism" of a political thesis which was rejected by the Bela Kun leadership of the Hungarian Communist party, complied even though he was "firmly convinced that I was in the right." But he knew that failure to comply meant expulsion from the party, and to him this "meant that it would no longer be possible to participate actively in the struggle against Fascism. I wrote my self-criticism as an 'entry ticket' to such activity as I neither could nor wished to work in the Hungarian movement in the circumstances." (George Lukacs, "Preface to the Ninth Edition," [1967], *History and Class Consciousness*, trans. Rodney Livingstone [Cambridge, Mass.], 1971, p. xxx).

31. Irving Howe, "The New York Intellectuals: A Chronicle and a Critique," *Commentary*, Vol. 46, No. 4 (October 1968), 33, 38.

32. Philip Rahv, "Our Country and Our Culture," *Partisan Review*, Vol. 19, No. 3 (May-June, 1952), 307.

33. Editorial "Our Country and Our Culture," *Partisan Review*, 284, 285. The responses were published in three issues: I, May-June, pp. 283–326; II, July-August, pp. 420–450; III, September-October, 562–597.

34. C. Wright Mills, II, p. 447.

35. William Barrett, "Our Country and Our Culture," II, p. 420.

36. William Phillips, "Our Country and Our Culture," III, p. 587.

37. Philip Rahv, "Our Country and Our Culture," I, p. 309.

38. Lionel Trilling, "Our Country and Our Culture," I, pp. 319, 320, 325.

39. Norman Mailer, "Our Country and Our Culture," I, p. 298.

40. C. Wright Mills, "Our Country and Our Culture," II, p. 447.

41. Irving Howe, "Our Country and Our Culture," III, pp. 580, 577.

42. Delmore Schwartz, "Our Country and Our Culture," III, p. 594.

43. "Jewishness and the Younger Intellectuals," *Commentary*, Vol. 31 (April, 1961), 307, 308, 309, 310.

44. "Run writer run," interview of John Updike with Matthew Nesvisky, *Jerusalem Post*, International Edition, November 14, 1978, p. 15.

45. John Updike, *Bech* (New York, 1970), pp. 71, 5–6, 143.

46. "Conversation on a Book," interview with Elizabeth Hardwick, *New York Times Book Review*, April 29, 1979, p. 61.

## 2. THE JEWISH DECADE: THE 1950S

1. Louis Harap, "Jewish Characters in Search of a Novel," *Jewish Life* (later *Jewish Currents*), Vol. 3, No. 8 (January, 1949), 12.

2. "A Vocal Group," *Times Literary Supplement* (London), November 6, 1959, p. xxxv.

3. Yuri Suhl, "Why I Wrote a Jewish Novel," *Mid-Century*, ed. Harold U. Ribalow (New York, 1955), p. 320.

4. Ben Hecht, *A Guide for the Bedevilled* (New York, 1944), p. 207.

5. Henry Popkin, "The Vanishing Jew of Our Popular Fiction," *Commentary*, Vol. 14 (1952), 46–55.

6. Arthur Miller, quoted in *This Land, This People*, ed. Harold U. Ribalow (New York, 1950), p. 4.

7. Laura Z. Hobson, *Gentlemen's Agreement* (New York, 1947), p. 183.

8. Dennis H. Wrong, "The Rise and Decline of Anti-Semitism in America," *The Ghetto and Beyond*, ed. Peter L. Rose (New York, 1969), p. 313.

9. Gertrude J. Selznick and Stephen Steinberg, *Tenacity of Prejudice* (New York, 1969), p. 3.

10. Wrong, p. 313.

11. Hortense Calisher, *Herself* (New York, 1972), p. 63.

12. Ibid., p. 62.

13. Ibid., pp. 57, 58.

14. Hortense Calisher, "The Old Stock," *Collected Short Stories of Hortense Calisher* (New York, 1975), pp. 263, 274.

15. Calisher, *Herself*, p. 57.

16. Hortense Calisher, "One of the Chosen," *Collected Short Stories*, pp. 384, 385.

17. Calisher, *Herself*, p. 66.

18. Hortense Calisher, *The New Yorkers* (New York, 1969), p. 148.

19. Sam Ross, *The Sidewalks Are Free* (New York, 1950), pp. 77–78.

20. Ibid., p. 301.

21. Beatrice Levin, *The Lonely Room* (New York, 1950), pp. 66.

22. Ibid., p. 118.

23. Stephen Longstreet, "Why I Wrote a Jewish Novel," *Mid-Century*, p. 327.

24. Sam Astrachan, *An End to Dying* (New York, 1958), p. 143.

25. Herbert Gold, *Therefore Be Bold* (New York, 1960), p. 227.

26. Sloan Wilson, *The Man in the Gray Flannel Suit* (New York, 1955), p. 149.

27. James Gould Cozzens, *By Love Possessed* (New York, 1957), p. 63.

28. Frederick Blacher, *The Novels of James Gould Cozzens* (Newport, Conn., 1959), p. 158.

29. Katherine Anne Porter, *The Ship of Fools* (Boston, 1962), pp. 50, 134, 244, 337.

30. Joan Givner, *Katherine Anne Porter: A Life* (New York, 1982), pp. 200, 261, 262, 268.

31. Ibid., pp. 450, 451, 458, 451, 450–51.

32. Irving Howe, "Our Country and Our Culture," *Commentary*, Vol. 19, No. 4 (July-August, 1952), 579.

33. Morris Dickstein, *Gates of Eden: American Culture in the Sixties* (New York, 1977), p. 57.

34. C. Wright Mills, *White Collar* (New York, 1956), p. 326.

35. Gerald Green, *The Last Angry Man* (New York, 1958 [c1952]), p. 589.

36. Ernst Pawel, *From the Dark Tower* (New York, 1957), pp. 17, 34.

37. Ibid., pp. 37–38.

38. Ibid., pp. 38, 87.

39. Ibid., pp. 101, 106, 51, 245.

40. J. D. Salinger, "Down at the Dinghy," *Nine Stories* (New York, 1953), p. 65.

41. Leslie Fiedler, "Zion as Main Street," *Waiting for the End* (New York, 1964), p. 86.

42. Mills, p. 347.

43. Herman Wouk, *Marjorie Morningstar* (New York, 1955), p. 44.

44. Ibid., p. 172.

45. Ibid., pp. 172–73.

46. Ibid., pp. 562, 469.

47. This account of *Exodus* and quotations from it are drawn from my article, "Another Look at Exodus," *Jewish Currents*, Vol. 14, No. 7 (July-August, 1960), 13–17.

48. Edward Lewis Wallant, *The Pawnbroker* (New York, 1961), pp. 31, 114–15.

49. Ibid., p. 207.

50. Ibid., pp. 278–79.

51. Ibid., p. 8.

52. Isaac Bashevis Singer, *A Crown of Feathers* (New York, 1973), "Author's Note."

53. Jacob Glatstein, "The Fame of Isaac Bashevis Singer," *Congress Bi-Weekly*, Vol. 32, No. 17 (December 27, 1965), 17.

54. Marshall Breger and Bob Barnhart, "A Conversation with Isaac Bashevis Singer," *Critical Views of Isaac Bashevis Singer*, ed. Irving Malin (New York, 1969), p. 39.

55. Isaac Bashevis Singer, *A Young Man in Search of Love* (New York, 1978), pp. 10, 107.

56. Singer, interview with Irving Howe, *Midstream*, July, 1973.

57. Glatstein, p. 17.

58. Jacob Sloan, "I. B. Singer and His Yiddish Critics," *Congress Bi-Weekly*, March 7, 1966, pp. 4, 5.

59. Singer, *A Young Man*, p. 38.

60. Isaac Bashevis Singer, "A Phantom of Delight," *New York Herald Tribune Book Week*, July 4, 1965.

61. Singer, *A Young Man*, p. 10.

62. Ibid., pp. 37, 39.

63. Gershom Scholem, "The Crisis of Tradition in Jewish Messianism," *The Messanic Idea of Judaism* (New York, 1971), p. 60.

64. Gershom Scholem, "Redemption through Sin," *The Messanic Idea*, p. 84.

65. Isaac Bashevis Singer, "The Destruction of Kreshev," *The Spinoza of Market Street* (New York, 1961), p. 101.

66. Singer, *A Young Man*, pp. 37, 135, 137.

67. Samuel H. Dresner, *Midstream*, Vol. 27, No. 3 (March, 1980), 445.

68. Irving Howe, Interview with Singer, *Midstream*, July, 1973.

69. Isaac Bashevis Singer, *Satan in Goray* (New York, 1955), p. 239.

70. Isaac Bashevis Singer, *The Magician of Lublin* (New York, 1960), p. 152.

71. Isaac Bashevis Singer, "Gimpel the Fool," *Gimpel the Fool and Other Stories* (New York, 1957), p. 5.

72. *Critical Views of Isaac Bashevis Singer*, p. 36.

73. I. L. Peretz, *Three Gifts and Other Stories*, trans. Henry Goodman (New York, 1947), pp. 24, 25, 26, 30.

74. Isaac Bashevis Singer, "Nobel Lecture," *New York Times*, December 9, 1978, p. 4.

## 3. THE CRITICS: TRILLING, RAHV, KAZIN, FIEDLER, HOWE

1. Lionel Trilling, "The Function of the Little Magazine," *The Liberal Imagination* (New York, 1950), pp. 90, 95, 95–96, 96.

2. Lionel Trilling, *The Middle of the Journey*, with a new introduction by the author (New York, 1975 [c1947]), pp. xx, xxi.

3. Lionel Trilling, "The Changing Myth of the Jew," *Commentary*, Vol. 66, No. 2 (August, 1978), 24, 25.

4. Lionel Trilling, "Afterword," in Tess Slesinger, *The Unpossessed* (New York, 1966 [c1934]), p. 321.

5. Diana Trilling, "Lionel Trilling, a Jew at Columbia," *Commentary* (March, 1979), 44. Sidney Hook, in "Anti-Semitism in the Academy: Some Pages of the Past," *Midstream*, January, 1979, 49–54, writes that Trilling came to him for advice concerning how to resist his projected dismissal from Columbia in 1936, and that Trilling followed his (Hook's) suggestion that he create a loud confrontation with the professors in his department to protest the dismissal. Mrs. Trilling does not mention in her article Hook's claim to this part in Trilling's reinstatement.

6. Lionel Trilling, "Some Notes for an Autobiographical Lecture," *The Last Decade*, ed. Diana Trilling (New York, 1979), p. 337.

7. Lionel Trilling, "Under Forty: A Symposium on American Literature and the Younger Generation of American Jews," *Contemporary Jewish Record*, Vol. 7 (February, 1944), 15.

8. Ibid., p. 17.

9. Lionel Trilling, "The Jewish Writer and the English Literary Tradition: A Symposium," *Commentary*, Vol. 8 (1949), 215.

10. Lionel Trilling, "The Poet as Hero," *The Opposing Self* (New York, 1955), p. 20.

11. Robert Gittings, *John Keats* (Boston, 1968), p. 25.

12. Lionel Trilling, *Matthew Arnold* (New York, 1949), p. 256.

13. Lionel Trilling, *The Liberal Imagination* (New York, 1950), p. 256. In his

essay, "Lionel Trilling" (*Midstream*, March, 1983), Edward Alexander suggests that "the single event in Jewish history which decisively influenced Lionel Trilling's thought was the Holocaust" (p. 50). He supports this view not only by his discussion of the 1950s essays on Wordsworth and Isaac Babel, but also Trilling's allusion in "Art and Fortune" to the Holocaust, which I have quoted. But it seems to me that his discussion tends to obscure the fact that Trilling had already begun his critique of liberalism and optimism and the simplistic in the first part of "Reality in America" in 1940. It is true, as Alexander notes, that the Holocaust drove Trilling to view that event as the logical conclusion of the critique of liberalism, namely that humanity is incurably depraved, in opposition to the assumption of liberalism that people have the potentiality for good. But in Alexander's discussion one tends to forget that the decisive influence on Trilling's thought was anti-Stalinism and his recession from radicalism of the post-Depression period.

14. Lionel Trilling, "Wordsworth and the Rabbis," *The Opposing Self*, pp. 123, 127, 129, 131, 135.

15. Lionel Trilling, "Isaac Babel," *Beyond Culture* (New York, 1965), pp. 120, 127, 138, 137, 143.

16. Trilling, *The Liberal Imagination*, pp. xi, xii.

17. Ibid., p. 3.

18. Ibid., pp. 19, 9, 15, 14.

19. Alfred Kazin, *New York Jew* (New York, 1978), p. 192.

20. Lionel Trilling, "Our Country and Our Culture," *Partisan Review*, Vol. 19, No. 3 (May-June, 1952), 319, 320, 322, 325.

21. Trilling, *The Opposing Self*, p. x.

22. Trilling, *Beyond Culture*, pp. xii, xiii.

23. Norman Podhoretz, *Breaking Ranks* (New York, 1979), p. 304.

24. Peter Steinfels, *The Neoconservatives: The Men Who Are Changing American Politics* (New York, 1979), p. 56.

25. Philip Rahv, *Literature and the Sixth Sense* (Boston, 1970), p. 190.

26. Ibid., pp. 280, 281.

27. Ibid., p. 282.

28. Ibid., p. 283.

29. Philip Rahv, "The Jewish Writer and the English Literary Tradition," *Commentary*, Vol. 8 (October, 1949), 361, 362.

30. Rahv, *Literature and the Sixth Sense*, p. 1.

31. Philip Rahv, "Our Country and Our Culture," *Partisan Review*, Vol. 19, No. 3 (May-June, 1952), 308, 308–309.

32. Alfred Kazin, *On Native Grounds* (New York, 1956 [c1942]), pp. 206, 204.

33. Alfred Kazin, "Under Forty," *Contemporary Jewish Record*, Vol. 7 (February, 1944), 9, 10, 11.

34. Alfred Kazin, "The Jewish Writer and the English Literary Tradition," pp. 367, 368.

35. Alfred Kazin, *A Walker in the City* (New York, 1951), pp. 98–99.

36. Alfred Kazin, *Starting Out in the Thirties* (New York, 1965), p. 82.

37. Ibid., p. 82.

38. Alfred Kazin, "The Jew as Modern Writer," *Commentary*, April, 1966, 37, 38, 39, 40, 41.

39. Alfred Kazin, "The Uses of Experience," *Contemporaries* (New York, 1962), p. 399.

40. Leslie A. Fiedler, "The Plight of the Jewish Intellectual," *Mid-Century: An Anthology of Jewish Life and Culture in Our Times*, ed. Harold U. Ribalow (New York, 1955), pp. 164, 166.

41. Leslie Fiedler, "The State of American Writing: 1948," *Commentary*, Vol. 15, No. 8 (August, 1948), 872.

42. Irving Howe, "The New York Intellectuals," *Commentary*, Vol. 46, No. 4 (October, 1968), 39–40.

43. Leslie Fiedler, "What Shall We Do About Fagin?" *Commentary*, Vol. 7 (May, 1949), 413.

44. Stanley Edgar Hyman, "The Jewish Writer and the English Literary Tradition," *Commentary*, Vol. 8 (1949), Pt. I, 214.

45. Robert Alter, "Jewish Dreams and Nightmares," *After the Tradition* (New York, 1969), pp. 20–21.

46. Leslie Fiedler, *The Jew in the American Novel* (New York, 1959), p. 7. This pamphlet was originally published in *Midstream* and was also reprinted in Fiedler's *Collected Essays*, 2 vols. (New York, 1971), vol. 1.

47. Fiedler, "Second Dialogue in Israel," *Congress Bi-Weekly*, Vol. 30, No. 12 (September 16, 1963), 24.

48. Ibid., p. 28.

49. Alter, "Jewish Dreams and Nightmares," pp. 21–22, 22.

50. Leslie A. Fiedler, *Collected Essays*, Vol. 2, p. xi.

51. Irving Howe, "The Lost Young Intellectual," *Mid-Century*, pp. 154, 163. This essay first appeared in *Commentary*, September, 1947.

52. Irving Howe, "The Stranger and the Victim: Two Jewish Stereotypes of American Fiction," *Commentary*, Vol. 8 (August, 1949), 147.

53. Irving Howe, "The Jewish Writer and the English Literary Tradition," Part II, *Commentary*, Vol. 8 (October, 1949), 364, 365, 364, 365.

54. "Our Country and Our Culture," Part III, *Partisan Review*, Vol. 19, No. 5, 577, 579, 580.

55. Raymond Williams, review of Irving Howe's *Steady Work*, *Commentary*, February, 1969.

56. Robert Alter, review of Irving Howe's *World of Our Fathers*, *Commentary*, April, 1976, 84.

57. Irving Howe, *The World of Our Fathers* (New York, 1976), p. 549.

58. For a reproduction of the postcard reply to the reader of the *Morning Freiheit* and its text, see the pamphlet by Paul Novick, *The Distorted World of Our Fathers* (New York, 1977), p. 7.

59. Howe, *The World of Our Fathers*, pp. 586, 588. For several detailed critiques of the book, see Morris U. Schappes, "Irving Howe's *The World of Our Fathers*: A Critical Analysis," *Jewish Currents*, September and October, 1977; also reprinted as a pamphlet (New York, 1978); and Louis Harap, "Irving Howe and Jewish America," *Journal of Ethnic Studies*, Vol. 4, No. 4 (Winter, 1978), 95–104.

60. Irving Howe, *Celebrations and Attacks* (New York, 1979), pp. 23, 23–24, 24.

## 4. A LITERATURE OF ALIENATION: SCHWARTZ AND ROSENFELD

1. Delmore Schwartz, "In Dreams Begin Responsibilities," *The World Is a Wedding* (Norfolk, Conn., 1948), pp. 194, 196.

2. Robert Martin Adams, *Nil: Episodes in the Literary Conquest of Void during the 19th Century* (New York, 1966), pp. 6, 7.

3. Delmore Schwartz, *Shenendoah* (Norfolk, Conn., 1941), p. 27.

4. F. O. Matthiessen, "A New York Childhood," *Responsibilities of the Critic* (New York, 1952), p. 14.

5. Delmore Schwartz, "Under Forty," *Contemporary Jewish Record*, Vol. 7 (February, 1944), 14.

6. Ibid.

7. Ibid., p. 13.

8. James Atlas, *Delmore Schwartz: The Life of an American Poet* (New York, 1977), p. 162.

9. Ibid., pp. 245, 287, 163.

10. Ibid., p. 164.

11. Donald A. Dike and David H. Zucker, eds., *Selected Essays of Delmore Schwartz*, with an appreciation by Dwight Macdonald (Chicago, 1970), p. 23.

12. Delmore Schwartz, "New Year's Eve," *The World Is a Wedding*, p. 88.

13. Schwartz, "America, America," *The World Is a Wedding*, pp. 110, 114, 119, 126.

14. Ibid., p. 128.

15. Schwartz, "The Child Is the Meaning of This Life," p. 187.

16. Schwartz, "New Year's Eve," p. 88.

17. Atlas, pp. 274, 235, 234, 235.

18. Delmore Schwartz, *In Dreams Begin Responsibilities* (Norfolk, Conn., 1938), p. 100.

19. Delmore Schwartz, *Genesis: Book I* (New York, 1938), pp. 103, 104, 121–22.

20. Schwartz, *Genesis*, pp. ix, 117.

21. Matthiessen, pp. 112, 113.

22. Delmore Schwartz, "Abraham," *Breakthrough: A Treasury of Contemporary American Jewish Literature* (New York, 1964), pp. 215, 216.

23. Editorial Note, *Commentary*, Vol. 10 (1950), 561.

24. Saul Bellow, "Isaac Rosenfeld," *Partisan Review*, Vol. 23, No. 4 (Fall, 1956), 565.

25. Ibid., p. 567.

26. Isaac Rosenfeld, "Under Forty," pp. 35, 36.

27. Karl Marx and Frederick Engels, *Literature and Art* (New York, 1947), p. 28. (The Marx passage is drawn from *Theories of Surplus Value*.)

28. Rosenfeld, p. 36.

29. Isaac Rosenfeld, *Passage from Home* (Cleveland, 1961 [c1946]), p. 1.

30. Ibid., pp. 262–63, 263.

31. Ibid., p. 94.

32. Delmore Schwartz, *Summer Knowledge: Selected Poems 1938–1958* (New York, 1959), p. 237.

33. Isaac Rosenfeld, "The Jewish Writer and the English Literary Tradition," *Commentary*, Vol. 5 (1949), 213, 214.

34. Isaac Rosenfeld, "Adam and Eve on Delancey Street," *Commentary*, Vol. 8 (October, 1949), pp. 386–87.

35. Jacob Blaustein, letter, *Commentary*, Vol. 8 (December, 1949), 594.

36. Isaac Rosenfeld, "King Solomon," *Breakthrough*, pp. 131, 132.

37. Isaac Rosenfeld, "America, Land of the Sad Millionaire," *Breakthrough*, p. 260.

38. Abraham Cahan, *The Rise of David Levinsky* (New York, 1960), p. 445.

39. Rosenfeld, "America, Land of the Sad Millionaire," *Breakthrough*, pp. 263, 264, 260.

## 5. FROM LIFE TO LIMBO: SAUL BELLOW

1. Herbert Gold, ed., *Fiction of the Fifties* (New York, 1959), p. 19.

2. Saul Bellow, "Isaac Rosenfeld," *Partisan Review*, Vol. 23, No. 4 (Fall, 1956), 565, 577.

3. Delmore Schwartz, "Jacob," *Breakthrough*, ed. Irving Marlin and Irwin Stark (New York, 1964), p. 216.

4. Saul Bellow, *Humboldt's Gift* (New York, 1975), p. 199. Strong influence of Max Weber is apparent here.

5. *Jerusalem Post Weekly*, July 13, 1970.

6. Abraham Chapman, "The Image of Man as Portrayed by Saul Bellow," *College Language Association Journal*, Vol. 10, No. 4 (June, 1967), 292.

7. Irving Howe, "Down and Out in New York and Chicago," in Saul Bellow, *Herzog*, text and criticism, ed. Irving Howe (New York, 1976), p. 397.

8. Milton Hindus, " 'Herzog': Existentialist Jewish Hero," *Jewish Frontier*, December, 1964, 12.

9. Joseph Epstein, "Saul Bellow's Chicago," *New York Times Book Review*, May 9, 1971, p. 12.

10. Saul Bellow, "Jewish Writers Are Somehow Different," *National Jewish Monthly*, April, 1971, pp. 51, 50, 51.

11. Meyer Levin, "Saul Bellow Crowned King of His Own Planet, in Which Jewish Survival Would Be Doubtful," *American Examiner-Jewish Week*, March 18, 1971, p. 6.

12. Rabbi David Polis, "Minority Report," *The Sentinel* (Chicago), Nov. 25, 1976.

13. "Bellow: Are the Miracles Ended?" *Jerusalem Post Weekly*, July 13, 1970.

14. Saul Bellow, "Jewish Writers Are Somehow Different," p. 51.

15. Saul Bellow, *Dangling Man* (New York, 1944), p. 9.

16. Ibid., p. 34.

17. Ibid., p. 12.

18. Ibid., p. 181.

19. Ibid., p. 39.

20. Ibid., p. 64.

21. Ibid., pp. 89, 92.

22. Saul Bellow, *The Victim* (New York, 1947), p. 41.

23. Ibid., pp. 116, 121.

24. Ibid., p. 154.

25. Gordon Lloyd Harper, "Saul Bellow: An Interview," *Writers at Work: Third Series* (New York, 1976), pp. 350, 351, 350. (First published in *Paris Review*, Winter, 1966.)

26. Ibid., p. 350.

27. Saul Bellow, *The Adventures of Augie March* (New York, 1953), p. 454.

28. Ibid., pp. 454, 455.

29. Ibid., p. 455.

30. Ibid., p. 485.

31. Saul Bellow, *Seize the Day* (New York, 1961 [c1956]), p. 66.

32. Ibid., p. 89.

33. Ibid., p. 98.

34. Ibid., p. 118.

35. Saul Bellow, *Henderson the Rain King* (New York, 1976 [c1959]), p. 12.

36. Ibid., p. 85.

37. Ibid., p. 132.

38. Hindus, p. 12.

39. Robert Alter, "Saul Bellow: A Dissent from Modernism," *After the Tradition* (New York, 1969), p. 108.

40. Bellow, *Herzog*, p. 49.

41. James Atlas, *Delmore Schwartz* (New York, 1977), p. 287.

42. Bellow, *Dangling Man*, pp. 34, 36.

43. Bellow, *Herzog*, p. 2.

44. Ibid., p. 231.

45. Ibid., p. 74.

46. Ibid., p. 75.

47. Ibid., p. 39.

48. Saul Bellow, *Mr. Sammler's Planet* (New York, 1970), p. 305.

49. Ibid., p. 313.

50. Bellow, *Herzog*, p. 68.

51. *Jerusalem Post Weekly*, July 16, 1970, pp. 10, 11.

52. Harper, "Saul Bellow: An Interview," p. 192.

53. *New York Times*, March 11, 1965.

54. *New York Times*, October 2, 1966.

55. *New York Times*, March 5, 1971.

56. *New York Times*, December 13, 1976.

57. Bellow, *Mr. Sammler's Planet*, p. 18.

58. Ibid.

59. Saul Bellow, *The Dean's December* (New York, 1982), p. 50.

60. Ibid., p. 86.

61. Bellow, *Herzog*, p. 68.

## 6. FROM *SHLEMIEL* TO *MENTSH*: BERNARD MALAMUD

1. Quoted in "The Quest of Bernard Malamud," *Jewish Chronicle* (London), April 4, 1967.

2. Quoted by Granville Hicks, "His Hopes in the Human Heart," *Saturday Review*, October 12, 1963, p. 32.

3. Ihab Hassan, *Radical Innocence* (Princeton, N.J., 1961), p. 161.

4. Robert Alter, "Bernard Malamud: Jewishness as Metaphor," *After the Tradition* (New York, 1969), p. 116.

5. Hicks, p. 31.

6. Ihab Hassan, "The Hopes of Man," *New York Times Book Review*, October 13, 1963, p. 5.

7. Bernard Malamud, *The New Life* (New York, 1961), p. 95.

8. "The Quest of Bernard Malamud."

9. Alter, p. 117.

10. Theodore Solotaroff, quoted by Robert Alter.

11. Earl Rovit, in "Bernard Malamud and the Jewish Literary Tradition," *Critique*, Vol. 3, No. 2 (Winter, 1960). Rovit discusses the "pattern of ultimate poetic resolution in metaphor" in Malamud's best stories. Theodore Solotaroff's essay cited by Alter is "Bernard Malamud's Fiction: The Old Life and the New," *Commentary*, Vol. 3 (March, 1962). On the tradition of the *shlemiel*, see Ruth R. Wisse, *The Shlemiel as Modern Hero* (Chicago, 1971).

12. Bernard Malamud, *The Natural* (New York, 1952), p. 158.

13. Sidney Richman, *Bernard Malamud* (New York, 1966), p. 38.

14. Bernard Malamud, *The Assistant*, paperback ed. (New York, 1958 [c1957]), p. 18.

15. Ibid., p. 133.

16. Ibid., p. 95.

17. Ibid., p. 71.

18. Ibid., p. 99.

19. Ibid., p. 192.

20. Ibid., p. 180.

21. Ibid., p. 70.

22. Ibid., p. 151.

23. Malamud, *The New Life*, p. 361.

24. Ibid., p. 362.

25. Alter, p. 122.

26. Bernard Malamud, *The Magic Barrel* (New York, 1958), p. 214. These stories were originally published in magazines each year from 1950 to 1956.

27. Ibid., p. 214.

28. Ibid., p. 15.

29. Ibid.

30. Ibid., p. 182.

31. Bernard Malamud, "A Pimp's Revenge," *Pictures of Fidelman* (New York, 1969), p. 113.

32. Bernard Malamud, "The Jewbird," *Idiots First* (New York, 1963), p. 113.

33. Bernard Malamud, "The German Refugee," *Idiots First*, p. 209.

34. "The Quest of Bernard Malamud."

35. Quoted by Ihab Hassan, "The Hopes of Man."

36. Philip Rahv, "A Note on Bernard Malamud," *Literature and the Sixth Sense* (Boston, 1969), p. 286.

37. Alter, p. 126.

38. "The Quest of Bernard Malamud."

39. Bernard Malamud, *The Fixer* (New York, 1966), p. 171.

40. Ibid., p. 104.
41. Ibid., p. 272.
42. Ibid., p. 273.
43. Ibid.
44. Ibid.
45. Ibid., p. 274.
46. Ibid., p. 314.
47. Ibid., p. 315.
48. Rahv, p. 286.
49. Malamud, *The Fixer*, p. 319.
50. Ibid., p. 314.
51. Ibid., p. 315.
52. Ibid., p. 17.
53. Ibid., p. 45.
54. Ibid., p. 335.
55. Alter, p. 129.
56. Bernard Malamud, *Dubin's Lives* (New York, 1979), p. 332.

## 7. CONFESSIONS OF PHILIP ROTH

1. Philip Roth, "Defender of the Faith," *Goodbye Columbus* (New York, 1959), p. 200.

2. Louis Harap, "An Anti-Semitic Short Story," *Jewish Currents*, Vol. 13, No. 5 (May, 1959), 9.

3. Philip Roth, "Writing about Jews," *Commentary*, Vol. 36, No. 6, (December, 1963), 448.

4. Irving Howe, "Philip Roth Reconsidered," *The Critical Point* (New York, 1973), pp. 145, 146.

5. Samuel Margoshes, Letter, *National Jewish Post and Opinion*, June 10, 1960.

6. "Second Dialogue in Israel," *Congress Bi-Weekly*, Vol. 30, No. 12 (September 16, 1963), 61.

7. Ibid., p. 35.

8. Ibid., p. 21.

9. Ibid., p. 37.

10. Philip Roth, "Goodbye Columbus," *Goodbye Columbus*, p. 17.

11. Philip Roth, *Letting Go* (New York, 1962), p. 432.

12. Ibid., p. 231.

13. Dwight Macdonald, review of *Our Gang*, *New York Times Book Review*, November 7, 1971, p. 31.

14. Philip Roth, "Imagining Jews," *New York Review of Books*, October 3, 1974, p. 23.

15. Philip Roth, *Portnoy's Complaint* (New York, 1969), pp. 36–37.

16. Ibid., p. 264.

17. Ibid., p. 266.

18. Philip Roth, *Zuckerman Unbound* (New York, 1981), p. 70.

19. Roth, "Imagining Jews," p. 22.

20. Ibid., p. 23.

21. Marie Syrkin, "The Fun of Self-Abuse," *Midstream*, Vol. 12, No. 4 (April, 1969), 65.

22. Marie Syrkin, quoted Philip Roth, "Imagining Jews," p. 28.

23. Syrkin, "The Fun of Self-Abuse," p. 65.

24. Ibid., p. 68.

25. Bruno Bettelheim, "Portnoy Psychoanalyzed," *Midstream*, Vol. 15, No. 6 (June-July, 1969), 5.

26. Ibid., p. 6.

27. Ibid., p. 8.

28. Ibid., p. 10.

29. Roth, "Imagining Jews," p. 22.

30. Ibid., p. 24.

31. Macdonald, review of *Our Gang*.

32. Murray Kempton, *New York Review of Books*, January 27, 1972.

33. Philip Roth, *The Great American Novel* (New York, 1973), p. 280.

34. Jean Stafford, "The Echo and the Nemesis," *The Collected Stories* (New York, 1969), p. 43.

35. Philip Roth, *Reading Myself and Others* (New York, 1975), p. 76.

36. Philip Roth, *My Life As a Man* (New York, 1974), p. 173.

37. Philip Roth, *The Professor of Desire* (New York, 1977), p. 94.

38. Ibid., p. 96.

39. Philip Roth, *The Ghost Writer* (New York, 1979), p. 179.

40. Ibid., p. 72.

41. Philip Roth, *Zuckerman Unbound* (New York, 1981), p. 54.

42. Ibid., p. 15.

43. Ibid., p. 137.

44. Ibid., p. 155.

45. Ibid.

46. Ibid., pp. 217–18.

47. Philip Roth, *The Anatomy Lesson* (New York, 1983), p. 44.

48. Ibid., p. 96.

49. Ibid., p. 204.

## 8. THE JEW MANQUÉ: NORMAN MAILER

1. Norman Mailer, "Responses and Reactions," *Commentary*, Vol. 34, No. 6 (December, 1962), 505. Mailer here conveys a "capsule of biography" relating to his early connection with Jewishness to justify his venture into comment of Hasidism. He did not reprint these autobiographical remarks in *Presidential Papers*.

2. Norman Mailer, "A Calculus at Heaven," *Cross-Section*, ed. Edwin Seaver (New York, 1944), p. 337.

3. Ibid., p. 340.

4. Mailer, "Responses and Reactions," p. 505.

5. Norman Mailer, *Advertisements for Myself* (New York, 1959), p. 271.

6. Norman Mailer, "Our Country and Our Culture," *Partisan Review*, Vol. 19, No. 3 (May-June, 1952), 298.

7. Ibid., p. 299.

8. Mailer, *Advertisements*, p. 94.

9. Mailer, "The Man Who Studied Yoga," *Advertisements*, pp. 184–85.

10. Ibid., p. 107.

11. Ibid., p. 205.

12. Norman Mailer, *The Deer Park* (New York, 1955), p. 374.

13. Norman Mailer, "The Time of Her Time," *Advertisements*, p. 495. (Other writers such as Paul Goodman, Isaac Rosenfeld, and even Saul Bellow were for a time influenced by Wilhelm Reich during the 1950s.)

14. Norman Mailer, "The White Negro," p. 347.

15. Mailer, "The Time of Her Time," pp. 487–88.

16. Ibid., p. 489.

17. Ibid., p. 502.

18. Ibid., p. 503.

19. Norman Mailer, *An American Dream* (New York, 1970 [c1965]), p. 37. For an elaborate and, in my view, overly-serious symbolized treatment of *An American Dream*, see Helen Weinberg, *The New Novel in America* (Ithaca, N.Y., 1970), pp. 124–40.

20. Mailer, *An American Dream*, p. 235.

21. Norman Mailer, "The White Negro," *Advertisements*, p. 233.

22. Ibid., p. 338.

23. Ibid.

24. Ibid., p. 339.

25. Ibid., p. 314.

26. Ibid., p. 340.

27. Ibid., p. 341.

28. Ibid., p. 349.

29. Ibid., p. 379.

30. Ibid.

31. Ibid., p. 380.

32. Norman Mailer, *Presidential Papers* (New York, 1963), p. 193.

33. Norman Mailer, *Advertisements for Myself* (New York, 1959), p. 381.

34. Mailer, "Responses and Reactions," *Commentary*, Vol. 34, No. 6 (December, 1962), 504, 505.

35. Mailer, *Presidential Papers*, p. 187.

36. Ibid., p. 189.

37. Ibid., p. 188.

38. Ibid.

39. Ibid., p. 189.

40. Ibid.

41. Ibid., pp. 190–91.

42. Ibid., pp. 191, 192–93.

43. Ibid., p. 192.

44. Ibid.

45. Ibid., p. 193.

46. Ibid.

47. Ibid., pp. 194, 195.

48. Norman Mailer, *The Armies of the Night* (New York, 1968), p. 23.

49. Ibid., p. 134.

50. Ibid., p. 180.

51. Ibid.

## 9. THE RELIGIOUS TREND

1. Charles I. Glicksberg, "The Religious Revival in Contemporary Literature," *Western Humanities Review* (Winter, 1957), 75.

2. Ibid., pp. 65, 67.

3. June Kramer, *Ginsberg in America* (New York, 1969), pp. 23, xvii.

4. J. D. Salinger, *Franny and Zooey* (Boston, 1961), p. 29.

5. Chaim Potok, contribution to a symposium on "The State of Jewish Belief," *Commentary*, Vol. 42 (August, 1966), 125.

6. For a speculation of why *The Chosen* became a best-seller, see Shelden Grebstein, "The Phenomenon of The Really Jewish Best Seller: Chaim Potok's *The Chosen*," *Studies in American Jewish Literature*, Vol. 1, No. 1 (Spring, 1975), 23–31, and Chaim Potok's, "Reply to a Sympathetic Critic," Vol. 2, No. 1 (Spring, 1976), 30–34.

7. Arthur A. Cohen, "Why I Chose to Be a Jew," *Breakthrough: A Treasury of American-Jewish Literature*, ed. Irving Malin and Irwin Stark (New York, 1964), p. 368.

8. Ibid.

9. Ibid., p. 371.

10. Ibid., p. 372.

11. Ibid., p. 375.

12. Ibid.

13. Arthur A. Cohen, *In the Days of Simon Stern* (New York, 1973), p. 72.

14. Ibid., p. 75.

15. Ibid., p. 73.

16. Ibid., p. 226.

17. Ibid., p. 347.

18. Ibid., p. 457.

19. Cynthia Ozick, "Envy; or, Yiddish in America," *The Pagan Rabbi and Other Stories* (New York, 1971), p. 82.

20. Cynthia Ozick, *Congress Bi-Weekly*, Vol. 38, Nos. 2–3 (February 26, 1971), 47.

21. Cynthia Ozick, "Preface," *Bloodshed and Three Novellas* (New York, 1976), p. 4.

22. Ibid.

23. Cynthia Ozick, "America: Toward Yavneh," *Congress Bi-Weekly*, Vol. 38, Nos. 2–3 (February, 1971), 53.

24. Ibid.

25. Ozick, "Preface," p. 9.

26. Ibid., pp. 9–10.

27. Cynthia Ozick, "Holiness and Its Discontents," *Jewish Book Annual*, Vol. 30 (1972–1973), 10.

28. Ozick, "Preface," p. 11.

29. Ozick, "America: Toward Yavneh," p. 48.

30. Cynthia Ozick, "Response to Josephine Knopp," *Studies in American Jewish Literature*, Vol. 1, No. 2 (Winter, 1975), 49–50.

31. Ozick, "Holiness and its Discontents," p. 11.

32. Cynthia Ozick, "Virility," *The Pagan Rabbi and Other Stories* (New York, 1971), pp. 254, 266.

33. Cynthia Ozick, "The Jewish Half-Genius," *Jerusalem Post*, international ed., August 8, 1978, pp. 10, 11.

34. Cynthia Ozick, "Notes Toward the Right Question," *Lilith*, No. 6 (1979), 19.

35. Ibid., p. 20.

36. Ibid., p. 29.

37. Ozick, *Bloodshed and Three Novellas*, p. 4.

38. Ibid., p. 15.

39. Ibid., p. 40.

40. Ibid., p. 41.

41. Ozick, "Preface," p. 4.

42. Ibid., p. 11.

43. Ozick, "Usurpation (Other People's Stories)," *Bloodshed*, p. 147.

44. Ibid., p. 177.

45. For a fuller treatment of Ozick's work, see my article, "The Religious Art of Cynthia Ozick," *Judaism*, Vol. 33, No. 5 (Summer, 1984), 353–63.

# Bibliographical Note

Since World War II research material relating to the Jew in American literature, including both studies of individual authors and surveys of various aspects or phases of the general subject, has proliferated in numerous books and periodical articles. A student entering the field should supplement the primary texts of literary works with political, social and economic histories of the period. One cannot otherwise understand the full socioeconomic life of fictional characters or the effect that life has had on their individual modes of thinking and feeling. An acquaintance with American-Jewish history is also essential in judging the authenticity of fictional Jewish characters in the United States. Useful background material is offered in Morris U. Schappes' *Jews in the United States: A Pictorial History, 1654 to the Present* (1958, 2nd ed. with corrections and a supplementary chapter updating the history to 1965, 1965). This book is based on original research. The readable *World of Our Fathers* by Irving Howe assisted by Kenneth Libo (New York, 1976) is also very useful although mainly drawn from secondary sources.

For an analysis of problems of ethnicity the student is referred to John Higham's classic *Strangers in the Land, Patterns of American Nativism 1860–1925.* Corrected, with a new Preface (New York, 1974). E. Digby Baltzell's *The Protestant Establishment* (New York, 1964) scrutinizes the effect of Anglo-Saxon dominance and recession of influence as that so strongly influenced the acculturation of Jewish immigrants. Milton M. Gordon's *Assimilation in American Life: the Role of Race, Religion and National Origins* (New York, 1964) offers a guide through the maze of ethnicity theories.

While the present volume covers only the post–World War II period it is essential for the serious student to become acquainted with the past treatment of the Jew in earlier literature and with *Creative Awakening*, the first book of this series. Some knowledge of the treatment of the Jew by English writers is also important since so much nineteenth century and early twentieth century American practice was derived from patterns developed in England. The most comprehensive work on this subject is Montagu Frank Modder's *The Jew in the Literature of England to the End of the Nineteenth Century* (Philadelphia, 1939; New York, 1960). More selective than Modder, and brilliantly written with irony and insight is Edgar Rosenberg's *From Shylock to Svengali* (London, 1961). The comparable American volume to Moddler's is Louis Harap's *The Image of the Jew in American Literature: From Early Republic to Mass Immigration* (Philadelphia, 1974; 2nd ed., 1978). Although the cut-off date for this work is 1900 it ends with a forty-page chapter surveying the entire English fictional achievement of Abraham Cahan, extending into the twentieth century. Sol Liptzin's *The Jew in American Literature* (New York, 1966) provides a short and rather spotty account concluding with the 1940s. A brief introductory view of the subject is contained in Leslie Fiedler's pamphlet, written for the Herzl Institute, *The Jew in the American Novel* (New York, 1959). This treats a small number of selected figures. A concise history of the Jewish religion in this country is presented in Nathan Glazer's *American Judaism* (Chicago, 1959). Finally, since so many of the novels are located in New York, and since the New York experience generally set the pattern of early immigrant experience for Jews, the student would do well to consult Moses Rischin's study in depth of that experience, *The Promised City* (Cambridge, 1962).

By far the best work on labor, socialist and "proletarian" fiction is Walter Rideout's *The Radical Novel in the United States* (Cambridge, 1956). His article on Jewish writers of the radical novel in "O Workers Revolution . . . The New Messiah," *American Jewish Archives*, Vol. II, No. 2 (October, 1959), pp. 157–175, is also valuable. Bernard Sherman's *Invention of the Jew: Jewish-American Novels, 1916–1964* (New York, 1969) is a useful study, and Marcus Klein's *Foreigners: The Making of American Literature* (Chicago, 1981) is an exceptionally stimulating one. One can, of course, also find a large number of works on special aspects of the Jew in literature.

There is still, to my knowledge, no comprehensive authoritative study of the history of anti-Semitism in the United States but sections of some of the books listed above, notably Higham's and Baltzell's, are informative on the subject for specific periods.

On anti-Semitism specifically during the post–World War II period we suggest Dennis H. Wrong's "The Rise and Decline of Anti-Semitism in America," in Peter B. Rose's anthology of essays, *The Ghetto and Beyond* (New York, 1969) and Gertrude J. Selznick and Stephen Steinberg, *The Tenacity of Prejudice* (New York, 1965), from which we can get a notion of the stubborn persistence of anti-Semitic beliefs in latent form, even when they do not reach the stage of overt behavior, and which exist even in time of recession of anti-Semitism.

By now the secondary materials on the Jew in American literature in this century, but most particularly in the postwar period, is already enormous and growing rapidly. The basic materials, however, the primary literary texts themselves discussed in this book, are provided with sufficient bibliographical information in the notes. However, a few suggestions are offered on secondary studies directly relating to the material in the present study. The concept of the *shlemiel* is so ubiquitous that familiarity with Ruth Wisse's *The Shlemiel as Modern Hero* (Chicago, 1971) can be helpful. It surveys the tradition of the *shlemiel* in the classic Yiddish writers and its continuation in English fiction by Jewish writers in the second half of our century. For the *Menorah Journal* as a precursor of the efflorescence of Jewish writers in this period, we suggest Alan M. Wald's comprehensive monograph, "The Menorah Group Goes Left," *Jewish Social Studies*, Vol. 38, Nos. 3–4 (Summer-Fall, 1976) and Mark Krupnick, "The Menorah Journal Group and the Origins of Modern Jewish-American Radicalism," *Modern Jewish Studies*, Annual III (1979), 56–67. For a detailed history of the *Partisan Review*, see James Burkhardt Gilbert, *Writers and Partisans: A History of Literary Radicalism in America* (New York, 1968).

The anthology of writing, which in a manner served as a widely heralded confirmation of the secure place in the literary mainstream achieved by Jewish writers, is the appropriately named *Breakthrough* (1968) with the subtitle, *A Treasury of Contemporary American-Jewish Literature*, edited by Irving Malin and Irwin Stark, containing the now famous stories, poetry, and nonfiction writing by leading Jewish writers.

The files of the monthly magazines *Commentary* and *Midstream* contain many studies of specific Jewish writers and of particular problems concerning the Jew in literature. Occasional articles also appear, in greater numbers of later years, in the general scholarly and critical journals.

The primary works of fiction of the post–World War II period are discussed in detail in the foregoing pages so that it would be redundant to list them here. A reader has only to consult the Index to ascertain where he will find all the necessary information about each of these, including date of publication, etc.

# Index

## About the Author

LOUIS HARAP received his A.B. and Ph.D. from Harvard University. He is the former editor of *Jewish Life* and is currently on the editorial board of *Jewish Currents*. He is the author of *In the Mainstream: The Jewish Presence in Twentieth-Century American Literature, 1950s—1980s* and *Dramatic Encounters: The Jewish Presence in Twentieth-Century American Drama, Poetry, and Humor and the Black-Jewish Literary Relationship* (both published by Greenwood Press, 1987), *Social Roots of the Arts*, and *The Image of the Jew in American Literature: From Early Republic to Mass Immigration* (1974). His articles have appeared in *Journal of Ethnic Studies, Science and Society, Jewish Currents*, and numerous other journals.